MINI[illegible]
LOCOMOTIVE C[illegible]RUCTION

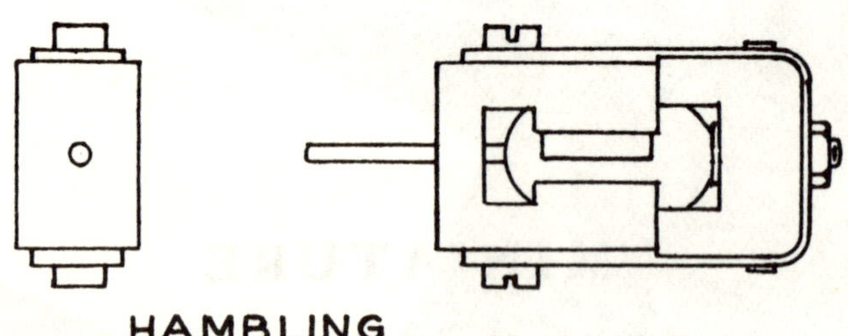

HAMBLING

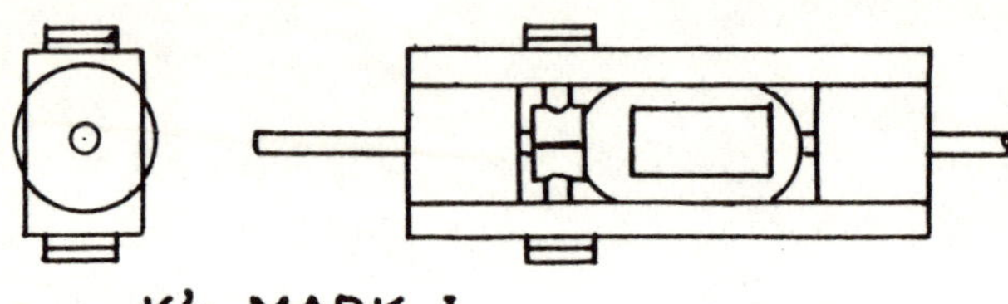

K's MARK I

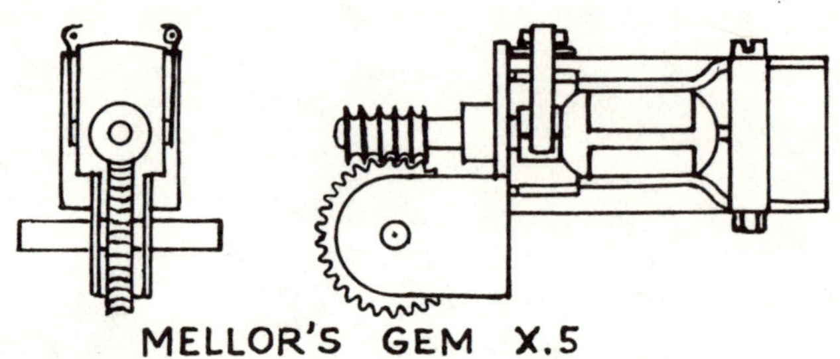

MELLOR'S GEM X.5

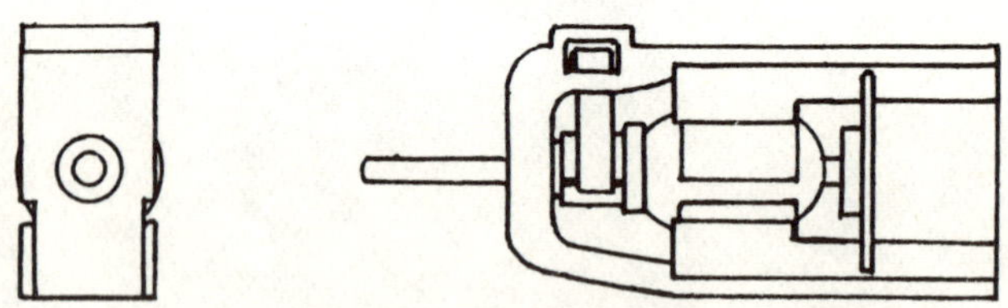

ROMFORD PHANTOM

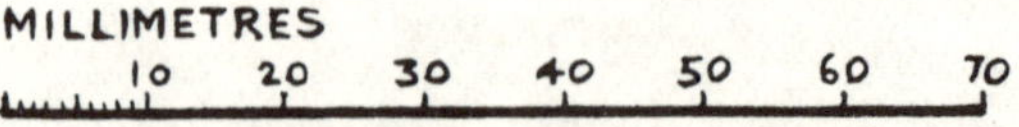

Some British motors for gauges "OO" and "HO"

MINIATURE LOCOMOTIVE CONSTRUCTION

JOHN H. AHERN

WITH A FOREWORD BY J. N. MASKELYNE, A.I.Loco.E.

MODEL & ALLIED PUBLICATIONS
ARGUS BOOKS LIMITED
14 St James Road, Watford,
Herts., England

Model and Allied Publications
Argus Books Limited
14 St James Road, Watford,
Herts., England

First Published 1948
Second Impression 1949
Second Edition 1956
Second Impression 1963
Third Impression 1969
Fourth Impression 1971
Fifth Impression 1973
Sixth Impression 1975
Seventh Impression 1977
Eighth Impression 1979

ISBN 0 85242 685 2

Printed by A. Wheaton & Co. Ltd., Exeter

PREFACE

I HAVE tried in this book to describe not only what is supposed to happen but also what often actually does happen ; not only what the modeller is *supposed* to do but also what in the heat of contest with more or less intractable materials he actually does do. To pretend that even experienced workers can predict in advance the exact method of every operation, and get everything dead right first time, would not be quite truthful, and would merely have the effect of burdening the beginner with an unnecessarily poor opinion of his own abilities. Even the " advanced worker " is subject to moments of something very like despair during the creation of a model locomotive. At least we learn more from such moments than from our easily achieved successes.

And I have not filled up precious space with photographic illustrations of *finished* model locomotives, which look pretty in a book but would contribute nothing to the beginner's knowledge of how to do likewise. It is hoped that the photographs which do appear in the following pages, of chassis and models in various stages of construction, will be more helpful.

John H. Ahern,

London, W.1.

PUBLISHER'S NOTE

This classic book by the late John H. Ahern remains a best seller and an essential part of the reference library of any miniature railway enthusiast. The reader will appreciate that since the book was written in 1948 there have been some changes in the material and supply situation. Plastics and more compact motors are just two examples of modern developments not covered in this book. Also some suppliers mentioned have moved on or changed. Essentially, however, all the contents of this volume are still valid today and we have not tampered with Mr. Ahern's style or comments. The modern reader will, however, be aware of items currently available.

FOREWORD

BY J. N. MASKELYNE, A.I.LOCO.E.

WHENCE comes the fascination of the miniature railway? The question occurs, time and time again, to the minds of uninitiated onlookers, who are intelligent enough to realise that the model railway hobby is not just a matter of " playing at trains." The many hundreds of complete model railway systems, be they large or small, each with its track, engines, rolling-stock, signals, stations, bridges, and other railway paraphernalia, all reproduced accurately to scale from the prototypes, represent technical skill and practical aptitude and knowledge applied to produce a result which can best be described as a scientific achievement, far advanced beyond the least suggestion of the " toy " stage. The mere effort required to produce such results is due to some urge, some irresistible enthusiasm, which is born in the minds of many boys—and even some girls—usually at an early age. In some cases, this enthusiasm later dies down, even to a point from which it can never be rekindled ; but in others it matures until it becomes a force potent enough to stimulate that natural craftsmanship which is in all of us, and urges on the desire to make something ; and the " something " is usually a locomotive in miniature !

To the question which opens the foregoing paragraph there is probably no one definite answer. But mention of the locomotive provides the clue to an answer that can be successfully given in the majority of cases ; it is that the steam locomotive is, itself, one of the most fascinating of all man's creations. Be it racing along at the head of an express train, or standing quietly ready to begin its allotted task, the locomotive induces an enthusiasm which, once it is assimilated, cannot be repelled.

There remains, however, the problem as to how the enthusiastic craftsman is to make his miniature locomotive. The process has often involved the expenditure of much time and patience in battling against limitations of workshop facilities or inadequate knowledge of the use and handling of the available tools. In this book, however, Mr. Ahern, writing obviously against a background of much personal experience, describes in detail methods which greatly reduce the difficulties of construction of miniature, electrically-propelled locomotives. The amateur constructor, with no technical knowledge or workshop experience, can easily apply these methods for himself, after a little practice in the use of a few comparatively simple tools.

It will be noted that, in his illustrations, Mr. Ahern stresses the building of small models of small prototypes. This is all to the good, if only for the reason that such models are the most difficult to construct ; but the methods employed are applicable to any class or type of railway engine.

Mr. Ahern is no novice to model railway engineering in the smaller and more difficult scales ; his prolific fund of ideas, artistic sense, and sound practical advice have been available to the hobby for years, through the medium of other books and periodicals devoted to the subject. But in this book is to be found a greater fund of information on model locomotive building than the locomotive miniaturist has ever before had readily available between two covers. All that remains is for the constructors to read this book, follow its advice and build as many locomotives as are required for operating the traffic on their miniature railways.

The fact that electricity is the source of motive power in practically all these tiny engines is purely incidental ; the important point is that it enables the miniature locomotive to move and to haul a train in a thoroughly realistic manner while under the control of the owner. In this way, much of the intrinsic fascination of the steam locomotive can be reproduced cleanly, conveniently and easily in any home. The guidance and instruction to be obtained from the following pages bring with them the added satisfaction of enabling the reader to build, simply and in miniature, any locomotive that he fancies.

CONTENTS

Other books by John H. Ahern

Miniature Building Construction

Miniature Landscape Modelling

A NOTE ABOUT TOOLS

I CALL this a note about tools, rather than a chapter, because I am not going to worry the reader with a catalogue of the ordinary tools which everybody may be presumed to know already. Here I shall simply mention a few things which may not be quite so obvious. And first we should place among the essentials a good supply of jeweller's files, of all shapes, and including some of the smallest obtainable. A few should be kept in a separate box for use on solder and lead only, and religiously segregated from those which are used on " clean " metals such as brass, nickel or steel. Next in importance we may place a small hand-vice, with jaws about ½ in. or ⅝ in. wide, and a toolmaker's clamp of the smallest size ; that is about 2 in. long. These, or at least one of them, must be classed among the necessities ; it is hopeless to attempt fine work without adequate means of holding it, and the ordinary bench-vice is sometimes by no means suitable. It is fixed in one position and cannot be turned about to get the best angle at which to work.

Taper taps, 6-, 8- and 10-B.A. and a suitable holder, are almost necessities. Plug taps and dies for the same sizes may be wanted occasionally, but are less important and can be obtained if the need should arise.

For the kind of work treated in this book, it is useless to think of drills in terms of the fractions-of-an-inch or " jobber's " sizes, except in a few obvious cases such as ⅛ in. The number drills are the most useful, and the most important are the tapping and clearance sizes for the screw threads mentioned in the last paragraph. These are :—

	Tapping	Clearance
6-B.A.	44	34
8-B.A.	51	43
10-B.A.	55	50

These are best kept, with the corresponding taps, in a box divided into compartments. It is a little difficult to advise as to the selection of drills apart from those named above. The worker should endeavour to obtain a selection ranging from about No. 28 (which is slightly larger than ⅛ in.) down to the size of a common pin, that is about size 68, which is 0.031 in. diameter. The smaller sizes at least should always be obtained in duplicate as they break very easily. To supplement the drills two or three fine broaches are a desirable acquisition, one of them being small enough to enter the smallest drill size which is likely to be used. A copy of the " Instantus " Standard Size and Thread Table, or some equivalent compilation, is almost a necessity, in the writer's opinion; it can be had from any good tool shop and gives drill sizes for every screw thread that could ever be required, inch and millimetre equivalents of all drill and Wire Gauge sizes, and much other valuable information. It may be mentioned that the Standard Wire Gauge sizes are used not only for wire but also for stating the thickness of sheet metal. Thus 28-s.w.g. sheet is 0.0148 in. thick. The most useful sheet metal sizes for locomotive bodies in " OO " and " HO " gauges are 33-s.w.g., which is 0.01 in. thick, and 36-sw.g. which is 0.0076 in. thick. The latter is quite stout enough for rolled boilers, cab sides, tank sides, etc., but seems rather difficult to obtain in nickel. For running-plates, thicker stuff is advisable, about 28- or 30-s.w.g.

A miniature hacksaw frame, the kind which takes a blade 6 in. long, is a necessary addition, and can be obtained anywhere. A larger one is unnecessary for the purposes treated in this book. A piercing-saw frame and blades should also be acquired. If possible, blades should be obtained in several sizes (that is different numbers of teeth to the inch.) They can be bought, I believe, as fine as 100 teeth to the inch, and some of the finest which may be available should be secured. The reason is that no piercing-saw will cut freely in sheet metal which is thinner than the distance between adjacent teeth. This can be overcome, to a certain extent, by clamping the work in the vice with a piece of waste wood behind it, and cutting metal and wood together. To attempt to saw thin metal without this precaution is a waste of time and can only lead to spoilt work, broken blades, and a frayed temper.

A good slide-gauge, with inch and millimetre scales, is almost a necessity. A micrometer is one of those things which people manage to get along without for years, but having once acquired one they wonder how they ever managed to survive without it. Unfortunately, it is a relatively expensive item and perhaps the best I can say is that the modelmaker will hardly feel the lack of it seriously until he has used one. Nevertheless, like a lathe, and some other special tools, it broadens the worker's outlook, and extends his range of activities and interests enormously.

Concerning lathes, all that can be said here is that every modelmaker should aim to possess one ultimately, however simple it may be.

A small power drill for use in the hand, of the type produced by Black & Decker, Wolf, Bridges, and other firms, is a very valuable acquisition. In addition to its more normal uses, it can be secured in a vice and made to fulfil some of the functions of a lathe for hand turning, the work being mounted in the chuck.

Several " attachments " are supplied by the manufacturers for use with some of these electric drills and details can be obtained from any good tool shop. By means of these moderately priced attachments the drill can be converted, when required, into a lathe, a vertical bench drill, and a circular saw table. This scheme is well worth the consideration of all those who do not feel able to afford a more elaborate workshop equipment. The lathe attachment should be adequate for all the small fittings, such as funnels and domes, which the model maker will require and the pillar bench drill is invaluable in all cases where holes have to be drilled strictly at right-angles to the work, as occurs when making locomotive frames for example. A drill of this type can also be used to drive a buffing wheel or a small grinding wheel for sharpening tools.

The reader is advised to make sure that any power tools, such as drills, are *properly* earthed, preferably to a water pipe which is known to go direct to earth, not to a cistern, and *not under any circumstances* to a gas pipe. I must add that within my personal knowledge presumably experienced professional electricians have been known to earth electrical apparatus to gas pipes through mental laziness or inability to distinguish them from water pipes. Hence the need for caution as the consequences could be very serious.

If I have occasion to use an electric drill when there is a doubt about whether it is properly earthed or not—or when it is known that there is no earth connection—I invariably put on a pair of leather gloves.

A magnifying-glass is really necessary sometimes. It can be used for such purposes as checking the accuracy of the mesh between worm and wormwheel teeth. In such cases, to be able to *see* what one is doing is more satisfactory than to rely on touch. It is also used to check the position of centres when drilling for axles, pinion-shafts and the like, where rather more than the normal degree of precision is necessary. If the reader can hold a watchmaker's eyeglass in his eye, well and good ; if (like the writer) he cannot, it is convenient to have the glass fixed on some sort of stand, either bought or improvised, so as to leave the hands free.

A miniature centre-punch should be included in the tool kit, and can be bought quite cheaply from good tool firms, or made from a piece of silver-steel rod about ⅛ in. diameter as described in Chapter VII. For a surface-plate, any odd piece of plate-glass will meet most requirements. For marking-out on metal, a pin chuck, which will grip a gramophone needle firmly, serves just as well as a regular scriber, and can be used for other purposes as well.

A small power grinder, with a wheel about 3 in. diameter, is the first machine tool the worker should consider. In this case also as with the micrometer, having once realised the utility of such a machine you wonder how you ever managed without it. At the time of writing, well made and compact little grinders can be obtained for about £3 10s. or £4. They are worth their cost many times over.

SOLDERING EQUIPMENT

It is to be hoped that electricity is available as electric irons are the only ones which are really convenient for this work. The ordinary copper bit, heated in the fire or over a gas flame, is satisfactory in large sizes but a nuisance in small ones. It overheats and cools off too quickly to be of much use. It is a convenience to have two electric irons, one of medium size and the other a small one with a pencil bit. As explained in a later chapter, there are occasions when the medium-size iron will hardly provide sufficient heat and a supplementary source of heat—a flame of some sort—is almost a necessity. Where gas is available one of the new miniature blowlamps, selling at about 2s. 6d. or 3s. 6d. is ideal as it gives a very small, hot flame. Means can be devised to clamp it to the bench, so that both hands are left free for the work and the soldering iron. Or the work can be held in the vice, or by other means, and the lamp manipulated with one hand while the iron is applied with the other. In the absence of a gas supply, a small methylated spirit lamp might be used. The writer uses one made from a glass cold cream jar with a screw-on metal top which is punched for the cottonwool wick. An extra pin-size hole should be made in the lid to serve as a vent. The ordinary paraffin or petrol blowlamp should be used only with the utmost discretion, as it is much too fierce for such small work as the building of miniature locomotives.

The writer admits he is prejudiced in favour of paste flux, rather than the liquid acid type. Acid fluxes are not very pleasant things in the vicinity of delicate and precision tools, and blueprint drawings should be kept out of the way when they are in use. If paste flux is used, a small bottle of carbon tetrachloride and a cheap stiff brush, such as an old toothbrush, should be kept on the bench for removal of the flux which sticks to the work. It is very useful to be able to undertake silver-soldering when required, with Easy-flo solder and the special flux which is provided for it. Contrary to popular supposition it is not more difficult than soft-soldering; in fact it seems to run just where it is wanted more easily and with the application of less skill on the part of the operator. It requires a much higher temperature, however. For very small work (such as joining two thin wires together) this can be provided by one of the miniature gas blowpipes which do not require a forced draught. This is rather exceptional, however, and for general work a regular gas blowpipe with an air compressor, or bellows, is the most satisfactory answer. The best form of Easy-flo for the modeller is wire about 16-gauge which can be obtained from toolshops. Full particulars are available from the makers, Johnson Matthey & Co. Ltd., 78, Hatton Garden, London, E.C.1.

A few remarks must be added for the encouragement of people who are obliged to manage as best they can without a regular workroom or even a permanent bench, but must carry on their model making in a living-room. It can be said that a permanent bench is not essential for building model locomotives in the smaller scales. The reader who is so situated should provide himself with a substantial board, measuring perhaps 3 ft. by 1 ft. 6 in., although the precise dimensions are not important. A large pastry-board or the top of a small kitchen table with the legs removed might serve. If this portable bench is to be used on a polished table top, felt pads should be glued underneath. A small vice should be screwed to one corner, and provided with removable jaws of a fairly soft metal which are not serrated. The board should be provided with a bench-hook, which is simply a strip of wood screwed to the front edge, on the underneath side, which engages against the front edge of the table and takes up the thrust of filing and sawing operations. In addition a partitioned box, or a nest of drawers, for tools, materials, and odds and ends, is required; it should be provided with a carrying-handle for convenience in handling.

Provided a lighting point is available for the soldering iron, the model-maker, equipped as described above, will be able to carry out practically every operation described in this book, except, of course, turning. Even as regards turning, however, small fittings can be produced by clamping the handbrace, or hand-power drill, in the vice and using it as an improvised lathe. Much excellent work has been accomplished in this way.

CHAPTER I

CERTAIN PRELIMINARIES

THE most important parts of a working model locomotive are the motor and frame, and satisfactory operation depends entirely on their efficiency and general suitability. Therefore, it is advisable to consider them first, leaving the superstructure, which calls for different methods and is in any case little more than a shell enclosing the working parts, for later chapters. We are, of course, concerned solely with electrically-driven models ; steam is outside the scope of this book, and is hardly practicable in gauges smaller than " O."

Broadly speaking, there are two courses open to the modelmaker : he can purchase a complete chassis, consisting of frame, motor, gears and wheels, and confine himself to the building of the superstructure, or he can " start from scratch " by building the chassis as well. In the latter case he will probably prefer to buy the wheels and also the motor (or at least the principal components of it) for electric motor construction is so highly-specialised a business that a book almost as large as this would be required to treat it adequately.

The reader is probably familiar with at least the general form of the commercially-made mechanism. It consists of a frame either built up in brass or cast in white metal alloy ; to this is fitted an electric motor, usually of the direct-current permanent-magnet type, with wheels, coupling-rods, and an arrangement of gears to transmit the power from the armature shaft to the driving-axle. Plastics are rapidly replacing metal for electric motor parts and the use of these materials may soon extend to frames as well. In fact it is possible that some such development may have taken place by the time these words are in print. Before the war, such units were usually wound for a 6-volt current supply ; but 12 volts has now become standard, with a marked improvement in running and general efficiency. Most readers will probably prefer to buy a complete chassis, at least for their first essay in locomotive construction ; but, for various reasons, the modelmaker may sometimes wish to build his own. It may be that no commercially-made mechanism is found to be entirely suitable for the particular job in hand. With some older locomotives, for example, it may not be possible to fit any ready-made mechanism into the restricted space afforded by a low-pitched boiler and firebox. The modelmaker, however, may wish to try out some idea of his own, perhaps in respect of transmission or springing, or he may quite simply desire the satisfaction of knowing that the whole of the finished model is his own creation.

The building of the chassis is treated in detail in the next chapter, but it may be said here that, assuming the motor has been obtained complete, the construction of a successful mechanism unit is not a difficult undertaking, even if only a few hand tools are available. It is assumed that wheels also will be bought, insulated on one side if the model is intended for two-rail operation, and, for preference, ready quartered on their axles. This is rather important to the beginner, because accurate quartering of cranks is not easy without proper facilities, and if the wheels are not correctly quartered there will be endless trouble with binding connecting-rods.

The application of plastics has now found an established place in the manufacture of wheels as well as motors. Messrs. Hambling supply a range of driving wheels with beautifully moulded plastic centres but with metal rims and hubs. These wheels are very strong and the user need not fear that the metal parts will ever work loose. A selection of them is shown in the photograph on this page. Driving wheels are available in sizes from 15 mm. to 26 mm. diameter and tender wheels of similar construction are also supplied. These wheels fit on axles with splined ends, one of which is also shown in the photograph.

Plastic wheels with metal tyres and centres by A. W. Hambling & Co. Ltd.

CHAPTER II

ADAPTING THE MECHANISM TO THE MODEL

THE prototype for the proposed model being chosen, the first, and one of the most important, steps is to make sure that the mechanism will fit into the boiler and firebox. This is equally true whether the mechanism is bought complete or is to be designed and made at home. It is obviously unwise to proceed with the construction only to discover, perhaps at an advanced stage of the work, that the motor will not fit inside the boiler. In the first place drawings should be obtained, or made, of the side and end elevations of the locomotive, full-size for the scale to which it is proposed to work. It may be advisable to make a plan also. Certain firms supply blueprint drawings of practically every locomotive in service in this country, and of many which are now obsolete. In addition, many excellent drawings can be found in the files of *The Model Railway News*, the *Journal of the Stephenson Locomotive Society*, and many other books and journals. If a drawing is obtained, which is to a different scale from that required, to re-scale it to the required dimensions is a simple matter.

Assuming that a drawing of the prototype has been made or obtained, full-size for the proposed model, and that a complete mechanism with the required wheel-spacing has been purchased, the next step is to measure up the chassis and motor very carefully, and to make side *and front* elevations of it on tracing-paper. These should show the frames and wheels and the outline of the motor, being careful to indicate the maximum height, the depth of wheel-flanges, as well as the tread diameter, *and any projections such as brush-gear which may stand up above the magnet or overhang at the sides.* A height-gauge and a slide-gauge are very useful here ; in fact, one or the other is practically essential. The mechanism should stand on a flat surface while height measurements are taken, and it is best to measure from rail-level by making a suitable deduction (0.75 mm. or 1 mm. in the miniature scales) for the depth of the flanges. It is convenient, also, to take all longitudinal measurements from the centre of the driving-axle, whether forwards towards the smokebox or backwards towards the cab. In effect, the driving-axle is treated as a fixed measuring point, and everything else is considered in relation to it. When complete, the side and front elevations of the chassis can be placed on top of the corresponding drawings of the locomotive so that the wheel centres coincide. As the chassis drawing is on tracing-paper, that of the locomotive will show through, and it will at once be evident whether the mechanism will fit into the superstructure or not. Even if all appears to be in order, it is better not to be in a hurry at this stage ; there is no harm, for example, in checking the leading dimensions again to be on the safe side. And the modelmaker should satisfy himself that no projection on the motor has been overlooked. The result, when the tracing of the mechanism has been laid in its correct position on the drawing, should appear something like Fig. 1. In this drawing I have, of course, shown only the outlines, and omitted everything which is not relevant to the point under discussion. The thick line indicates the outline of the chassis and motor. Considering Fig. 1A, comparison of the side and end elevations shows that the motor does come within the limits of the boiler and firebox as it should, and construction may proceed.

But in Fig. 1B we see what should *not* happen. If the side elevation alone is considered, everything appears to be in order ; but the end view tells a very different story. The corners of the magnet would foul the firebox, and the superstructure would not be able to sit down on the chassis. The reader should be on his guard against this insidious little trap. It is useless to proceed with the model until some solution of the difficulty has been found. Either a mechanism in which the motor is mounted lower on the chassis must be obtained, or the boiler and firebox must be raised slightly or enlarged in diameter. In some cases, this is possible—strictly within limits—without the appearance of the model being very seriously affected, but it should be avoided if any other means can be devised ; it is a risky thing to take liberties with the dimensions of a locomotive. Generally speaking, it may be suggested that, in 4-mm. scale, two millimetres is the *absolute maximum* by which a boiler should ever be raised above its proper position. If this is exceeded the appearance of the model will almost certainly be so much affected that it will cease to be a satisfactory reproduction of the original. In any case, it is obvious that as soon as one takes liberties of this sort the result must cease to be a faithful model, and how far one can dare to go is best determined by making a drawing of the locomotive with the boiler and firebox in the proposed modified position, and comparing the result with the original.

A third remedy is to grind a little off the edges of the magnet on a power grinding-wheel, to enable it to clear the firebox. If this is attempted, it is most important that the motor should be completely covered, except that part which is actually being ground, to ensure that no particles of metal or of carborundum get into the armature or the shaft bearings. If it is thought undesirable to take the motor to pieces the best thing is to stuff paper between the armature and the pole-pieces of the magnet, to pack any odd corners with paper or cotton wool, and then to cover the motor with adhesive medical tape. Proceed slowly with the grinding, touching the magnet against the wheel slightly, and only for two or three seconds at a time. Do not let the magnet become hot on any account or the magnetism may be adversely affected.

From the foregoing, it is clearly advisable to obtain the dimensions of a chassis from the manufacturer before purchase. When ordering it is always necessary to specify the wheelbase, to correspond to that of the original.

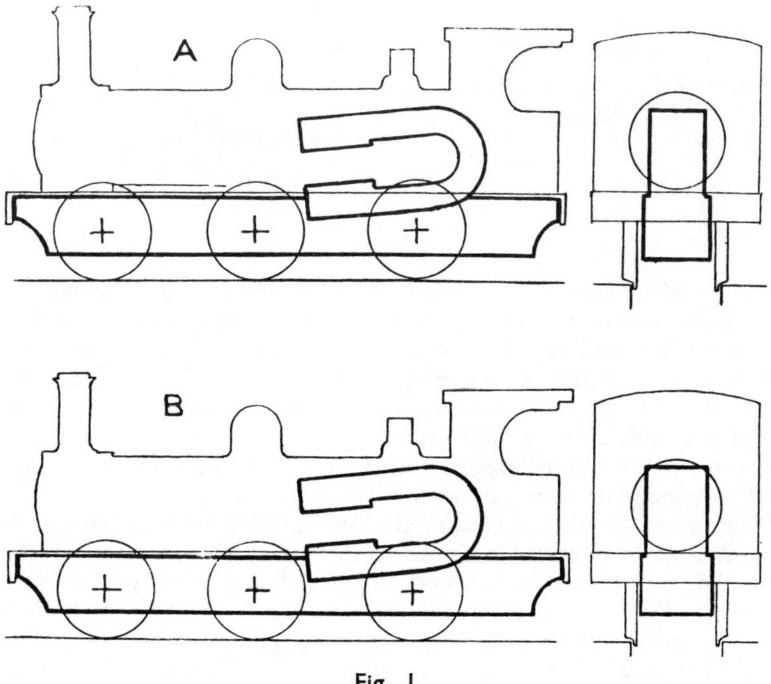

Fig. 1

JOINING THE CHASSIS AND SUPERSTRUCTURE

This is a matter that should be settled before construction commences. The two parts of the model must be rigidly and securely united, but must be easily and quickly separated for oiling and adjustment. It is usual for the mechanism to have two holes drilled vertically through the centres of the cross-members, one close to each end of the frame. The normal method of attachment is by means of screws pushed up from below through these holes into corresponding ones which have been drilled and tapped in the running-plate of the superstructure. The screws may be 8- or 10-B.A., but the larger size should be used, if space permits, for additional strength. It is clear that we cannot, as a rule, tap the running-plate itself as it is usually of quite thin sheet metal. It is therefore necessary to provide the required thickness for a screw thread by soldering a nut, or a small piece of metal which has been drilled and tapped, to the running-plate. It seems to be a fairly common practice to solder it above the running-plate, as in Fig. 2A, which, for obvious reasons, must be done before the boiler and smokebox are mounted. This arrangement cannot be recommended because if the nut should ever become loose, or if the thread should become stripped or damaged, it is well-nigh impossible to get at it without pulling the model to pieces. The nut should always be below

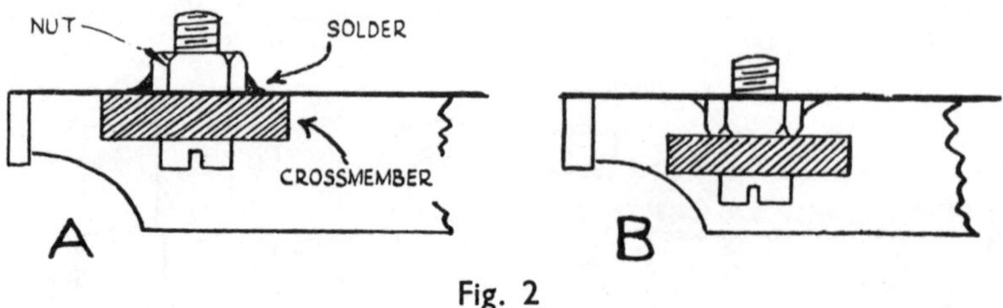

Fig. 2

the running-plate, as in Fig. 2B, where it can be removed if necessary with no more serious consequence than the risk of slight damage to the paint from the heat of the soldering iron. The chassis cross-member, or lug, must, of course, be lowered to allow room for the nut, which will be located between the side-frames. It will be found that some commercially-made mechanisms are designed with this in view, and the cast white-metal chassis, which enjoyed considerable popularity before the war, had the end lugs dropped below the normal running-plate level presumably for this reason.

If the reader should have acquired a chassis which is not so fitted, it should not be difficult to alter the positions of the lugs. The method will depend on how the chassis is made, but that shown in Fig. 3 is likely to be the most satisfactory. First, a new cross-member is soldered across the frames, below the existing one, as shown at *B*. Then the original one is either unsoldered or cut and filed away, taking care that none of the filings find their way into any part of the motor. The reason for fitting the new lug or cross-member before removing the old one is that there is then no danger of the side-frames

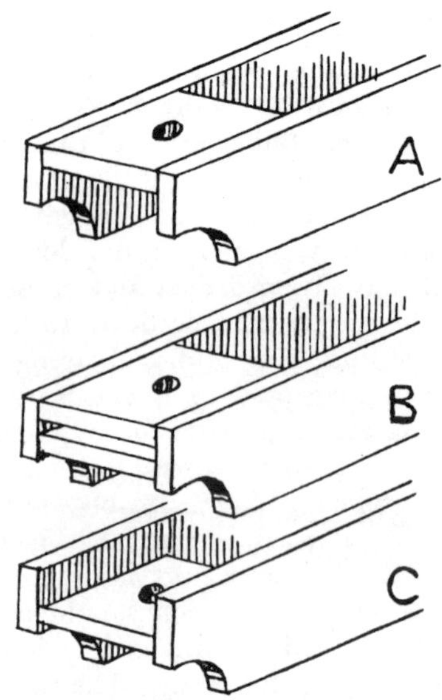

Fig. 3

moving out of alignment while unsupported, which would cause binding of the axles and other troubles.

The writer sometimes arranges to join the mechanism and superstructure by one screw only, usually at the forward end. At the other end there is a form of " housing," which may be filed from $\frac{1}{16}$-in. brass and soldered to the back of the buffer-beam, as in Fig. 4. A projecting tongue on the end of the chassis engages in this housing. It must be a good tight fit or there will be slight movement between chassis and superstructure. The best way is to file the slot

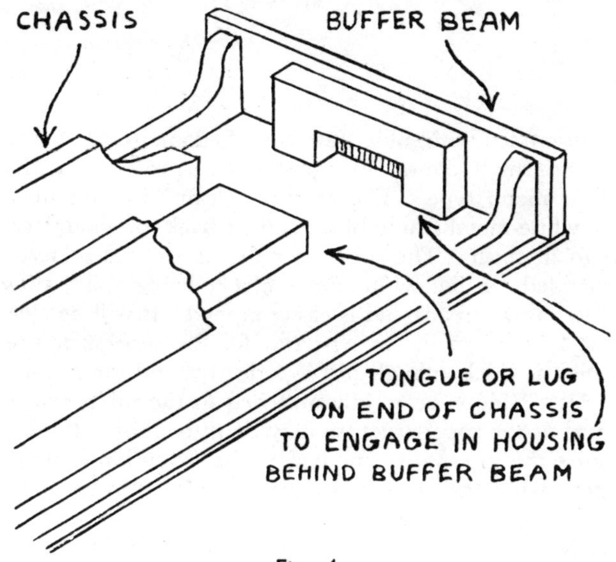

Fig. 4

in the housing slightly small for the tongue, and then file the tongue until it will just enter. This arrangement is very convenient and satisfactory.

EXTENSION-FRAMES

The frames of commercially-made mechanisms seldom agree exactly in length and shape with those of the prototype, unless specially ordered for the particular job. The usual practice is to leave them rather short, so that the modelmaker is free to make such additions as may be required. It is therefore necessary, in most cases, to build on what may be termed extension frames. This can be done in two ways : they can be built on to the chassis, which is undoubtedly the more workmanlike proceeding, or they can be soldered to the superstructure, under the running-plate, so that they *appear* to be integral with the main frames. The second method may possibly give better results in inexperienced hands. The first method is shown in Fig. 5. Diagram *A* shows how a chassis with built-up frames can be treated. A new extended cross-member is fitted, and to this the short extension side-frames are attached.

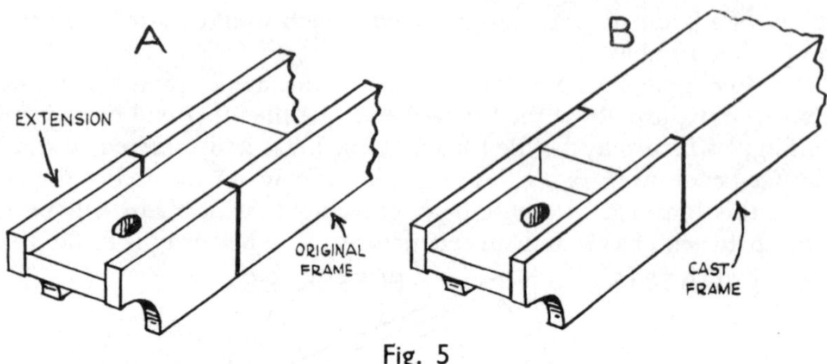

Fig. 5

The parts are assembled with solder (an iron of adequate size being necessary), and reinforced with small screws. Fig. 5B shows the procedure with mechanisms of the cast white-metal type. The extension frame is built up as described above, but the white-metal frame block is filed back, or shouldered, to enable the extension to fit flush. The use of screws, as well as solder, for fixing is to be recommended, as the white-metal block, being solid, provides ample thickness for the screw threads and is easily tapped. It will be clear that if the extension-frame is to carry the fixing-screw for the superstructure it must be of material which is thick enough to be perfectly rigid, and $\frac{1}{16}$-in. strip brass is suggested. Also, it must be rigidly attached to the main chassis, and must be perfectly level or the superstructure may be thrown over to one side.

Fig. 6 shows the alternative method : the extension-frames in this case are cut from somewhat thinner metal and are soldered to the underside of the running-plate, to come into line with the mechanism frame when the parts are assembled. It is advisable to cut the extensions slightly long, and to adjust

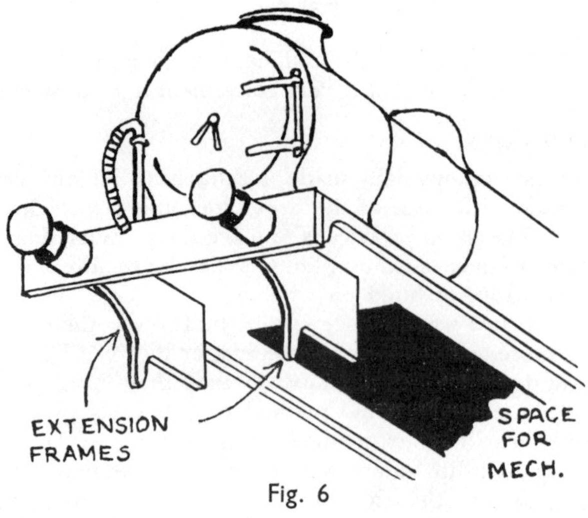

Fig. 6

by filing until a good fit is obtained. In certain cases it may be expedient to mount the extension-frames slightly closer together than the normal width of the mechanism frames in order to allow extra side movement for a bogie or pony truck. This little subterfuge is not likely to be noticed as parts such as brakes and sandboxes, as well as the wheels, will conceal it.

Six-coupled chassis by the author with Romford motor parts

The Romford motor bogie with flywheel

CHAPTER III

BUILDING MECHANISMS

WHEN the mechanism is to be built at home, the preliminary drawing-board work will be much the same as described in the last chapter, except that in this case we should first make accurate full-size drawings on tracing-paper of the motor—front and side views. We cannot start by laying a tracing of the mechanism on our prototype drawing since, at this stage, there is no complete mechanism but only a motor, and our first concern is to design a chassis which will fit both the superstructure of the proposed model and the motor. To accomplish this, the tracing of the motor should be pinned down on the prototype drawing so that it comes within the outline of the boiler and firebox, *not forgetting any snags which may lie concealed in the end elevation.* We can thus satisfy ourselves that the motor, including any projections such as brush-gear, can be housed within the shell of the superstructure, and we can now trace the outline of the main frames on to the tracing-paper drawing of the motor. The position of the motor must be adjusted as may be necessary to obtain the correct spacing between the worm and worm-wheel ; in other words, between the centre of the armature-shaft and the centre of the driving-axle. The positions of the axle-centres should also be transferred to the tracing, making sure that no part of the motor will get in the way of any of the axles or wheel-flanges. These successive stages are illustrated in Fig. 7. Diagram *A*, we may assume, is the tracing-paper drawing of the motor, and *B* is an outline drawing of the projected model. In *C* the motor drawing has been correctly placed on top of that of the locomotive. In *D* we have the motor drawing after the outline of the frames and the positions of the axles have been transferred to it. The outline of the frames is indicated by a thicker line, and it will be seen that part of them must be cut and filed away to enable the motor to be lowered to assume the correct position in relation to the worm-wheel on the driving-axle. We shall return to this subject later.

At this point, we must determine the position and shape of the cross-members, and decide where the screws for attaching the superstructure to the mechanism are to be located. If the model is intended for three-rail operation, the position of the insulated block for the current collectors must be settled also. In the particular case illustrated, it might be located as shown by the dotted line in Fig 7c.

The subject of current collection for two-rail and three-rail systems, can be considered at a later stage ; but, before dealing with the construction of the actual frame, something must be said concerning the form of gearing

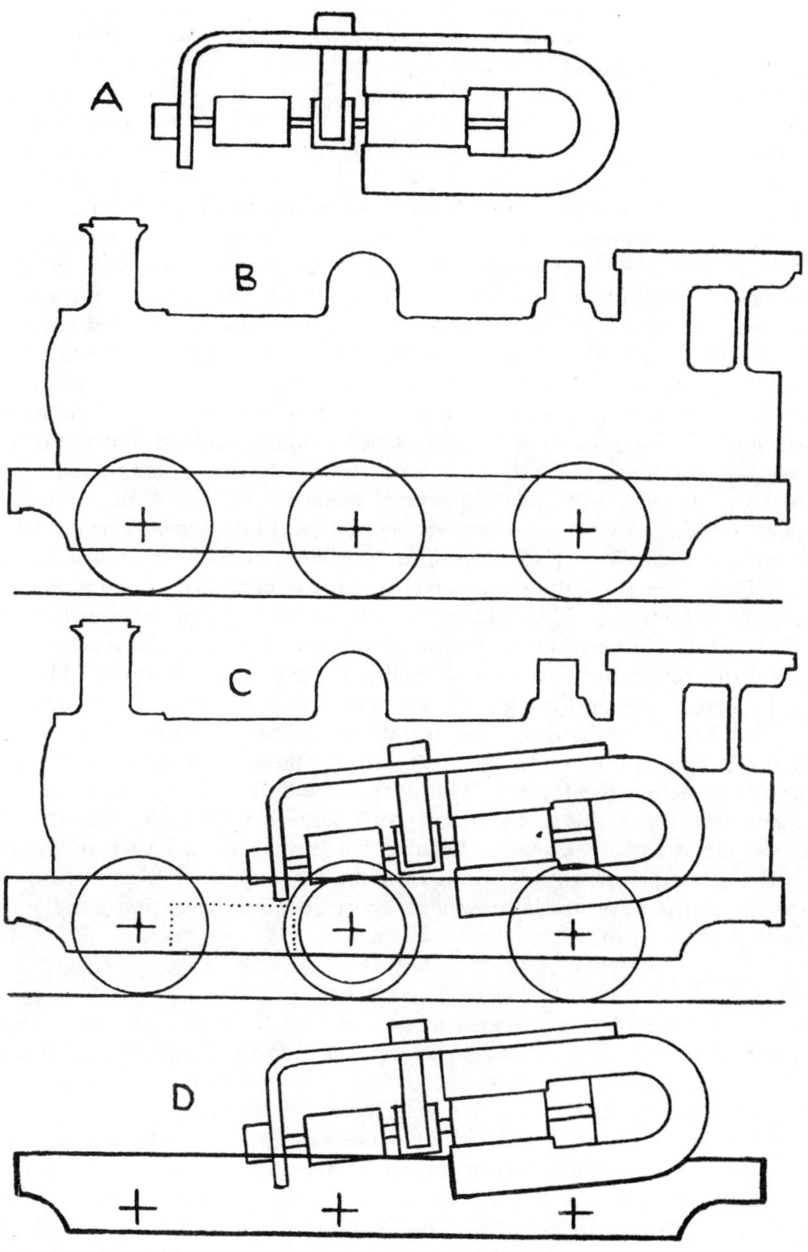

Fig. 7

between the armature-shaft and the driving-wheels. The worm and worm-wheel is by far the most widely used, at least in " OO " and " HO " gauges. The worm, which is usually of steel, is mounted on the armature-shaft, and the worm-wheel, of brass or bronze, is a force fit on the driving-axle. Suitable gears are usually supplied with the motor. The ratio of the gearing is very important to the good performance of the model. In the writer's opinion it should never be less than 30-to-1 in " OO " and " HO " gauges, which means that the motor must make thirty revolutions to turn the driving-wheels through one complete revolution. These little motors develop their power at such high speeds that if lower gearing, such as 15- or 20-to-1, were employed it would be difficult or impossible to make the model run at a reasonably slow speed, such as is needed for shunting and stopping in a realistic manner ; and its ability to start a heavy train would be impaired. A " OO "-gauge motor has been timed at over 14,000 revolutions per minute, running without load, and it seems that speeds of 6,000 r.p.m. may be regarded as quite normal. Gearing of 25-to-1 may be deemed just permissible provided that the driving-wheels are not more than 18-mm. diameter ; but the writer favours 35- or 40-to-1 in all cases, and has built several mechanisms incorporating a second stage of reduction by means of spur-gears. Multiple-stage gear-trains probably offer the most satisfactory solution of the problem, and are treated in Chapter XII. There are difficulties attached to the manufacture of worm-gears for very high reductions. The diameter of the worm-wheel is necessarily limited by that of the driving-wheels, and the higher the reduction (for a worm-wheel of given diameter) the lower the overall efficiency of the gearing. That is to say, the loss of power through friction increases with the ratio of reduction.

The Essar mechanism, illustrated elsewhere in this book, differs from others in employing spur gears and in having the armature shaft disposed transversely across the frame. The gear reduction ratio is 25 : 1. I said a moment ago that ratios of less than 30 : 1 should not be used but the Essar may be taken as an exception because the armature is larger in diameter than that on other motors, $\frac{3}{4}$ in. against the usual $\frac{1}{2}$ in. For this reason it is probable that it develops its power at lower revolutions so that a higher gear ratio should be in order.

THE FRAME

The method of chassis construction used by the writer combines several desirable features : correct alignment of the side-frames is secured automatically, and, with ordinary care, there is no risk of them being " in winding " with consequent binding and lack of parallelism of the axles. If the keeper-plate method, described later, is adopted, the wheels can be dropped out of the chassis at any time, without the necessity of removing one of them from each axle. For main frames the most usual and convenient material is $\frac{1}{2}$-in. by $\frac{1}{16}$-in. strip-brass, although nickel-silver would be better if obtainable.

When the outline of the side-frames and the positions of the axle-holes have been determined by the methods described in the last chapter, two pieces

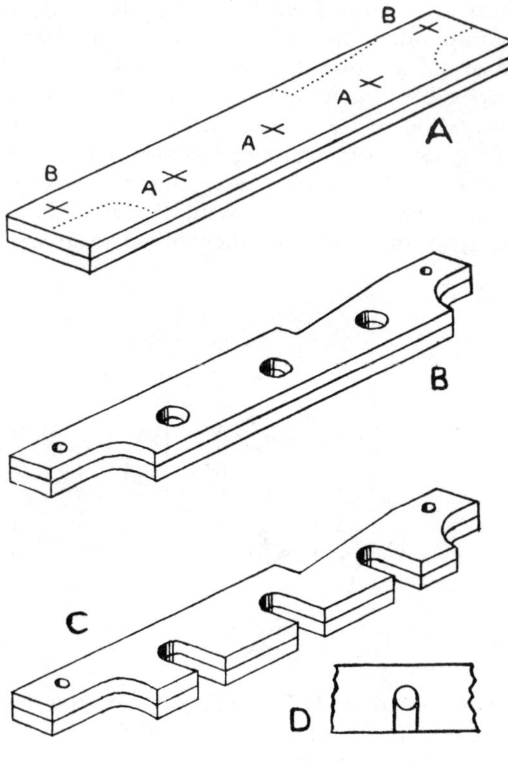

Fig. 8

of the material are cut to the required length, leaving a margin of about half a millimetre for trimming. To ensure that they are identical in length they should be clamped together in the vice while the ends are squared up with a file. The frame outline, and the centres for all holes which are to be drilled, are transferred to one of them from the drawing, with a steel rule and scriber, and the centres for drilling popped with a small centre-punch. It is very important that all axle-holes should be dead in line, and to ensure this a line should be scribed with a steel straight-edge parallel to one of the edges of the frame member, and long enough to include all the axle-holes. Next, the two frames should be soldered together round the edges so that subsequent cutting and drilling operations can be performed on both at once. It is essential that they should be in perfect alignment ; they should be securely clamped together while the soldering iron is applied. With care, a strong office paper-clip can be made to serve as a clamp, but it is more satisfactory to use a vice. The frames should be protected against the jaws by strips of card, or thin wood (Fig. 9). This serves a double purpose : to protect the frames against abrasion, and to stop the heat of the iron from being rapidly dissipated into the vice. If this precaution is omitted the heat will be drawn away from the place where it is wanted so quickly that the solder will refuse to melt properly, and it will be all but impossible to unite the frames securely. The writer has known them to break apart while drilling, due to defective soldering, at the moment when the point of the drill was breaking through out of one into the other. It is not necessary to solder the two frames together all round the edges ; if they are securely joined at a few points that should be enough. It is not easy to solder two pieces of $\frac{1}{16}$-in. thick brass together with an ordinary domestic electric

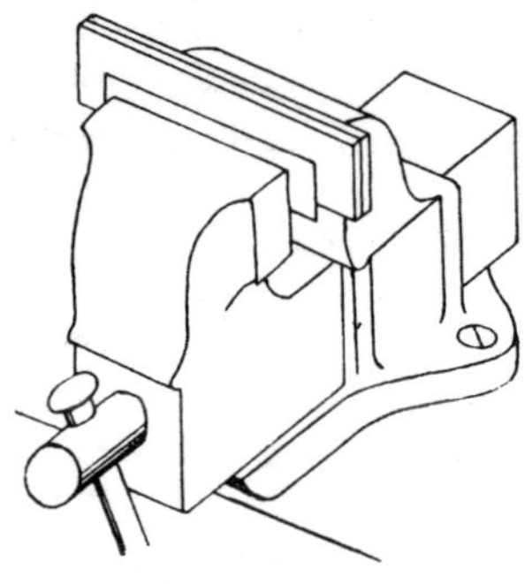

Fig. 9

soldering iron ; it hardly provides enough heat for this bulk of metal. I nickel-silver is used, matters will not be quite so difficult, for this metal does not dissipate heat so rapidly as brass. It may be preferable to use a large copper bit heated over a gas-ring, a blowlamp or a bunsen burner. Or a small blow-lamp or bunsen may be used to supplement the heat of the electric iron by allowing the flame to play on a portion of the work which is not covered by the vice jaws or other clamp. It will be seen that a small highly-concentrated flame is required. If a small electric iron is used alone, it may be necessary to hold it in contact with the work for as long as two or three minutes before the material will be hot enough for the solder to run freely. The iron should be held quite still in one place and not moved about, and it is advisable to add a little flux from time to time during such protracted operations.

After soldering, the appearance of the job should be something like Fig. 8A, which represents the frames for an 0-6-0 type loco. The parts indicated by dotted lines are to be cut and filed away. Note the wedge-shaped portion at the top which must be removed in order to lower the motor so that the worm can mesh with the worm-wheel. The holes marked *AAA* are for the axles, and *BB* are for cross-members to hold the side-frames together. And there may be other holes for various purposes : screws to hold in place a block of insulation material upon which to mount current collectors, for example, or for dummy brake gear or cylinders.

DRILLING THE FRAMES

If the holes for the axles, etc., can be drilled on a lathe or bench drill, there will be no difficulty about keeping the drill perpendicular to the work ; but if it must be done with an ordinary hand-drill, the important thing is that it should be held upright so that the holes in the two frames will be in line. It is not easy to hold a hand-drill perfectly vertical, and it is advisable to obtain the help of an assistant to keep a check and to warn the worker if the tool is allowed to stray from its proper position. This applies to the holes marked *B* in Fig. 8 quite as much as to the axle-holes, because if they are out of true there will be a slight tendency for the frames to be thrown out of alignment,

The axles should be a close fit in their bearing-holes ; they must turn. freely and without the least suspicion of binding, but there should be no trace of side-play. Up and down play is a different matter and is considered later. " OO "-gauge driving-wheels are usually mounted on axles ⅛ in. diameter ; if a ⅛-in. drill is used for the holes they should be just the right size, and require no adjustment. Ordinary twist-drills usually produce a hole two or three thousandths of an inch larger than their nominal size, and this will be just enough to give the required clearance. If, by any chance, the axles are a shade tight in the holes, they can be opened out *very cautiously* with a broach. This tool, unfortunately, produces a slightly conical hole, and to neutralise this as far as possible it should be worked alternately from both sides. It is recommended that the holes *BB* in Fig. 8 be drilled size 55, the tapping size for 10-B.A., for the screws which will be used later in the assembly of the frames.

THE " KEEPER-PLATE " METHOD OF FRAME ASSEMBLY

If the reader wishes, he can use the side-frames just as they are. When fitting the wheels to the chassis, he will have to remove one of them from each axle, push the axles through the appropriate holes in the chassis, and replace the wheels. Many workers think it is more satisfactory to hold the axles in the frame by what is usually called a keeper-plate, which is simply a strip of brass, or other metal, bolted to the underside of the chassis. This is most conveniently done by means of two 10-B.A. screws which enter holes drilled and tapped in the cross-members. It involves a little extra trouble but the advantage is that if it should be necessary to remove the wheels for any reason they can be slipped out from below by the quick and simple expedient of removing the two screws and dropping the keeper-plate. There is no need to disturb the fitting of the wheels on the axles, or to remove the connecting-rods.

This method has obvious advantages if it is proposed to undertake any work of an experimental nature, as regards springing or gearing, for example. The first procedure is to cut away the metal between the axle-holes and the lower edges of the frames, as in Fig. 8C. This should be done with a miniature hacksaw or a piercing-saw. Scribe where the cuts are to be made, Fig. 8D, and be careful to keep the cuts well inside these lines. The slots thus formed should be opened up to the marked lines with a jeweller's flat file and finished with a strip of the finest emery-cloth folded over a thin piece of metal or wood.

The axles should be tested in the slots frequently while filing ; when the work has been finished, they should slide in the slots quite freely but without the least suspicion of side-play. The frames should now resemble Fig. 8C, and if everything has been done which is common to both, it is time to unsolder them. This is best done with a gas-flame or blow lamp. It is not very practicable to attempt it with a soldering-iron, unless a very large one is available. Loop a piece of wire through one of the holes and hold them in the flame ; they will separate in a few seconds. Have an old screwdriver or a strip of metal handy to keep them apart while they cool as otherwise they may stick together again.

But before separating them consider carefully whether any more holes—common to both frames—are wanted for any purpose. One should have settled before this how the current collectors, for example, are to be mounted, and what form of fixing they will require. Although, if the keeper-plate form of construction is to be used, it may be more convenient to mount the collectors on this part, rather than on the side-frames.

THE CROSS-MEMBERS

After they have been separated the side-frames should be cleaned up with emery-cloth, and we are ready to consider the cross-members by which they are to be joined together. The outside width of the frames of a 16.5-mm. gauge model should be about half-an-inch, or 12.5-mm., and since we usually make them of strip material $\frac{1}{16}$ in. thick, the side-frames together will account for $\frac{1}{8}$ in. The cross-members then must have a width of about $\frac{3}{8}$ in. to make up the total of $\frac{1}{2}$ in. If the model is for 18-mm. gauge track, the overall width should be increased to 14- or 15-mm. by using slightly wider cross-members.

As already stated, the holes *BB* are for the 10-B.A. screws which will hold the side-frames together until we are ready to solder everything up. It may be noted, however, that if the frames are well and securely assembled with screws it is not absolutely necessary that solder should be used. In one of our side-frames the holes *BB* should be tapped 10-B.A., taking care that the tap goes through at right-angles and does not wander to one side. In the other side-frame, the hole should be opened out with a No. 50 drill, to clear the screw, and countersunk so that the head will be flush with the outside surface of the frame. As a matter of fact, it is preferable to tap both frames together before they are unsoldered, because the extra thickness will render it easier to keep the tap perpendicular. One of them is subsequently opened out as described above. The cross-members can take alternative forms : they can be lengths of $\frac{1}{8}$ in. or $\frac{3}{16}$-in. outside diameter brass tube, as in Fig. 10A and B, carefully squared off at the ends by facing in a lathe if possible, or they can be cut and drilled from square or rectangular section brass and combined with the lugs which must be provided to join the chassis to the superstructure, as in Fig. 10C. The size of the holes through them for the 10-B.A. holding screws is not critical, *provided they allow considerable clearance to the screws.* A drill about 3/32 in. or 40 Morse might be used. The importance of this will be clear from Fig. 10E, where a possible fault has been much exaggerated for clarity.

A
TUBE
TUBE
B
HOLE FOR FIXING SCREW
TO SUPERSTRUCTURE
C
D
SCREWHOLE
FOR KEEPER
PLATE
E
F
G

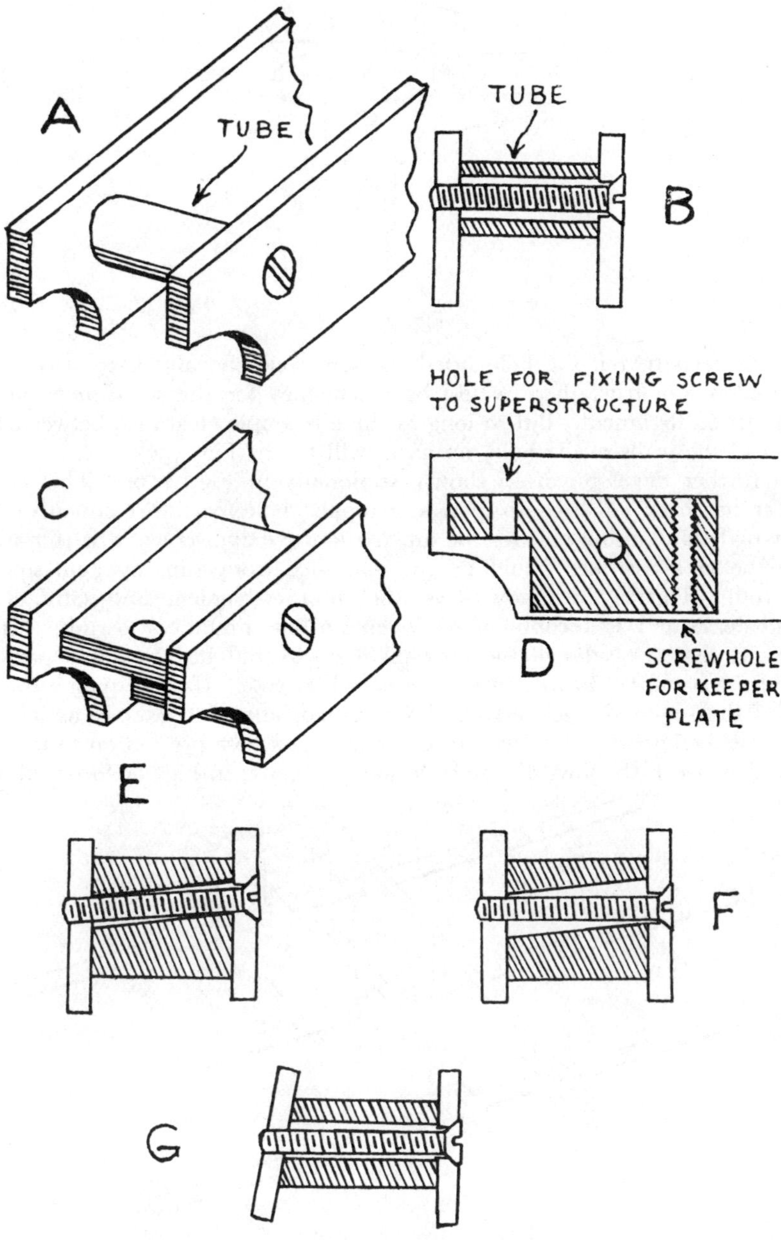

Fig. 10

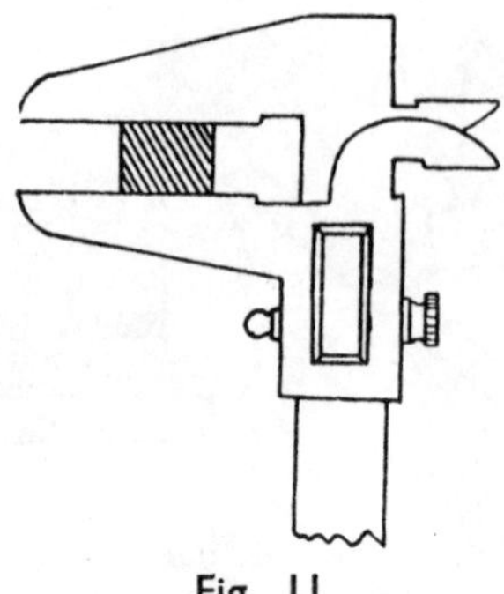

Fig. 11

It will be seen that if the hole fitted the screw closely, and if the drill had wandered out of true, there would be a tendency for the side-frames to be pulled out of alignment. But so long as there is ample clearance between the screw and the walls of the hole, no harm will result (Fig. 10F).

A further development is shown sectionally in Fig. 10D. The cross-member has been enlarged to include a tapped hole for the retention of the keeper-plate, and also a hole for the superstructure fixing-screw. For 16.5-mm. gauge the cross-member could be cut and filed from $\frac{3}{8}$-in. by $\frac{3}{8}$-in. square brass rod. This is, in many ways, the most convenient and satisfactory arrangement, and is recommended whenever circumstances permit. It is important that the sides of the cross-members should be absolutely parallel or the frames will be drawn out of true as in Fig. 10G. If good quality drawn brass of the required thickness can be obtained, and used exactly as it is, it will be perfectly true ; but even in this case it is a wise precaution to test the material between the jaws of a reliable slide-gauge, as in Fig. 11 to reveal any

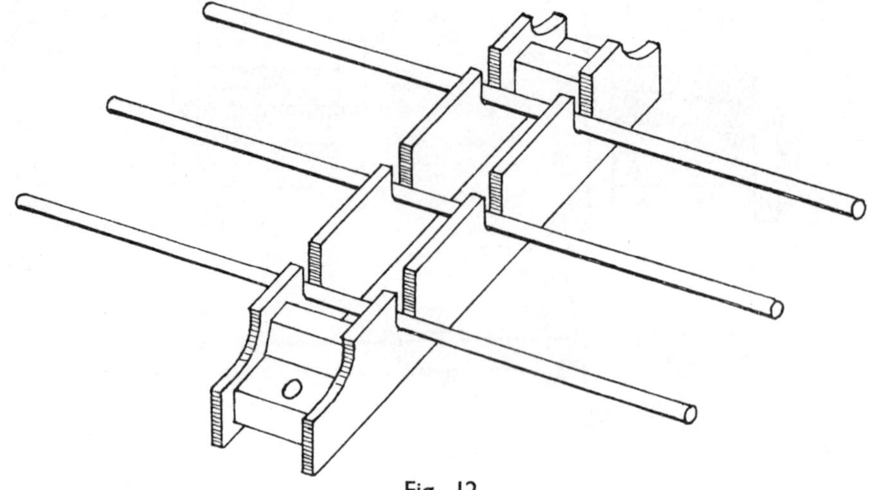

Fig. 12

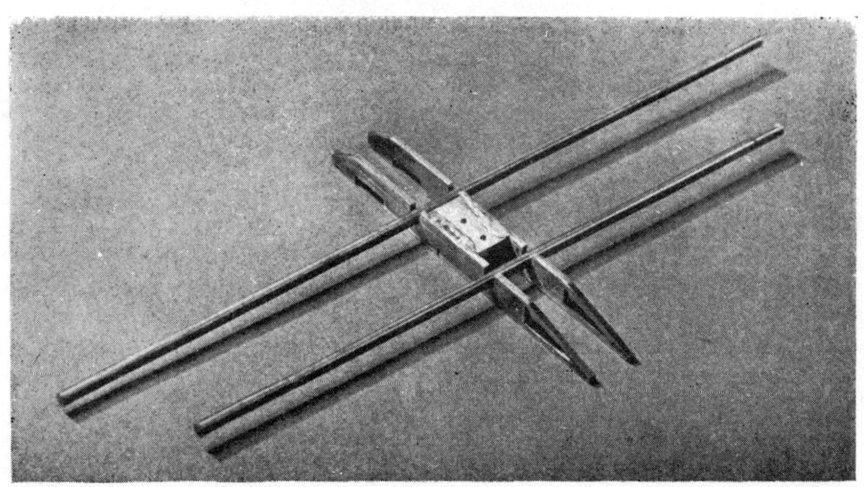

Testing a chassis for parallelism of the axles by means of rods as in Fig. 12. The shadows reveal that the near rod is true and that the far one is " up " at the right end

high spots which might be present. If thicker material must be filed down by hand, it should be tested very carefully with the slide-gauge, both vertically and horizontally.

The frames are assembled by passing the 10-B.A. screws through the holes which have been opened out to clearance size in one of the side-frames, then passing the cross-members over the screws, and finally screwing on the other side-frame. Before passing the assembly as ready for soldering, it should be tested for parallelism. Place the frame upside down on a sheet of plate-glass, or other flat surface. If the frames are not in contact with the flat surface at all points—if they can be made to rock, however slightly, in a diagonal direction when touched with the finger—the frames are not properly lined up ; the fault should be corrected by partly releasing one of the fixing-screws and coaxing the side-frames until they are truly parallel and touch the flat surface at all points.

The next test is to establish that the axles will be truly parallel. For this, lay pieces of dead straight metal rod in the axle-holes so that they project an equal distance on each side as in Fig 12. If the holes have not been slotted and opened for keeper-plate fitting, the procedure will be exactly the same except that the rods will be pushed through the holes instead of being laid in them as shown in the photograph. If all is well, and the holes have been drilled true, the rods should lie parallel to one another and to the flat surface. The best material for the purpose is silver-steel rod of a size which is just a comfortable fit in the holes. Knitting-needles or hand-drawn brass may be used but should be tested for straightness. A convenient length for " OO " gauge is about 6 in., for " O " gauge about 10 in. If the rods do not lie parallel, and it is known that the frames are in alignment, then the fault must be due to the holes having been incorrectly drilled : the drill was not perpendicular. If this unfortunate state of affairs should arise the worker must use his discretion as to whether it is practicable to correct the trouble by cautious filing of one or more of the axle-holes with a small round file, followed by the finest grade of emery, or whether a new pair of frames should be cut. The latter course may well prove to be most satisfactory in the long run. The truing up of the frames, needless to say, should be left until one is ready to solder the parts together (assuming that solder is to be used). If anything remains to be done to them—any filing or drilling—it should be done first, in order to avoid any possibility that they might get out of alignment again, through the unintentional application of pressure in some way, before being soldered.

When soldering up the frames, some additional source of heat to supplement the iron, will make the work easier and quicker. If the reader has a large copper bit, or a so-called "industrial" electric iron, no additional source of heat may be necessary ; failing that, a bunsen, or almost anything, will help.

When the soldering is complete, we can try the wheels temporarily in place, and test the chassis on a length of level track to see that all the wheels run freely, and that they are all in contact with the track.

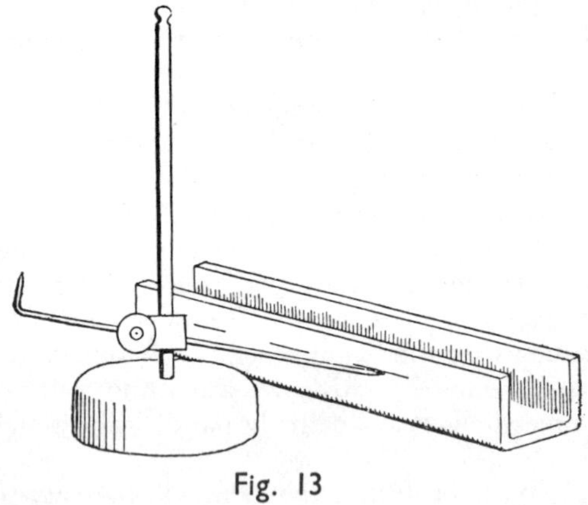

Fig. 13

MAKING CHASSIS FROM CHANNEL-SECTION BRASS

Some people like to make "OO" and "HO" gauge chassis from ½-in. by ½-in. drawn brass channel-section, so we may pause to consider the merits of this method. It possesses the slight advantage that the frames are already aligned at the correct distance apart without the need for separate cross-members. The writer, however, hesitates to recommend it, at least for the beginner, although it is quite reliable for commercial production when specially-made drilling jigs are available. The disadvantage, from the amateur's point of view, is that it is more difficult to locate the axle-holes with the necessary degree of accuracy to bring the axles into perfect alignment. If this type of frame is used, the method of locating the axle-holes illustrated in Fig. 13 provides the best safeguard. The frame is placed on a flat surface—such as a sheet of plate-glass. The height of the axle-holes is then established with a rigid height-gauge. By this means the worker is assured that all the holes will be on a line parallel with the top surface of the frame, and, therefore, that the superstructure will sit level. It is assumed, of course, that the subsequent centre-popping and drilling is very carefully carried out. To establish the positions of the holes on the horizontal line, one end of the frame should be filed dead true. Then, measuring always from this prepared end, the positions of the axles can be scribed on the chassis with a steel rule. The holes are then drilled and the work tested for accuracy as described above.

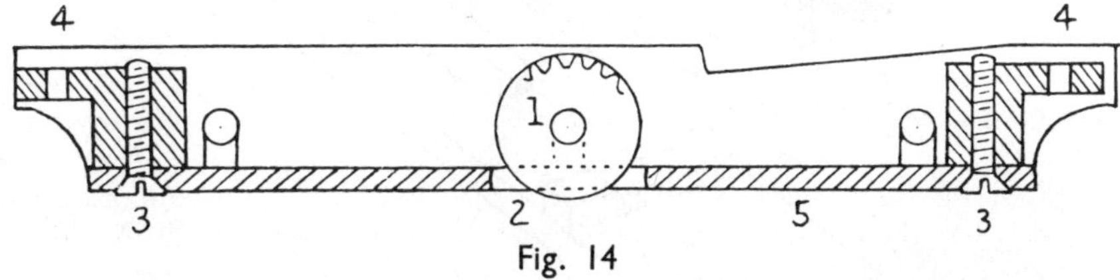

Fig. 14

When making frames from channel-section it is a very wise precaution to drill the axle holes, in the first instance, to a smaller size than the final one. If, for example, the axle holes are to be $\frac{1}{8}$ in. diameter use a 3/32 in. drill. At this stage check for parallelism by the method shown in Fig. 12, using rods of appropriate diameter for the holes. If it is found that the holes lie parallel, both vertically and horizontally, well and good; you can proceed to drill out to the final size. If they are not, there is a chance of filing one or more of them to one side, with a rat-tail file, so that the final drill will find a new centre and thus secure better alignment. Naturally it is a tricky business for the inexperienced, but in any case the result should be better than if no adjustment had been made and, even if the first attempt is not successful, this is a branch of the art of fitting in which it is worth the modeller's while to make himself proficient.

KEEPER-PLATES

If this method of assembly is to be used,* we may next consider the keeper-plate itself, which is to hold the wheels in the frame. It is quite a simply fitting, and for " OO " and " HO " gauges can usually be made of $\frac{1}{2}$-in. be $\frac{1}{16}$-in. strip brass. The length must be rather more than the rigid wheelbase of the locomotive, to cover all the axle slots and also the tapped holes for the fixing screws which are to secure the keeper-plate to the frame. It will be necessary to cut a hole in the keeper-plate below the driving-axle to clear the worm-wheel, as shown in Fig. 14. This is most easily done by drilling two

* See page 19.

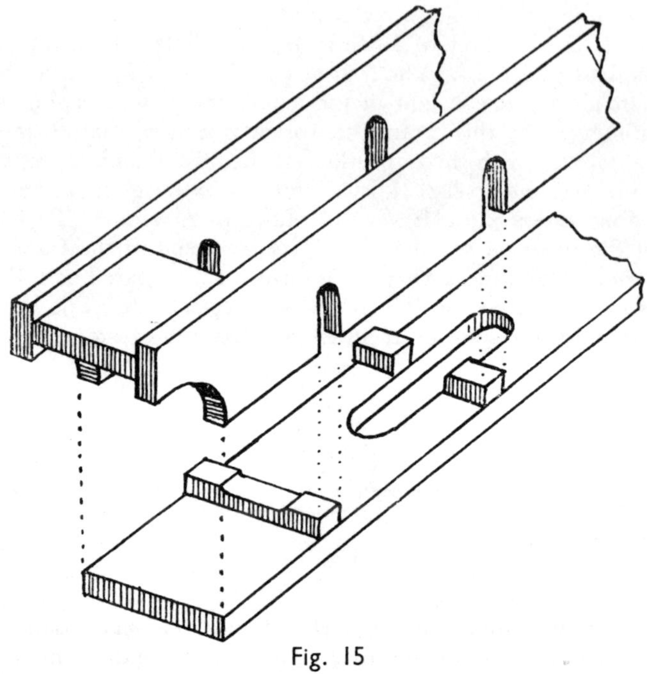

Fig. 15

$\frac{1}{8}$-in. holes in the centre-line of the plate and uniting them with a piercing-saw. In this drawing, 1 is the worm-wheel, 2 is the slot to clear it, 33 are the screws (preferably 10-B.A.) which secure the keeper-plate in position.

It will be noted that in Fig. 14 the axles are represented as being free to move up and down to the full extent of the depth of the slotted axle-holes. If the axles are to be sprung, as discussed in a later section, this movement may not be excessive, except, of course, for the driving-axle, which cannot be sprung or permitted to have any vertical play since it must be in mesh with the worm. For axles which are not to be sprung, it is necessary to solder little strips of metal to the keeper-plate to take up this movement, and hold the axles at the top of their bearings. This is shown in Fig. 15. It is advisable to make these packing-pieces slightly " high " to start with, and to adjust by filing, after they have been soldered in place, until the axles turn freely.

It is a good idea to fit a little gear-box under the worm-wheel slot. It is very easily made from thin sheet metal, soldered in place, and helps to exclude dirt from the gears and to retain lubricant.

MOUNTING THE MOTOR IN THE FRAME

It will be clear from the illustrations that part of the side-frames must be cut away in order to lower the forward end of the motor so as to bring the worm and worm-wheel into mesh. This may cause the beginner some

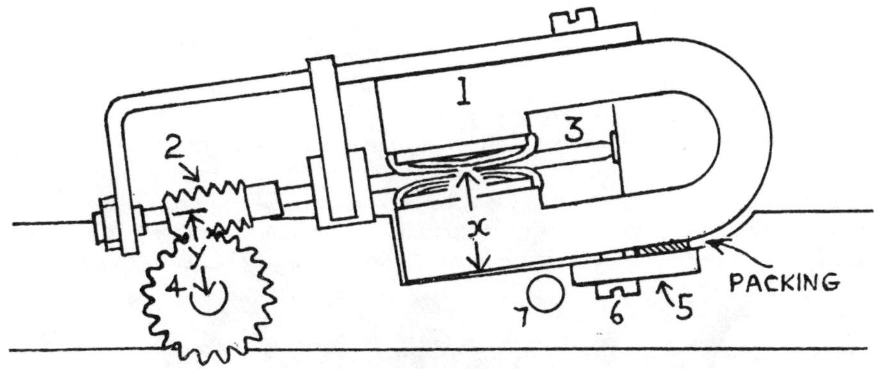

Fig. 16

perplexity. How is he to establish, with the necessary degree of accuracy, what amount of the frames must be cut away to bring the motor shaft to the required position? It may as well be said at once that it is extremely difficult to accomplish this with such accuracy as to render any subsequent fine adjustment unnecessary. Since the meshing of the worm and worm-wheel is very critical, it is possible that, to obtain the final fine adjustment, it may be necessary to insert a packing-piece or " shim " of thin sheet metal between the magnet and the frame, finding by trial and error the correct thickness to allow the necessary play between the gears. This is shown, somewhat exaggerated, in Fig. 16. Naturally, the constructor should endeavour by careful work to avoid the need for such makeshift methods. Certain motors have been marketed in the United States with some form of adjusting screw to facilitate the accurate meshing of the gears, and it is possible that, by the time this book is in print, British units with a similar refinement may be available.

Naturally, the exact arrangement will be governed to some extent by the particular motor used, but the general procedure suggested here will hold good in most cases. In Fig. 16, 1 is the permanent magnet; 2 is the worm and 3 is the armature-shaft ; 4 is the worm-wheel mounted on the driving-axle ; 5 is a $\frac{1}{16}$-in. thick metal plate soldered between the frames and drilled for the screw, 6, which secures the motor to the chassis. There is a hole through the magnet, usually tapped 6-B.A., and a suitable fixing-screw is supplied with the motor.

The reader may be uncertain how to mark and cut the side-frames for the reception of the motor so that the minimum of adjustment will be needed when the parts are assembled. The two measurements which fix the position of the motor in relation to the frame and worm-wheel are indicated in Fig. 16 by *x* and *y*. The first is the distance from the lower edge of the magnet to the centre-line of the armature-shaft. This is easily obtained, for it will be evident that it is half the height of the magnet. One has only to measure this and divide by two, and the edge of the side-frames, where the motor rests on them, will be parallel with the armature-shaft. Thus we have two useful guides to use in setting out the position of the motor. The other measurement, *y*, is the more difficult to establish with accuracy. Actually, the distance from the centre of the armature-shaft to the centre of the axle should be half the sum of the pitch diameters of the worm and worm-wheel ; or, to put it in a slightly different form, the pitch radius of the one gear plus the pitch radius of the other.

Most readers probably understand the term pitch diameter, but it may be as well to append an explanation for the benefit of beginners. In Fig. 17A the broken lines indicate approximately the pitch diameters of the two gears. It will be seen that they are located about half-way between the summits

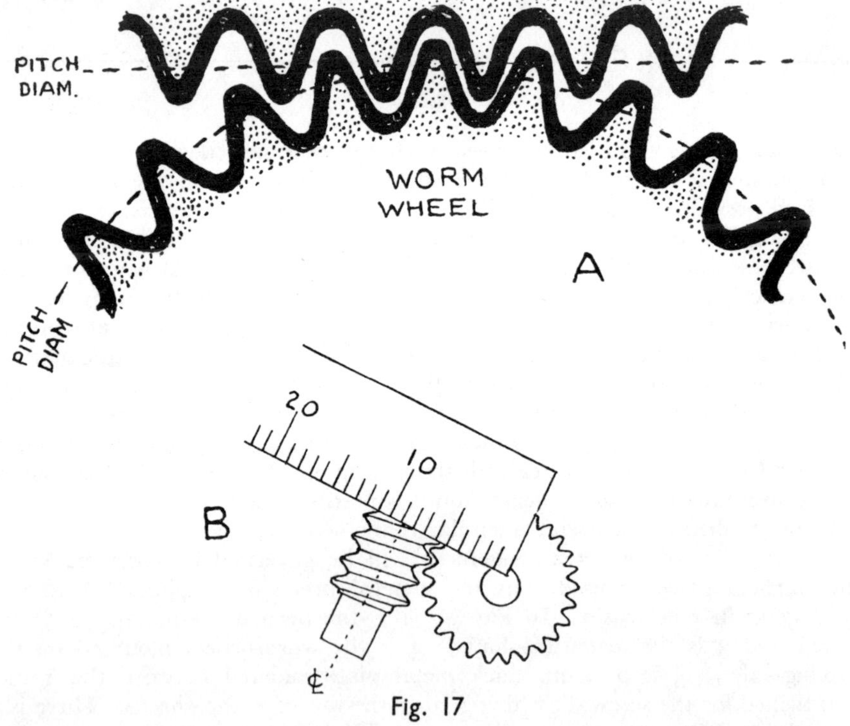

Fig. 17

of the teeth and the valleys between them. The reader can hardly expect to obtain these with theoretical accuracy with the facilities for measurement which are likely to be available, but by measuring the outside diameter of the gears with a slide-gauge and the diameter at the base of the teeth with a steel rule, and taking the average of the two, he should be able to arrive at the pitch diameter with sufficient accuracy for practical purposes. Another method, which should be used to provide a check, is to lay the two gears on a flat surface so that the teeth engage but do not quite " bottom." A magnifying glass will be necessary to do this properly. Now measure as accurately as possible from the centre of one gear to the centre of the other. The result will be our measure-

Marking off the portion of the main frames to be cut away with the motor, or, as here, the magnet and armature located so that the worm meshes with the wormwheel. Note the packing used to raise the armature to the same level as the wormwheel

ment *y*. This is fairly simple with a pair of spur gears, but when a worm and wheel are being measured the worm-wheel must be packed up to bring it to the centre-line of the worm, Fig. 17B.

When setting out on paper the relative positions of the motor and frame, it is good practice to work to twice full-size by doubling all measurements. This gives more room to see clearly what one is doing, and should have the

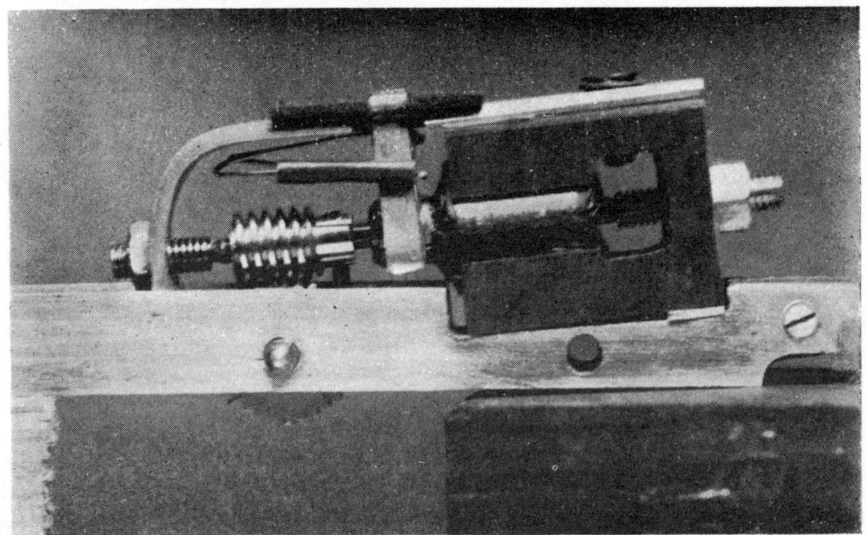

The motor mounted on the chassis, before fitting of driving wheels. Note the packing under rear end of magnet to secure correct mesh

effect of halving any errors. We thus arrive at a diagram something like Fig. 16, from which the line that indicates the part of the frames to be cut away can be transferred to the metal. In the first place, cut just above the marked line to leave a margin for adjustment by trial and error after the frames have been assembled and the worm-wheel is in place. The motor can then be " offered " and the frame gradually filed down until correct mesh is obtained.

The upper photograph opposite illustrates a method of locating the motor which eliminates all calculation and drawing-board work, and gives good results if used with care. It can be used alone or to apply a check to the method described in the preceding paragraphs. The frames, before being separated, are laid on the bench, or on an odd piece of wood. The driving-axle with the worm-wheel fitted is placed in the axle-hole, the projecting end of the axle being accommodated in a hole drilled in the wood support. The motor, or the magnet and armature as shown in the photograph (if this unit has not yet been completed) is placed and firmly held on the frame so that the worm meshes correctly with the wheel. Then, without allowing the motor to move, its position is marked with the point of a scriber on the frame. This will indicate the part which is to be cut away.

FLYWHEEL DRIVE

The addition of a flywheel improves the running of a model locomotive very much, particularly the starting and stopping. When a flywheel is fitted it becomes necessary to learn stopping distances and to cut off the power some distance before the point where the locomotive is required to stop, as on a real train. It is a pity that on many models it seems all but impossible to find space for this excellent addition. It is quite practicable, however, on most

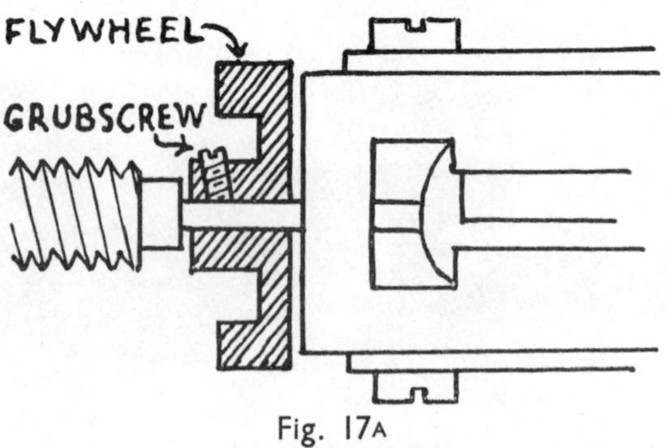

Fig. 17A

large boilered locomotives and on some with side tanks. Several of the motors which are illustrated in this book can be fitted with flywheels, but it may be necessary to arrange for the motor to be supplied with a slightly longer shaft than is usual. The constructor who has a reasonably accurate lathe can make up a flywheel for himself from brass rod. It should be attached to the shaft by means of a grub-screw through a central boss as in Fig. 17A. It should be

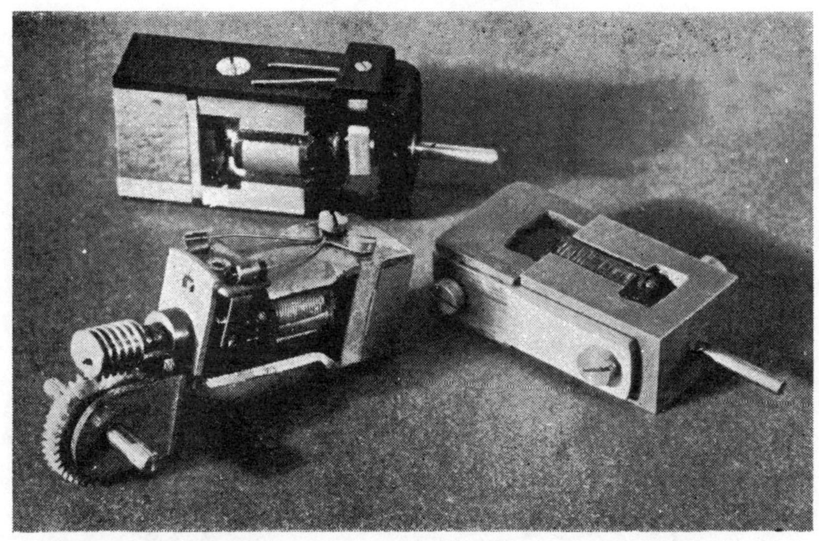

A group of representative motors for the miniature scales. Top : Romford Phantom. Left: Mellor Gem X5. Right : Hambling.

A popular commercial product for " OO " gauge, the Gnat locomotive with diecast body and Essar spur gear driven motor which is here shown removed from the body

as thick as space permits at the periphery; the thickness nearer the centre is of no importance.

On K's Mark I and Mark II motors the shaft projects beyond the frame at both ends and it is, therefore, possible to fit a flywheel at the far end from the wormgear. Hence it may be housed in the cab, where there is plenty of space and it is out of the way.

The only rule I know governing the diameter of a flywheel is that it should be as large as possible.

CURRENT COLLECTORS

We have now almost completed the chassis part of the model, except for current collectors—which are necessary in some form on two-rail as well as three-rail models.

The reader is probably aware that collectors, whether two-rail or three-rail, must be electrically insulated from the frame, and all metal parts of the model,

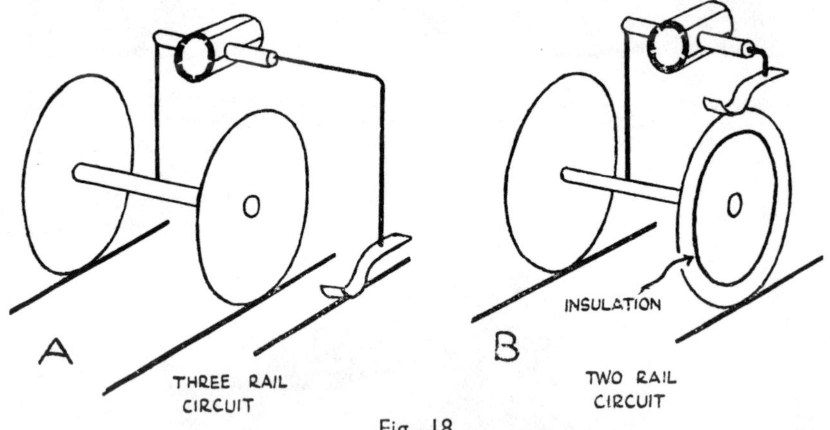

Fig. 18

by means of fibre, ebonite, mica, wood, or other non-conducting material, and connected to one brush of the commutator, which must, of course, itself be insulated. The wire used for this connection should be of large enough gauge to carry the maximum carrent the motor will take. Ordinary bell-wire may be used, but copper wire enclosed in a " Systoflex " sleeve (obtainable from wireless shops) makes a neater job. If the wire is soldered direct to the brush itself, and not to a brush-holder, fine flex should be used so as not to impede the free movement of the brush. The circuit for three-rail is shown in Fig. 18A. That for two-rail is given in Fig. 18B. The so-called " return " path of the current is usually by way of the motor, the frame of the locomotive, the axles and wheels to the running-rails. There is a weakness in this procedure, however ; the writer believes that poor running is often due to the film of oil, which should always be present between the axles and bearings, acting as an insulator and increasing the total resistance of the circuit. It is suggested that when possible a separate collector should be fitted on the "return"* side. It may assume much the same form as the two-rail collectors described later : a light phosphor-bronze or steel wire spring, bearing against the tread of the wheel, or, if preferred, against the running-rail. The latter may be thought preferable from an electrical point of view, as it has the effect of by-passing a possible source of poor contact and inefficiency, namely the contact between the treads of the wheels and through the bearings to the frame. It seems certain that poor running is sometimes due to the current having to get past the semi-insulating film of oil in the wheel bearings. Fig. 19 shows a collector of this type.

Fig. 20 shows several forms of third-rail current collector. The simplest arrangement, *A*, consists of a strip of phosphor-bronze about 0.012 in. thick and $\frac{3}{8}$ in. or $\frac{7}{16}$ in. wide, with soldered transverse shoes of nickel-silver or brass wire. The length of the phosphor-bronze strip must be determined to suit the chassis, so that the collectors will not foul the wheels or other parts. It is best to arrange matters so that the collectors are outside the coupled wheelbase where they cannot get in the way of the coupling-rods. The overall length of the collector shoes should be about 38 mm. for 16.5-mm. gauge, and it will be noted that the tips are bent upwards so that they can ride up on the third-rail without catching when approaching it obliquely as occurs when the locomotive is traversing points.

The weakness of this arrangement is that sometimes, when the collector is raised on one side by the third-rail, it inclines downwards on the other and

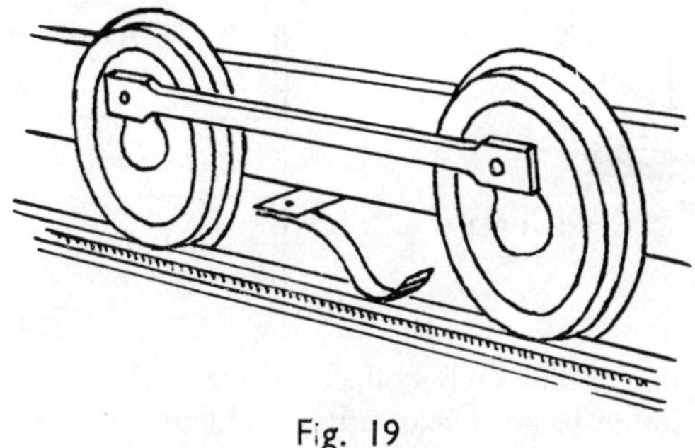

Fig. 19

touches the running-rail as in *B*, the result being, of course, a short circuit. This can be overcome by dividing the shoe and spring with a fine saw, Fig. 20 *C* and *D*, so as to allow independent movement. Do not attempt to do it with tinsnips as this will distort the metal hopelessly ; lay the collector flat on a waste piece of wood and go through with a miniature hacksaw or piercing-saw, cutting the wood at the same time.

* The use of this term is rather arbitrary since, with permanent-magnet motors, the direction of flow of the current changes when the direction of travel of the locomotive is reversed Hence the "way out" side of the circuit becomes the "way in."

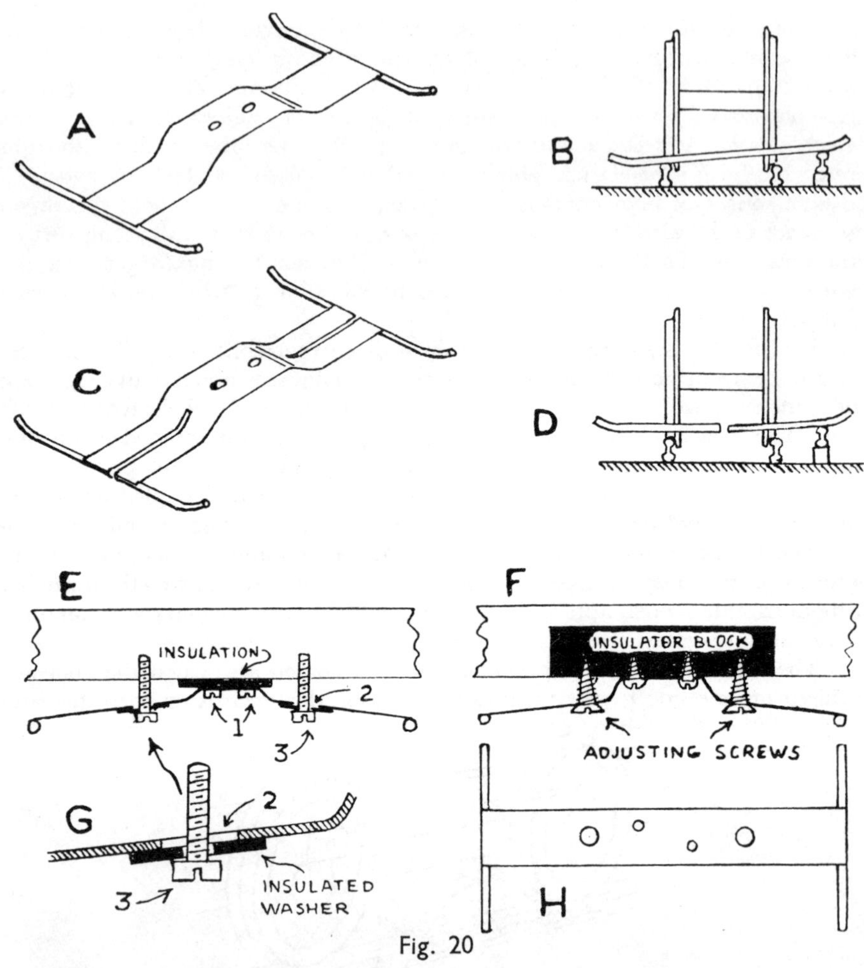

Fig. 20

The fact remains that such collectors are rather difficult and fiddling things to set, and liable to get out of adjustment in use. Further, no means of regulating the tension of the collector on the third-rail is provided, and this may prove to be hardly sufficient for good electrical contact. The adjustment must be made by careful bending with pliers or with the fingers.

Fig. 20E shows a modification used by the writer. In this drawing, 1 are the screws by which the collector is attached to the locomotive frame (with, of course, adequate insulation) ; 2 are holes for adjusting screws, 3, which are secured into tapped holes in some convenient part of the frame. The holes, 2, must be large enough to ensure that the screws, 3, can never in any circumstances touch the collector spring and, before they are inserted in the frame, small washers of sheet fibre, card treated in shellac, or other insulating material, are slipped under the heads. This will be better understood from the enlarged detail, *G*. The collector shoes should be so adjusted that, if unrestrained by the screws, 3, they would drop just low enough to touch the running-rails. The screws are adjusted up until the shoes are lifted between 1/32 in. and $\frac{1}{16}$ in. clear of the running-rail. It will be seen that the adjustment can be made with greater accuracy and far less trouble than when it is necessary to rely on bending the phosphor-bronze spring : in use this form of collector has been found very satisfactory. The only weakness about it is that the screws, 3, are rather liable to work out of adjustment through vibration when the model is running. To cure this, the shanks of the screws should be sealed by painting with shellac varnish or oil paint where they emerge from their holes on the upper surface of the frame. This will prevent movement, and if it should be necessary to alter the adjustment at any time, it is the work of a moment to renew the broken seal with fresh varnish or paint.

Diagram *F* shows an essentially similar arrangement, except that the adjustment is provided by small wood-screws, which are inserted into a block of hard wood or fibre. In this case, there is no need for insulating washers, since the screws themselves are not in electrical contact with the frame. They are not likely to work out of adjustment, as wood or fibre exercises a more effective grip than can be expected with a metal screw in a tapped hole. Diagram *H* shows the collector in plan.

It seems advisable to insert a word of caution concerning the *bending* of hard sheet-metals such as phosphor-bronze. If the surface of such metal is examined closely it will be seen that it has a distinct grain, running in one direction and suggestive of the grain of wood. It has greater strength, and is

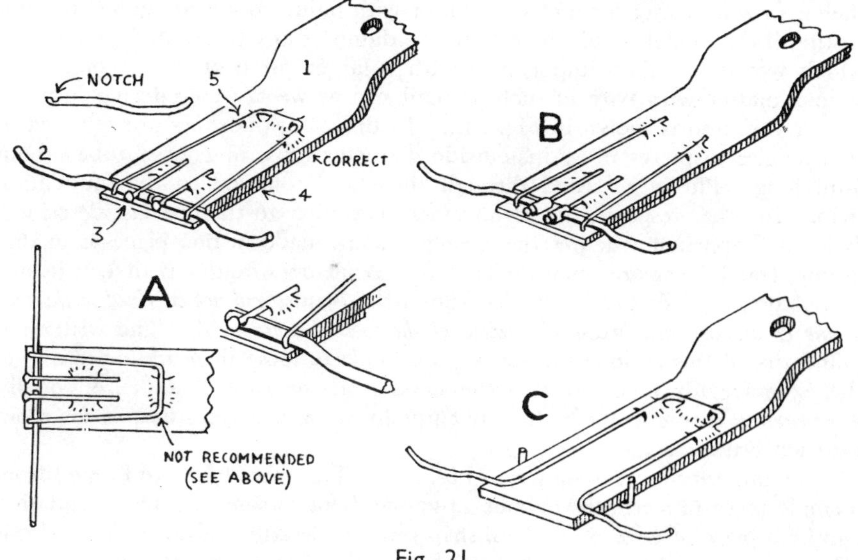

Fig. 21

less liable to break, if bent at right-angles to the direction of the grain than if bent with it (i.e. parallel to it). If bent to form a sharp corner in the same direction as the grain it will almost certainly fracture. Hence the direction of the grain should be ascertained before marking out, and the metal cut so that any sharp bends will be across the grain.

Fig. 21A shows a different type of collector in which the actual shoes are pivoted or hinged to a more rigid form of support and actuated by small separate springs. The foundation, 1, can be a piece of strip brass $\frac{3}{8}$-in. wide by 1/32-in. thick for "OO" gauge. The shoes, 2, are 18-gauge nickel-silver wire. They are bent as shown in the enlarged detail drawing and a notch is filed about half-way through and as close as possible to the inner end. This is to accommodate an ordinary pin, 3, which acts as a pivot and allows the shoe to move up and down with reasonable freedom but no suspicion of sloppiness. A piece of thin sheet brass, 4, is soldered underneath the foundation-strip so as to overlap the end by about $\frac{1}{16}$ in. This is to form a shoulder against which the shoe rests, and by which it is held from dropping beyond a predetermined point. The pin, 3, is soldered to the foundation so that its shank lies in the notch in the shoe, and with its head butting up against the shoe to prevent it slipping off. Lastly, the spring, 5, is bent from steel wire of about 26-gauge and soldered to the foundation to press down on the shoe. It will be noted that the ends of the springs are bent down at right-angles for about $\frac{1}{16}$ in. to check sideways movement of the shoes. A collector of this kind has the advantage that once it has been correctly adjusted there should never be any need to touch it afterwards.

Whenever steel wire is used for springs it is advisable to treat it with shellac or some other form of varnish, or with paint, to guard against possible rusting if the model should be exposed to damp at any time. A degree of rust which would be of no importance with a larger piece of metal could be a serious matter with wire of such a small size as we are considering here.

A variation is shown in Fig. 21B. In this case, the shoes are soldered at right-angles to pieces of $\frac{1}{16}$-in. outside diameter brass or copper tube, about $\frac{1}{8}$-in. long. Pins are passed through these and soldered to the foundation strip. In other respects, the arrangement is similar to the one last described. It is not important whether the springs, 5, are made in one piece as in diagrams *A* and *C*, or are separate as in *B*. What does matter is that, if in one piece, the solder should be carried round the bends, *and not confined to the base of the U as suggested in the plan view at the foot of diagram A*. The writer has found that if this is done the springs are liable to loose their resilience due to the excessive torsional stress at the bend. In the case of an exceptionally long spring, it might not matter, but usually we are rather cramped for room for such fittings.

Yet another form is shown in Fig. 21C. The shoes here are formed from a single piece of steel wire, about 24-gauge, bent as shown. The foundation can be a piece of $\frac{3}{8}$-in. × 1/32-in. strip brass as described above. The wire is soldered at the fulcrum end, but left free at the sides to provide the necessary

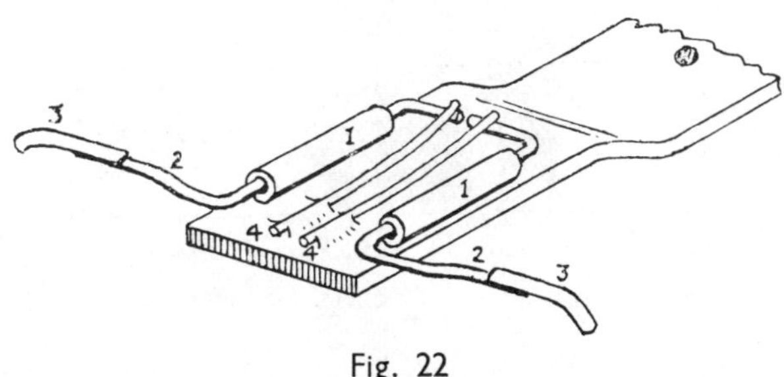

Fig. 22

movement when the shoe comes in contact with the third-rail. It is advisable to provide stops, as shown, which can be made from a single piece of wire, to check side movement. This collector is simple to make and inconspicuous, and should give very satisfactory results when correctly adjusted. There is no reason why short pieces of nickel wire should not be soldered to the steel wire shoes if it is thought that the former will provide better electrical contact.

The collector shown in Fig. 22 was described to the writer by Mr. Vacy-Ash. The writer has not tried it, but the idea is obviously so good that it would be a pity to omit it. It should be noted that the drawing, unlike the others to this section, shows the collector as it would appear if turned upside-down. Two pieces of $\frac{1}{16}$-in. outside diameter tube, 1, can be employed, or alternatively, a strip of thin sheet-metal can be bent to form a channel section. These are soldered to the foundation strip and should be as long as possible.

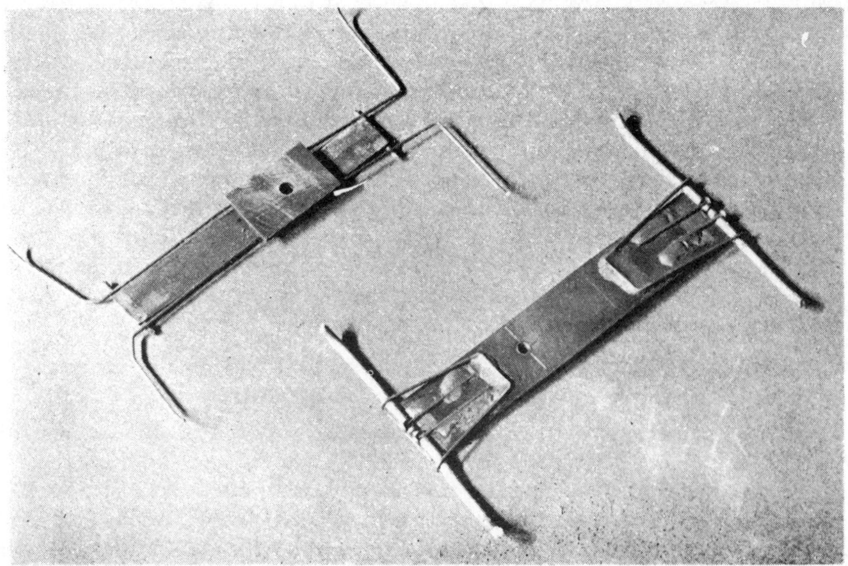

Two forms of third rail collector shown in Fig. 21. "C" is on left and "A" on right

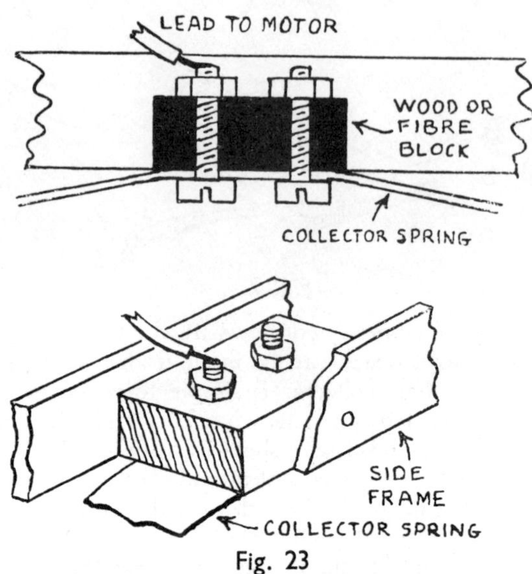

Fig. 23

Steel wire must be obtained for the shoes which is an easy fit within the tube or channel. Pieces of this material, 2, are passed through the tubes (with a drop of thin oil), and bent as indicated. The actual shoes can be nickel wire of a slightly larger gauge, as shown, or can be provided by the steel wire itself. Two pieces of steel wire, 4, or one bent to a U shape, are soldered to the foundation strip so as to exert pressure on the turned-in ends of the collectors. The action is obvious and should need no explanation. This might well prove to be the most satisfactory form of collector here described.

The four collectors last described are adjusted by bending the brass foundation-strip with long-nosed pliers so as to position the shoes at the correct height above rail level, normally about 3/64 in. This implies that if the third-rail is $\frac{1}{16}$ in. above running-rail level the shoe will be lifted about 1/64 in. Naturally, some attention should be paid to the tension of the springs which hold the shoes in contact with the third-rail. If the pressure is excessive the shoe will tend to lift the wheels off the rail, with consequent loss of adhesion. If too weak, imperfect electrical contact may result.

FITTING COLLECTORS TO THE LOCOMOTIVE

The method of fitting must depend on the design of the frame, the disposition of the various parts, motor, gears, and wheels, and also on whether a keeper-plate has been provided or not. When there is no keeper-plate, the best way, probably, is to instal a block of fibre or hard wood between the side-frames, as in Fig. 23. It can be held in place with Durofix and pins, or very small wood-screws, passed through holes in the side-frames. If pins are used they should be filed off flush on the outside ; if screws, the holes should be countersunk. The collector is attached to the block by two small screws as shown, or, alternatively, by one screw, plus a pin to prevent the collector turning sideways on the screw as on a pivot. The lead to the insulated brush of the motor can be soldered to the shank end of the fixing-screw, or to one of them when two are provided. It is advisable to solder the head of the screw which conveys the current to the motor to the collector for better electrical contact. If a wood block is used, in conjunction with two screws, it is as well to note that the holes for them should be staggered, as in Fig. 20H, to bring them out of alignment with the grain as a safeguard against splitting. As a further precaution, the wood should be held in the vice while any necessary holes are drilled.

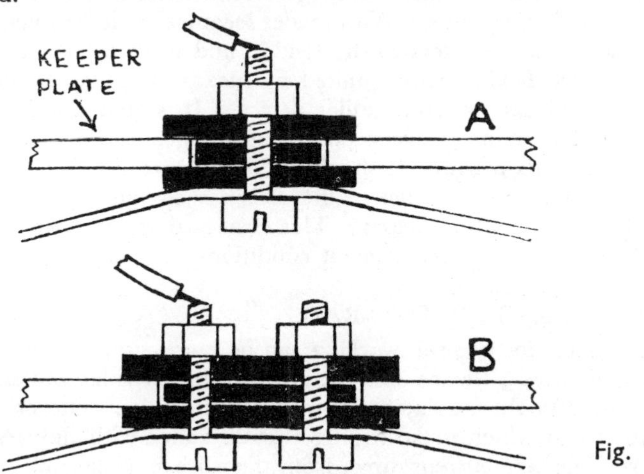

Fig. 24

The method suggested when a keeper-plate is used is shown in the two sectional diagrams, Fig. 24A and B. Considering *A*, first a hole about 7/32 in. or ¼ in. diameter is drilled through the keeper-plate. A round fibre washer is cut which will just fit snugly in the hole. It should be the same thickness as the keeper-plate, or slightly thinner. In place of sheet fibre, a thin slice of tube or rod could be used if a suitable size happens to be available, and should be easier to shape. Two more fibre washers are wanted, somewhat larger than the hole in the keeper-plate. These will not necessarily be circular; in fact the one between the keeper-plate and the collector should be of a shape to provide a good firm bearing surface for the latter. The parts are assembled as shown: first, the collector; then a large washer; next, the small washer (within the thickness of the keeper-plate), the other large washer, and finally the nut which holds all secure. It may be found necessary to add a small metal washer under the nut to prevent excessive distortion of the fibre.

The lead to the motor can be soldered to the shank of the screw, and should be allowed a certain amount of slack so that the keeper-plate can be dropped sufficiently to allow removal of the wheels without the necessity of unsoldering the connection to the brush. To prevent the collector pivoting sideways it should be soldered to the head of the screw, and, as a further precaution, the nut can be sealed with paint or varnish. If space permits, two screws can be used to provide a complete safeguard against this. The hole in the keeper-plate, and the small washer, can be elongated to provide room for the additional screw as shown in Fig. 24B. If the small washer is a good fit in the hole, movement will be impossible.

In difficult and unusual cases, it may be necessary to modify both the form of the collectors and the method of attachment to the chassis. It might be expedient, for example, to make the front and rear collectors as separate units instead of in one piece as suggested hitherto, and to attach them to the chassis at different points. With tender locomotives it is sometimes convenient to fit one of the collectors to the tender, and to connect it to the locomotive with insulated flexible wires, united by means of a snap fastener of the kind used for necklaces, or some similar device. It is obviously impossible here to suggest means to meet every possible contingency, and each case must be considered on its merits. It should be added that the form the collectors are to take should be settled before the chassis is assembled ; indeed, before the two side-frames are unsoldered. This ensures that any necessary holes can be drilled under the most convenient conditions.

COLLECTORS FOR TWO-RAIL

Collectors for two-rail working can be much simpler, and are more easily made and fitted ; hence this section will be considerably shorter than the foregoing. On the insulated side of the locomotive* one or more collectors must be fitted which make wiping contact either with the tread or flange of the wheel, or take current direct from the surface of the rail. Which of these alternatives is preferable is a matter of opinion ; a track collector necessarily takes a small amount of adhesive weight off the drivers, just as a third-rail collector does, whereas one which makes contact with the wheel must constitute a slight brake. A track collector eliminates one source of electrical inefficiency—the contact between the wheel and the rail. It is not a very serious matter either way if the collectors are reasonably well adjusted. A rail collector can take the form shown in Fig. 19, except that it must be insulated from the frame. It is so simple that no further comment seems to be needed, except to point out that no part of it should be located behind the flanges where there might be a chance of it shorting against the opposed point blade when traversing points. This assumes, of course, that the point blades are electrically connected, and will have the same polarity.

The wheel collector can be similar in form, except that it is arranged to bear against the flange as shown in Fig. 25. The spring should be about the same width as the tread, or slightly more, provided it will not foul the connecting-rods, and can be soldered or riveted to its support. The writer makes

* The accepted practice is for the wheels on the left-hand side of the locomotive to be insulated. That is to say they would be on the left hand of an observer stationed behind the locomotive and looking forward towards the smokebox.

these springs of phosphor-bronze about ten "thous." thick. If thicker stuff must be used, it should be adjusted so that the pressure is very light in order not to absorb an excessive amount of power. Since writing this I have been led to think that phosphor-bronze or steel wire may make more satisfactory wheel collectors than strip material. The gauge should be about 24 or 26. They are certainly less conspicuous. Some people may prefer a collector bearing against the flange, but the writer thinks that a tread collector should tend to exercise a cleaning action on the wheel, and retard the formation of the deposit which ultimately produces uncertain electrical contact. Needless to say, collectors should be fitted to at least two wheels to ensure continuous electrical contact. It is obvious that such collectors could easily be modified to resemble brake shoes and hangers. The attachment to the chassis would have to be at a point near the top of the frame, and might be through a fibre bush. The spring would then simulate the hanger, and a brake block, filed from nickel or brass, would be added. Any reader who is attracted by the idea should have no difficulty in working out details to suit the particular model.

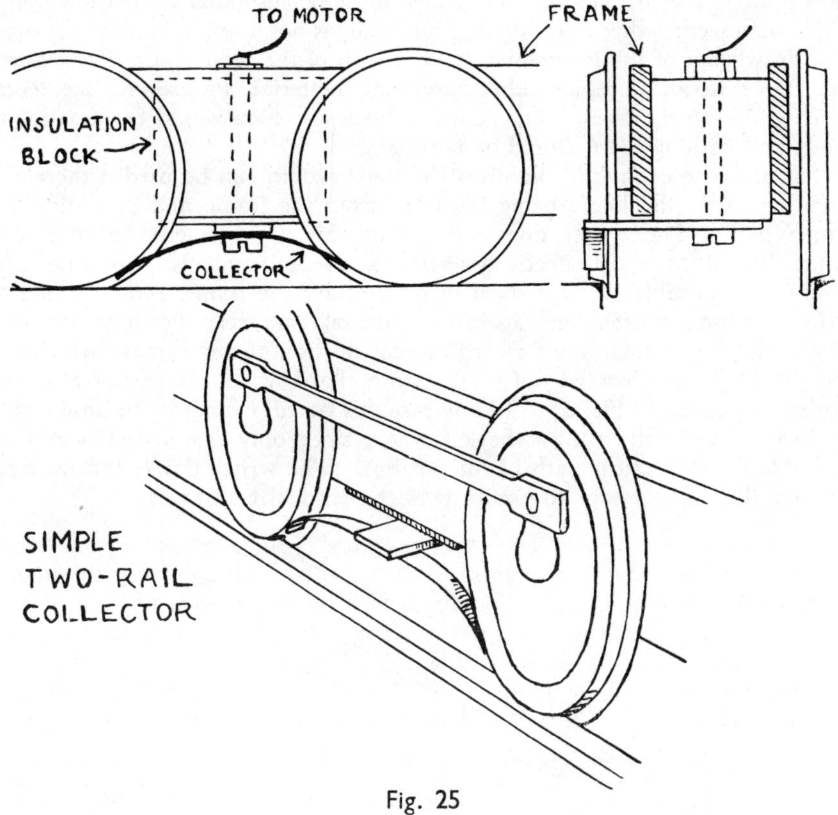

Fig. 25

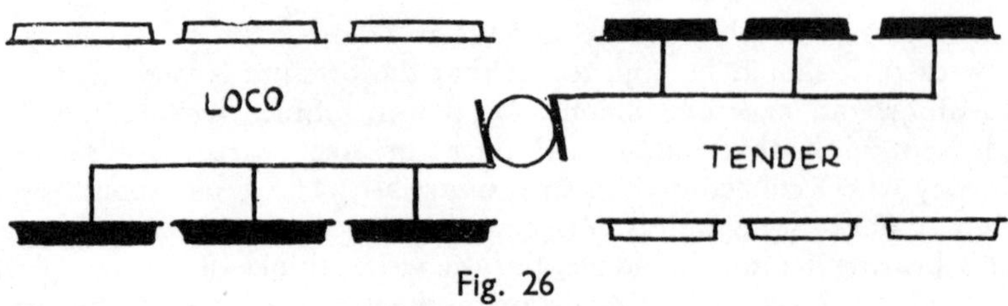

Fig. 26

Some workers dispense with the use of collectors by the device of insulating the locomotive wheels on one side and those of the tender on the other. By this system current passes from the earthed wheels on the locomotive, *via* the motor, to the earthed wheels on the opposite side of the tender. The circuit is illustrated in Fig. 26, in which the wheels shown solid black are the earthed ones and in electrical contact with the frames of the respective units. A flexible lead is taken from the *insulated* brush of the commutator to the earthed frame of the tender by means of a dress fastener, or similar device. It will be seen that the locomotive and tender must be insulated from each other, which may seem rather intimidating, but really is not at all difficult to arrange. The drawbeam of the locomotive (and the sill of the tender also if necessary) can be of wood, fibre, or other insulating material, to prevent accidental shorting on sharp curves. The coupling hook and loop would be attached to these, and nothing more should be necessary.

In the case of tank locomotives the same system can be used if there is a bogie or truck, the bogie being insulated from the frame and providing the return path. The writer does not favour this arrangement because it is rather difficult to guard effectively against accidental contacts. In some cases it might be possible to fix a sheet of fibre under the frame, large enough to form an absolute safeguard against accidental contacts. Possibly, the best way would be to make the forward or rear portion of the frames—whichever end the bogie was located—of solid fibre or hard wood, somewhat after the manner suggested in Fig. 27. In any case this system cannot be recommended for locomotives with a two-wheeled truck, since only one wheel would be available for the return path of the current. The writer thinks that at least two wheels are necessary to ensure perfect electrical continuity.

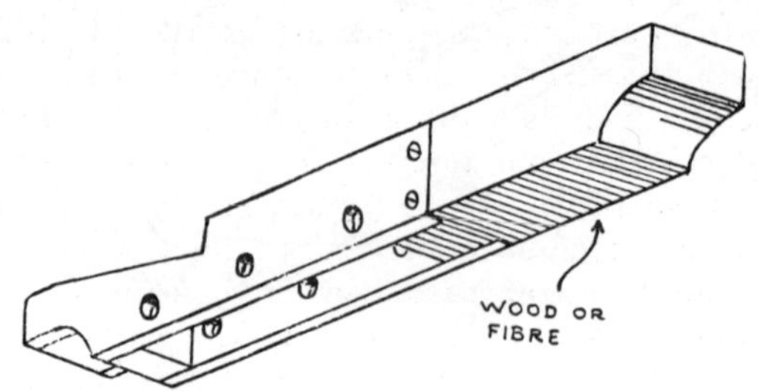

Fig. 27

THE STUD-CONTACT SYSTEM

The stud-contact system of current collection has gained considerable popularity in recent years and has many points in its favour ; the wheels of locomotives and vehicles do not have to be insulated and as regards all essentials it may be regarded as a special form of the old three-rail system. On the other hand the permanent way is not burdened with a third rail which, in the opinion of many people, spoils the appearance of nicely laid track and in some cases is definitely out of place. We may say, therefore, that the stud-contact system makes the best of both worlds in a very satisfactory manner.

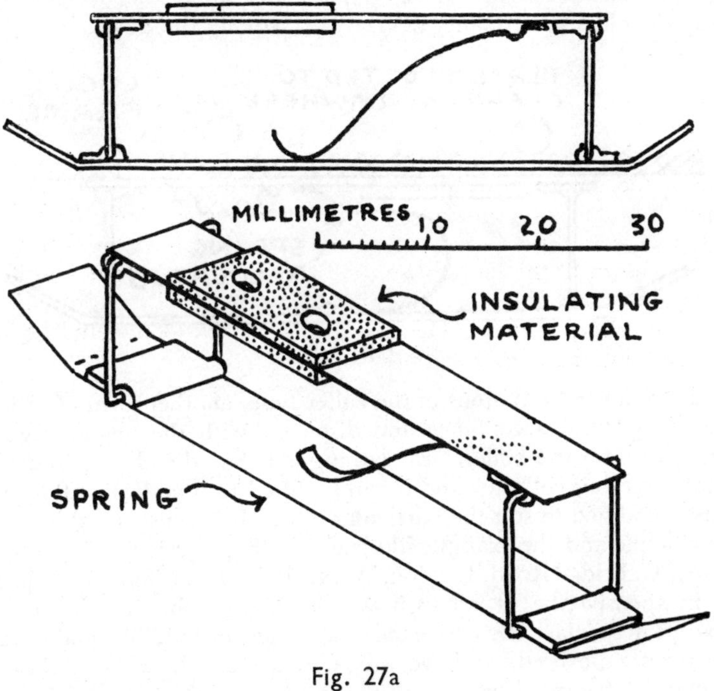

Fig. 27a

It seems that the only serious objection to stud-contact is that it requires a rather special form of current collector and the mounting of this fitting on some locomotives presents considerable difficulties and may tax the ingenuity of the constructor. The difficulty arises from the fact that the collector must be long enough to bridge the interval between any two studs, to ensure continuity of current supply, and that it must be able to rise and fall, to accommodate itself to studs of unequal heights, in a strictly vertical plane. In other words, it must be constructed so that it cannot tip fore and aft when moving from a low stud to a higher one, or vice versa. If this condition were not fulfilled it is almost certain that it would make contact with the running rails when passing over points, causing a short circuit.

As far as the writer knows the first stud-contact collectors were mounted on long, spring loaded, vertical guides. Hence they could rise and fall but the shoe was maintained in a horizontal plane relative to the track by the guides, which had to be constructed with the minimum possible clearance to exclude side-play. The snag inherent in this form of collector, apart from the fact that the construction was fairly intricate, was that the guide, or guides, had to project upwards into the body of the locomotive, almost to the full extent of the height of the boiler and firebox. Considering the limited space inside a " OO " gauge locomotive, it is hardly surprising that in many cases there simply was not room for it. Thus many interesting locomotive types, especially the older and smaller ones, were virtually ruled out.

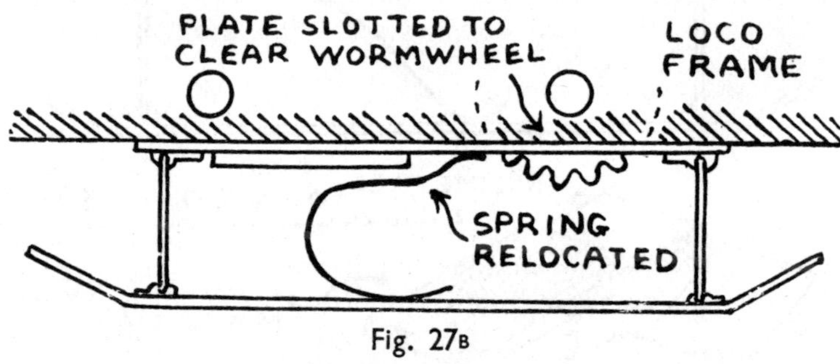

Fig. 27B

Because of the limitations of the ealier type, another form of collector has now gained general acceptance and dispenses with the ungainly guide rods projecting up into the boiler. Everything is below the chassis frame, as with a normal three-rail collector and it can be fitted to practically all locomotives, if suitably modified to suit the particular case. It is constructed on the pantograph principle and the example illustrated in Fig. 27A is marketed by Messrs. K's of 197, Uxbridge Road, London, W.12. It is a beautifully made little fitting and so inexpensive that it is hardly worth while for the modeller to make his own, except in special cases where the design must be modified and the standard pattern cannot be used. I have prepared a scale drawing of this collector which may be regarded as typical of the best practice. It consists of a thin metal plate, 7.5 mm. wide, which is attached to the underside of the locomotive frame by two small screws but effectively insulated from it by a conventional arrangement consisting of two strips of fibre. On the undersurface of this plate there are mounted two double arms or stirrups, of thin, hard, wire which are free to swing freely in a fore and aft direction and carry the collector shoe, also 7.5 mm. wide, at their lower extremities. Thus the shoe can swing, to a limited extent, either towards the front or rear of the locomotive when passing over studs of varying height, but it will be clear from examination of the drawing that it remains at all times horizontal and parallel to the surface of the track. It is maintained in tension by a phosphor-bronze leaf spring. A lead can be taken to the insulated brush of the motor from whatever point on the collector may happen to be most convenient. It will be seen that the practical difficulty which may arise is to find room for the collector where it will be out of the way of the axles and the wormwheel. In fairness it must be pointed out that such difficulties are by no means unknown in ordinary three-rail work. In the case of tender locomotives it may be best to mount it under the tender and take the current to the motor by a flexible lead but in some cases, particularly on tank locomotives, it might be necessary to cut a slot in the mounting plate for the wormwheel to project through. It might also be necessary to relocate the spring to clear the wormwheel. In the case of K's collector this should be quite easy as the spring is soldered to the mounting plate and could be detached and refixed in another position, Fig. 27B.

If the constructor makes up the collector himself he cannot do better than to follow the example illustrted as closely as possible, but the following points should be noted.

The mounting plate which is attached to the locomotive could, if necesssary, be shorter, the shoe remaining the same length. This should not be done unless it is necessary to clear some obstruction on the locomotive for if the pantograph base is relatively short, and the ends of the shoe project some distance beyond it, there is likely to be some slight loss of precision. The pantograph base should always be as long as possible but it must be remembered that the length of the shoe is governed by the distance between adjacent studs. It is probable that many workers have placed the studs too far apart for efficient operation and the writer thinks that better results would be obtained with studs not more than an inch apart.

To provide the bearings for the pantograph arms the home constructor will not necessarily reproduce the type of fitting shown in the illustration. He could solder lengths of small diameter brass or copper tube at right angles across the fixing plate and the shoe. Tube of $\frac{1}{16}$ in. o.d. will take 20 gauge wire very nicely and this is quite thick enough for " OO " gauge.

An alternative form of pivot bearing is shown in Fig. 27C. In this case the bearings are made of 16-gauge brass, across which a sawcut has been made to a depth of about half the thickness of the material. One of these little pieces is shown separately on the left to reveal the sawcut. They are soldered in the appropriate positions to the mounting strip and to the shoe. It will be evident that the wire pantograph arms must be in position in the bearings before the latter are soldered to the mounting strip. To prevent the wire becoming soldered up solid it should be smeared with a *very little* grease, but care must be exercised to prevent the grease coming off onto either of the surfaces where the solder is required to run freely. A better way, which would overcome this difficulty, would be to paint the part of the wire which is enclosed in the bearing with shellac varnish and to let it dry before undertaking the soldering.

The form of the pantograph arm, of hard brass or nickel wire, is also shown separately on the left of Fig. 27C. It is important that the right and left-hand arms of the stirrup should be exactly the same length or the shoe will lean to one side. The wire should be bent as nearly as possible to the final shape, and carefully checked, before being assembled to the mounting plate. The ends are then pressed inwards, with small pliers, until they are fully engaged in the bearings of the shoe and no perceptible side-play remains.

In difficult cases, where the wormwheel has to project through a slot in the mounting plate, it might be necessary to bend the spring back on itself in the form of a U in order to leave the necessary unobstructed space. In such cases the use of a small helical spring in place of the leaf spring is worth consideration. To keep it in place it would probably be necessary to devise means of securing it to the shoe as well as to the mounting plate. This might be done by passing its ends through very small holes drilled or punched in these parts and making them secure with solder. Such a spring, being in a vertical position, would not occupy so much space as a leaf spring.

Needless to say, it is desirable that the spring—whatever form it may take—should bear on the shoe, as nearly as possible, at its middle point.

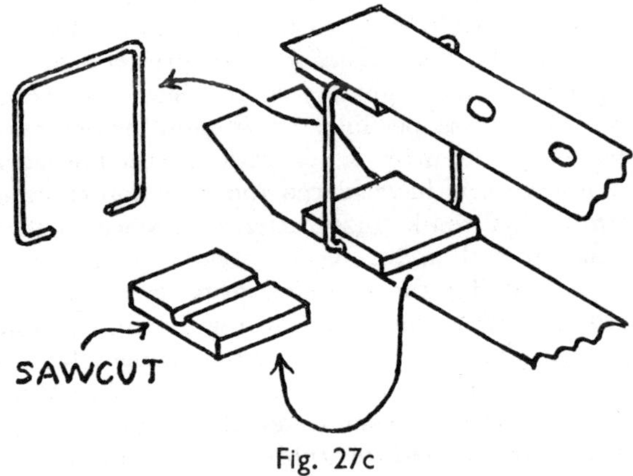

Fig. 27c

CHAPTER IV

SPRINGING

IT is not essential that the wheels of miniature locomotives should be provided with springs, and many—in fact at present the majority—manage to get along fairly well without. Nevertheless, it is certain that adhesion, which means hauling-power, is improved thereby because all wheels are in firm contact with the track all the time, regardless of irregularities of surface level. Locomotives with sprung wheels are less liable than others to derailment, because the wheels can adapt themselves to places where the track is not so evenly laid as it might be. Hence when sprung motive power and stock is in use the worker is not obliged to be quite so precise with his track work. This consideration should carry weight, for experience shows that nearly all derailments are due to low spots in the track level. Those who are adopting "OO" gauge scale dimensions should regard full springing as essential, or the task of maintaining the track in a fit state for the fine treads and flanges prescribed for this gauge may, in time, prove rather burdensome.

Another argument for springing of locomotive wheels is that better current collection can be expected. This applies particularly to two-rail when, as is usually the case, the wheel treads are relied on exclusively to pick up current.

In most cases an adequate system of suspension is not difficult to instal. It would be quite an undertaking to spring the driving axle (meaning the one on which the worm-wheel or other gear is mounted) since that would entail a special form of mounting for the motor to allow it to float with the axle, but if all the other wheels of the rigid wheel-base are sprung, one fixed axle is not a matter of any great importance. The form of spring suggested by the writer is illustrated in Fig. 28, but it will of course need modification to suit particular cases. There is not much room for refinements in "OO" gauge chassis and, in some cases, considerable ingenuity may be required.

The springs can be cut from sheet phosphor-bronze, preferably about 0.007 in. thick, and nearly the full between-frame width of the chassis. They are screwed or pinned to the cross-members, or to special cross-members provided for the purpose. They should be as long as space permits to provide maximum flexibility, and should be split for the greater part of their length to permit independent movement of the ends of the axles. Adjustment of pressure is effected by careful bending, or they can be made more resilient by drilling a few small holes as suggested in Fig. 31. It is essential to the proper working of the system that the degree of resilience should be such that *the weight of the locomotive is sufficient to depress the springs, and to push the axle to the top of the slotted holes as in* Fig. 28A.

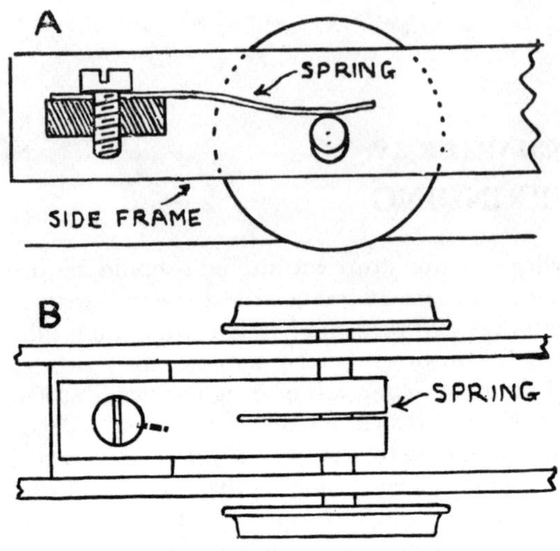

Fig. 28

Some explanation is necessary as to the action of the springs for it will be clear that when the model passes over irregularities of track level all movement of the axles must be downwards, which is contrary to full-size practice of both road and rail vehicles, where springs are adjusted to have movement both upwards and downwards. The reason for this difference from full-size practice is that it would be very difficult, if not almost impossible for most workers, to adjust such tiny springs with the necessary delicacy to enable them to act in quite the same way as larger ones. Fortunately, it is found in practice that it does not seem to make much difference whether the wheels move both up and down from the normal position or down only. The important thing is that they should be free to move *independently* one way or another. What is wanted is that when the locomotive passes over a low spot in the track level

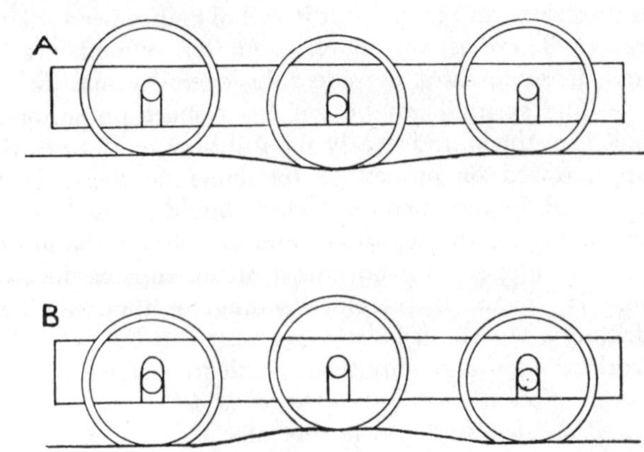

Fig. 29

each wheel as it reaches that spot should be able to dip momentarily to maintain contact with the rail, Fig. 29. But it may be asked how it works when the locomotive encounters a "high spot." I think this is answered by the diagram Fig. 29B. In the first case, axles 1 and 3 will be up while axle 2 will be in some lower position. In the second case, axles 1 and 3 will be down, while axle 2 will be up. It is agreed that when the position of one axle has to be fixed, because it takes the drive, it cannot always (in the case of a six- or eight-coupled chassis) adapt itself to the track, but in practice this seems to be of little account, and in any case the behaviour of such a locomotive will be better than that of one without any springs at all.*

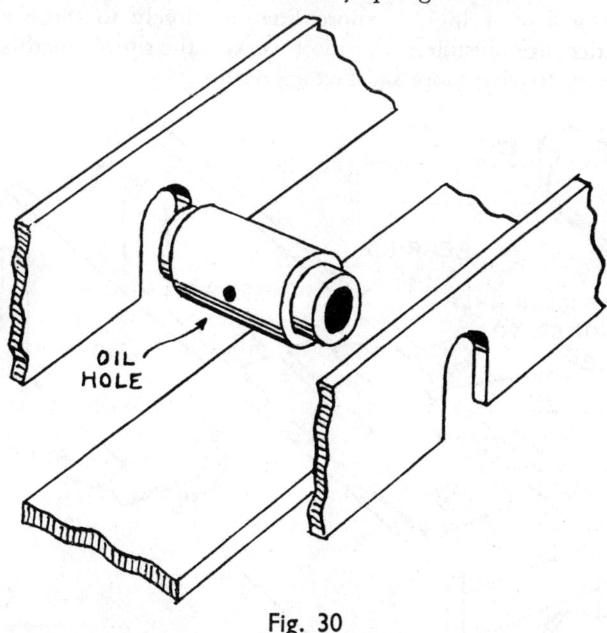

Fig. 30

In Fig. 28, it is suggested that the springs bear direct on the axle itself, without the intervention of any form of journal-box. This simple arrangement is quite satisfactory, but some people may think it worthwhile to adopt the slightly more elaborate method shown in Fig. 30 and Fig. 31A. Here the axles are enclosed in brass tubes with shouldered down ends which move in the guides and check side movement. A hole should be drilled for lubrication purposes, Fig. 30, and any burr which may be left inside by the drill should be carefully removed with a reamer or broach. These "journal-boxes," as we may call them, are a very simple piece of turning, but in the absence of a lathe an acceptable substitute could be produced by using thick walled tube

* In six or eight-coupled chassis it is essential that the coupling rods be divided, as in full-size practice, to enable the axles to function independently.

and filing a pair of parallel guide surfaces at each end as in Fig. 31F. A chassis frame incorporating a keeper-plate is shown in Figs. 30 and 31A.

An alternative form of spring, made of steel wire, is shown in Fig. 31B, C, D and E. To obtain sufficient flexibility, the wire should be twisted into a loop, like the end of a safety-pin, as shown in the drawings. If necessary two or more loops can be formed as at *E*. The method of forming the loops is similar to that employed in making coil-springs. A nail, or a piece of rod of about 16- or 14-gauge, is fixed upright in the vice and the wire is drawn firmly round it by hand.

For the few who possess the necessary skill and patience much more elaborate systems of springing, approximating closely to those employed in full-size practice, are possible. For most workers the simple methods described above are likely to give more satisfactory results.

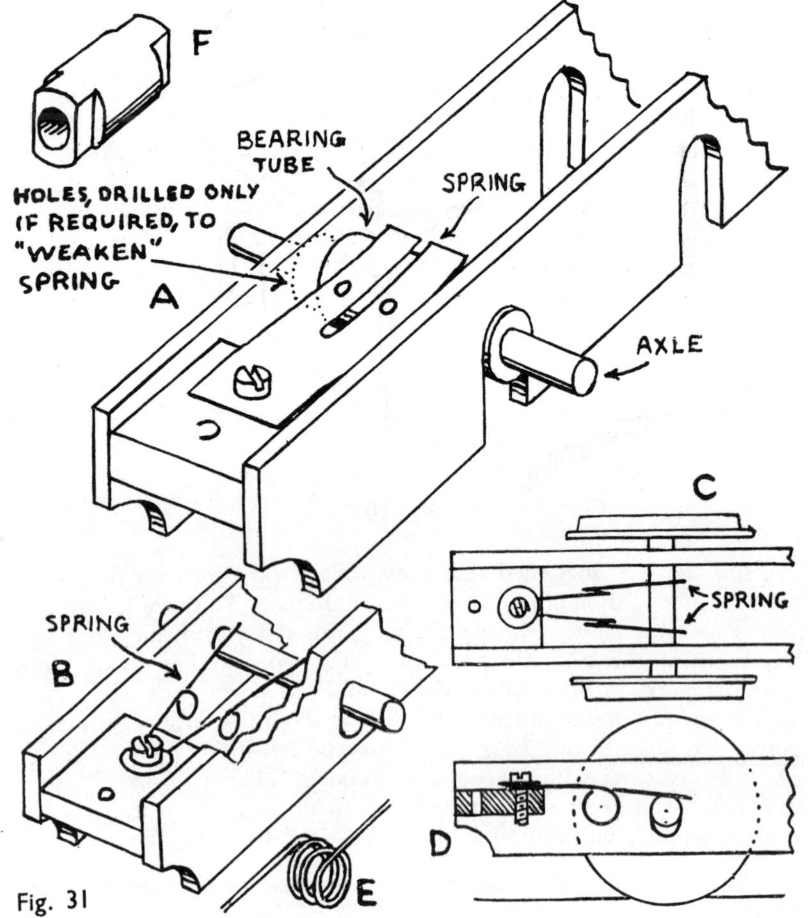

Fig. 31

CHAPTER V

BOGIES AND PONY TRUCKS

LEADING and trailing trucks, both two- and four-wheeled, should always be made as heavy as possible to reduce the risk of derailment. For the same reason, it is desirable in the case of four-wheeled bogies that one of the axles should have some form of springing. There could be little advantage in springing both axles. It is extremely difficult to devise any sort of effective springing in the limited space afforded by the bogie-frame, since as much of the space as possible should be filled up solid with lead or other metal to obtain the maximum weight. If the holes for one of the axles are slotted vertically, as described when discussing driving-wheels, the advantages of springing will result to a limited extent, although no springs are fitted. The wheels will at least be free to drop by their own weight to conform to track irregularities. It must be admitted that this method is likely to be more effective at low speeds than when the locomotive is running fast, since, in the latter case, the wheels, with nothing to guide them but their own weight, may not react quickly enough to track unevenness. The weight of the wheels should be increased as much as possible by slipping a piece of tube or drilled rod over the axle before assembling it in the bogie-frame.

If it is thought practicable to use an actual spring, it might take the form of a piece of steel wire arranged to press down on the axle ; it should be light enough to allow the axle to stand normally at the top of the slotted guide-holes for the reason discussed in the last section.

An alternative expedient to increase adhesion between the bogie and track is to fit a light spring to the chassis, designed to press downwards on the bogie bolster. Two forms are shown in Fig. 32. Since little work is involved in their preparation, the modeller may care to experiment with both. The spring in *A* could be either a piece of steel wire or a strip of phosphor-bronze, about $\frac{3}{16}$-in. or $\frac{1}{4}$-in. wide. The writer prefers the latter as it offers a larger rubbing surface and should be less likely to impede the free sideways movement of the bogie on curves. It is important that the pressure should be quite light or the spring will take needed adhesion away from the driving-wheels, and the normal movement of the bogie might be impeded. The reader must be prepared to undertake a certain amount of experimental work, and he should not be discouraged by possible failure in the early stages. The subject is still a long way from the cut-and-dried stage where it would only be necessary to follow on well-tried lines.

The construction of the bogie-frame can be somewhat similar to that of a locomotive-frame, although on a smaller scale. The side-frames can be drilled while soldered together; they may be cut from $\frac{1}{16}$-in. or even 3/32-in. metal, for the thicker they are the greater the weight. The sides can be soldered to a bolster of similar material which, if the sides are $\frac{1}{16}$ in. thick, can be strip brass $\frac{3}{8}$ in. wide. The bolster should run the full length of the frame and should be extended backwards to the pivot point by which the bogie is anchored to the chassis. The extension should be tapered as shown in Fig. 33. Care is required when soldering the bogie parts together, to ensure that the

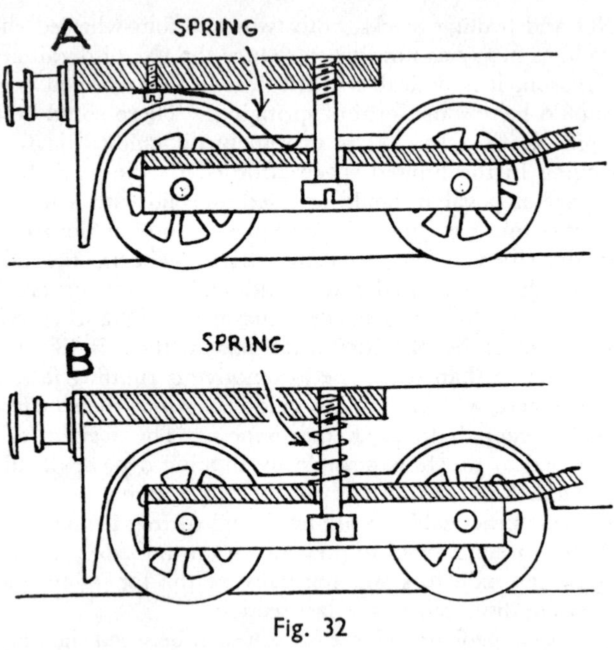

Fig. 32

axle-holes are properly aligned. The simplest way perhaps is to clamp the parts with drawing pins or small nails in the angle of a mitre-block, as in Fig. 34, so that the side and bolster are at right-angles to each other and cannot slip while the iron is being applied. When the parts have been assembled they should be tested for parallelism of the axle-holes by applying a pair of straight rods as described in connection with locomotive-frames and illustrated in Fig. 35. Probably the best way to make sure that the axles will be parallel is to drill the holes, in the first place, with a rather smaller drill than the required finished size. Then if any error is discovered after assembly, any of the holes can be drifted quite appreciably with a rat-tail file to correct the misalignment. Finally, the holes are opened out with a drill of the correct size. It may be mentioned here that the drill size required for standard "OO" gauge axles (other than driving axles) is No. 49. This will normally allow just the amount of clearance necessary for free running.

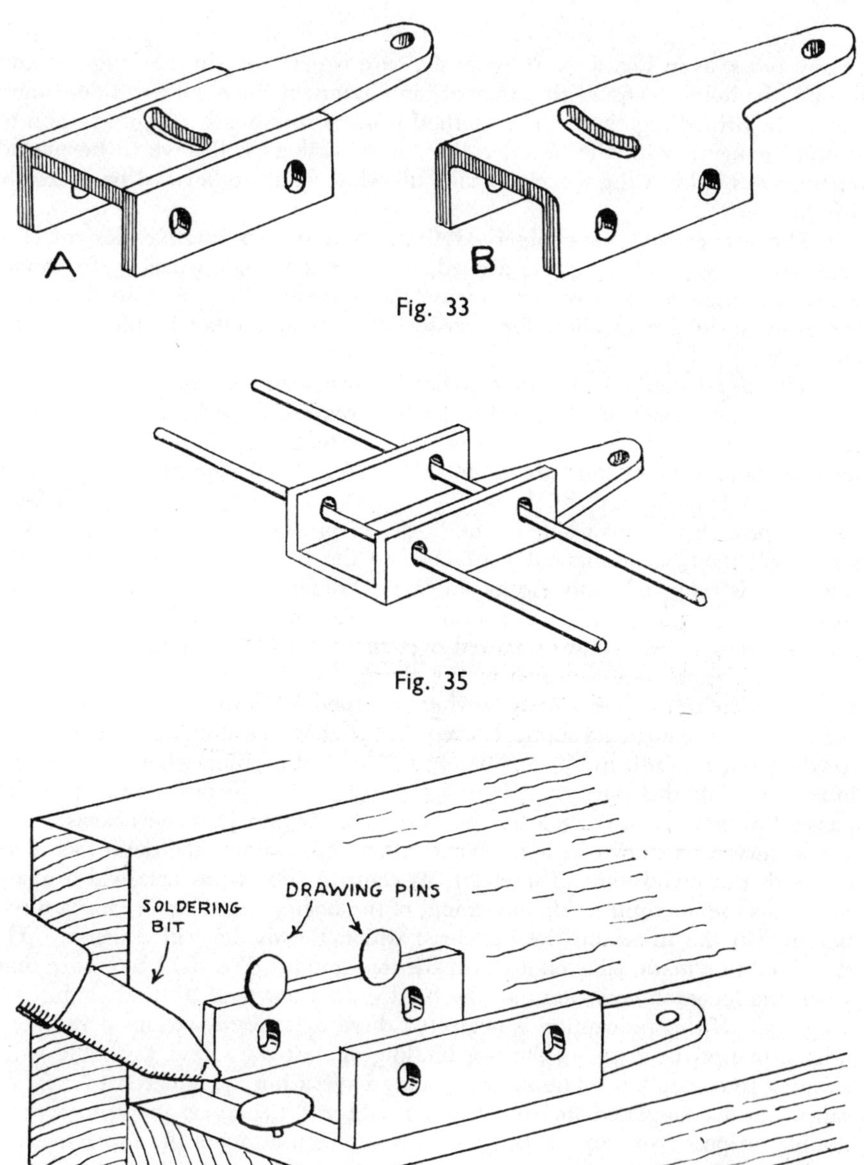

Fig. 33

Fig. 35

Fig. 34

Alternatively, the frames can be made in one piece from ½-in. channel-section brass, as in Fig. 33B. Obviously, care is necessary in marking-out and drilling the holes to ensure that they are in alignment since the two side-frames cannot be drilled together. The method is more suitable to 16.5-mm. than to 18-mm. gauge ; with the latter, rather thick washers will have to be placed on the axles behind the wheels to take up what would otherwise be excessive side play.

The reader will have observed that, in many locomotive designs, the main frames are cut away, or arched, to clear the bogie-wheels. In model work, it is usually necessary to increase the dimensions of these arches above the exact scale size to allow for over-size flanges and unavoidable side- and end-play.

The usual method of fitting bogies is illustrated in Fig. 36. The pivot is the screw, 1, which may be 8-B.A. ; it will require a special cross-member if the chassis does not offer any convenient point for its attachment. The bogie must be able to pivot quite freely on this screw. It is suggested that the nut, 2, which acts as a stop, should be soldered to the screw, 1, after it has been passed through the pivot-hole in the bogie, to prevent it working loose. The screw will then be permanently attached to the bogie, and cannot get lost if the bogie is removed from the locomotive. Solder should be kept out of the thread above the nut, or it will prevent the screw going right home. If necessary, a circular die should be passed over the thread to clear it.

If the bogie were attached to the chassis by the screw, 1, only, it would flop about in an exasperating way whenever the locomotive was removed from the rails. An additional support is required which will allow the bogie perfect freedom but retain it in approximately the normal position when the model is lifted up. For this purpose it is usual to introduce a second screw, 3, which passes through a slotted hole in the bogie bolster and into the chassis. The slot is curved as shown in Fig. 36 and other illustrations, the curve being set out with the pivot-point of screw, 1, as centre. The transverse width of the slot limits the maximum side movement of the bogie, and therefore has a direct bearing on the minimum radius curve which the model will traverse. The slot should be made wide enough (in the fore and aft direction) to ensure that, when the locomotive is running, the bolster does not tend to bind against the screw, 3. If this precaution is neglected there may be mysterious derailments due to one of the edges of the slot binding against the screw, probably when running into a curve. The screw, 3, may have a nut, 4, soldered to it in the same way as suggested for the screw, 1. Screw 3, can be made to serve a double purpose—it can be the fixing screw which attaches the superstructure to the chassis, as shown at 5, in Fig. 36.

The bogie-frame should, of course, be modelled to correspond to the prototype in appearance as closely as possible ; visible details such as springs, guard irons, etc., will be added by the usual methods. But there is one type of bogie which requires special consideration, that fitted to the Great Western Railway " King " class. In this bogie, as most readers will be aware, the

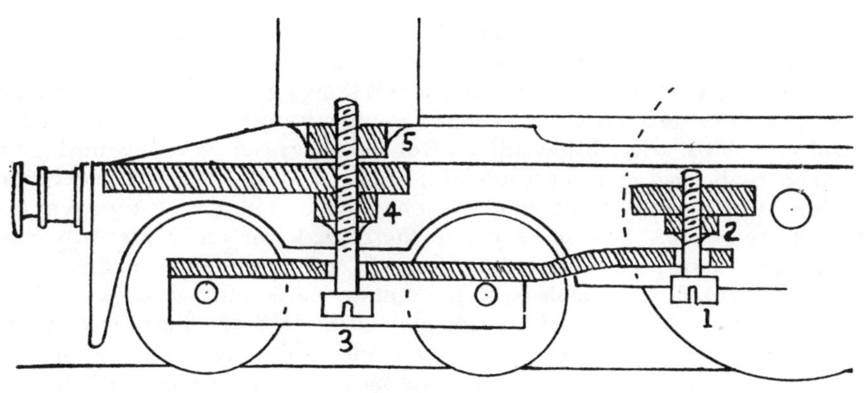

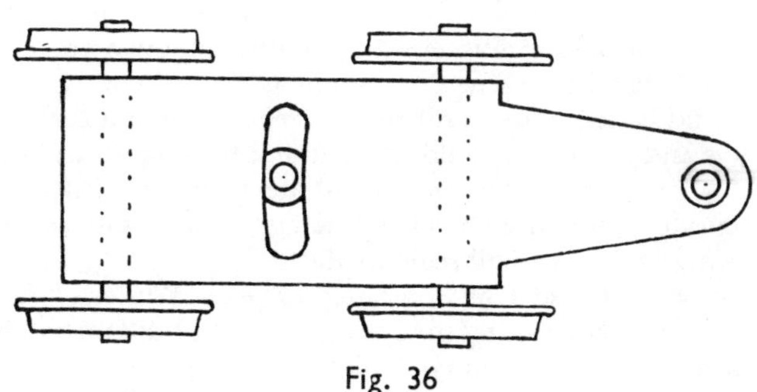

Fig. 36

Fig. 37

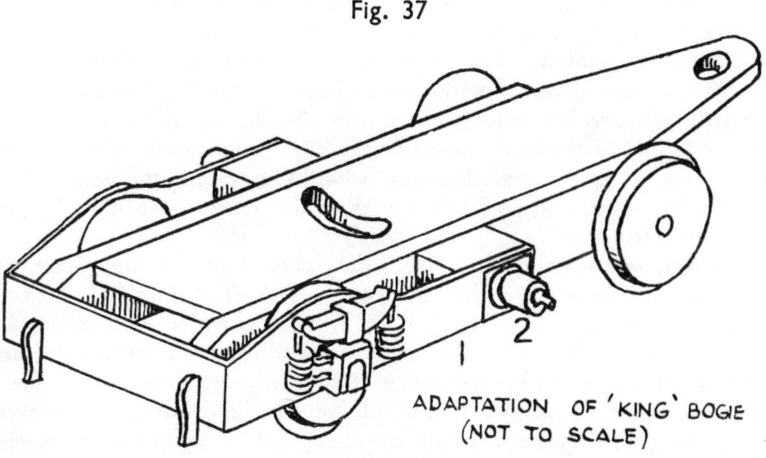

trailing wheels have inside bearings but forward of them the frames swing wider apart to enclose the leading ones. The form of construction which the writer considers best in the miniature scales is shown in Fig. 37. Basically, it is exactly as described above, but *dummy* outside frames of quite thin sheet-metal are added. The bogie side control spring, 2, can be represented by a small cheese-headed screw or a special turning. Two thin washers, one round and the other square, are placed under it and soldered in place to represent the base of the fitting. It is screwed into the bogie-frame and serves to secure the dummy frame, 1. The dummy frame is attached also by solder at the front end. It will be possible to fit the dummy outside frame more closely—and nearer to scale width—if the side-play of the leading wheels is restricted to a minimum by the use of washers on the axle. If the model is intended for two-rail operation it is essential that side movement should be restricted, so that the wheel on the insulated side cannot touch the bogie-frame, unless, of course, the wheel itself is made of an insulating material. If there is any doubt on the subject, it would be advisable to attach a piece of insulating material to the inside of the frame with suitable adhesive such as Durofix. Hard, red fibre can be obtained as thin as 0.01 in. and would be very suitable. Empire cloth could be used but might require renewal after a time.

The springs and axleboxes could be filed and built up from brass or other metal, or cast alloy commercial ones might be adapted. Fig. 37 is not, of course, an accurate representation of a "King" bogie, but shows only the main details as applied to a small-scale model.

Outside-frame bogies, such as were fitted to Great Western "Badminton" and "City" class locomotives, and many others, can be built up if desired on the same general principle as the prototype. That is to say, the outside frames will provide the actual bearings for the axles. The writer thinks, however, that readers who have had little experience may find a modification of the method described for the "King" class simpler and more satisfactory. It is suggested that the actual frame be made up in the normal way, with *inside* bearings. Then, after the bogie has been tested and found to run satisfactorily, dummy outside frames are added. They can be soldered or attached with 10-B.A. screws with spacing-washers to make them clear the wheels. Since the spacing-washers will increase the total weight they should be as large as possible. In fact, the whole of the free space between the wheels may as well be filled up solid. In some cases, it might be possible to adapt commercial cast bogie sides for this purpose, and so avoid the laborious business of building up the axleboxes and springs.

In all that has been said so far, it has been assumed that the bogie is purely ornamental and that it does not carry any part of the weight or contribute to the running of the locomotive. In full-size practice, of course, a bogie has two very definite functions—it carries a certain part of the weight, and it helps to guide the front of the locomotive when entering a curve. In the case of a small-scale model it is hardly desirable for a bogie to carry any substantial part of the weight, because as much of it as possible is wanted for adhesion.

But the second function—the possibility of regulating the bogie so as to ease the locomotive when entering a curve—is at least worth consideration. If a light steel wire spring could be arranged to come into action against the bogie on curves, tending to pull it back to the normal position, this might be achieved. It will be seen that if the sprıng tends to bring the bogie back to the normal position it also tends to ease the front of the locomotive round into the curve, and reduces the friction of the driving wheels against the outside rail by transmitting some of it to the bogie. A possible basis for experiment is suggested in Fig. 38. The spring is rigidly attached to the chassis, at a point near the bogie-pivot. When the bogie moves out of the straight ahead position the spring engages with one or other of two pins or stops on the bolster and tends to make the locomotive follow. The action is illustrated in Fig. 38B, which shows a 4-4-0 locomotive on a curve.

If any reader cares to experiment on these lines, it is quite likely that,

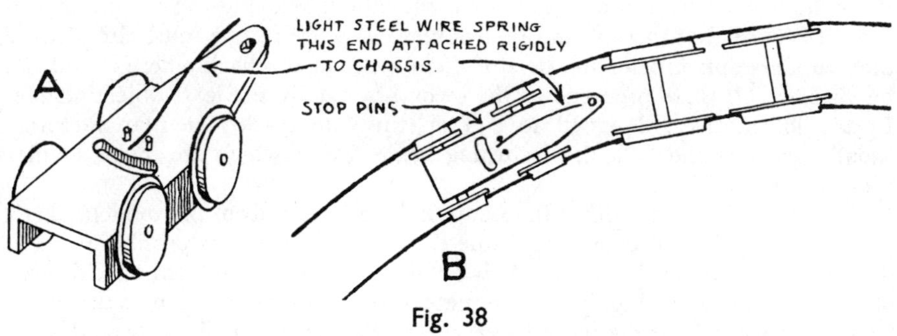

Fig. 38

in the early stages, the spring will do nothing but pull the bogie off the track. It is a matter of discovering by trial and error the correct strength for it. It will be seen that since the spring must press downwards on the bogie it can be made to perform the function shown in Fig. 32 at the beginning of this section.

It is one of the major difficulties of miniature locomotive design that curves on model railways are always proportionately sharper than any which would ever confront full-size ones. For this reason the side-swing of bogies and pony trucks must always be greater than would be required of the prototype. Unless certain departures are made from the prototype design, it may be found that, on sharp curves, the bogie will foul outside cylinders or some part of the frames. It is advisable to investigate these unpleasant possibilities before construction is undertaken, so that any modifications may be made at once rather than later, perhaps after the model has been painted. The best way is to make a plan, preferably full-size, to show the relative positions which the rigid wheelbase, frames, bogie, and cylinders, will occupy when the locomotive is on the sharpest curve it will be required to traverse. The rails can be drawn with an improvised compass or trammel, consisting of a piece of stripwood,

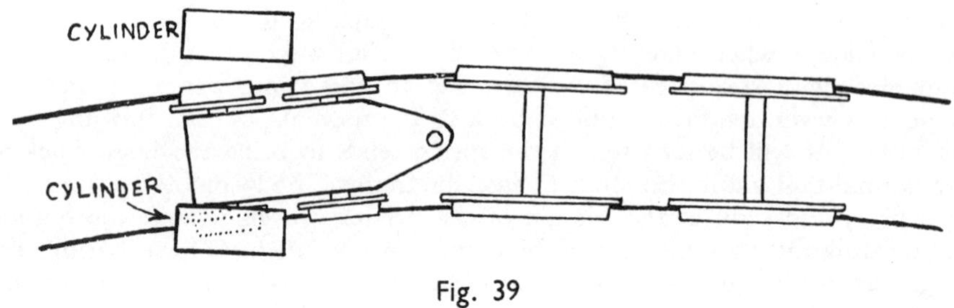

Fig. 39

with a pencil inserted in a hole at one end and a nail for a pivot at the other the distance from the pencil to the nail being equal to the radius of the curve Next, draw the coupled wheels, and from these obtain the positions of the frame and cylinders. It will at once be evident if the bogie wheels will foul the cylinders. The result should look something like Fig. 39 ; and in this case, it is clear that there would be trouble. To cure it, one must either move the cylinders outwards or file part of them away at the back where it will not be visible. Of these proceedings the second is usually the least objectionable. In toy locomotives, designed to run on tin-plate track, the manufacturers usually get over the difficulty by fitting bogie wheels which are much smaller then they should be.

Pony trucks do not differ in essentials from bogies, from the modelmaker's point of view. In all cases, the frame should be as heavy as possible to assist the wheels to stay on the track. It is usual to saw and file it from a solid piece of metal, as shown in Fig. 40. The method of mounting is much as described for bogies, except that the second screw (3, in Fig. 36) is usually dispensed with. It appears that no advantage would be gained by the fitting of springs, provided the truck is fairly loose on its pivot so that it is free to tip slightly to one side or the other, on uneven track. If the truck frame is solid, as suggested above, it is advisable to drill a small oil hole down into the axle bearing.

The question remains to be considered at what point on the chassis the

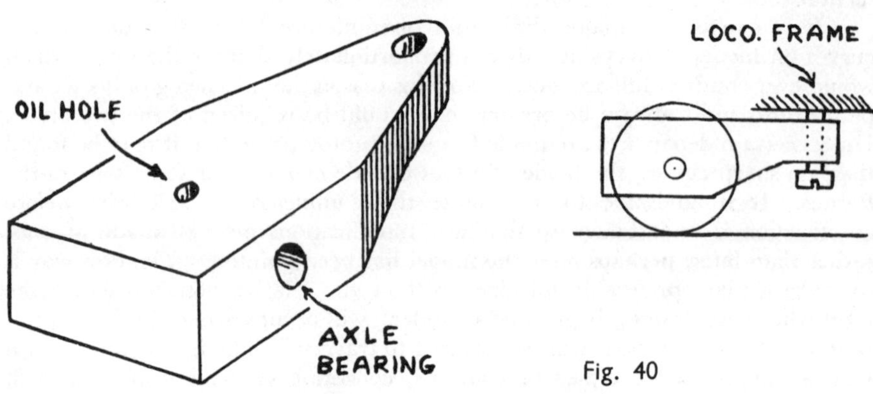

Fig. 40

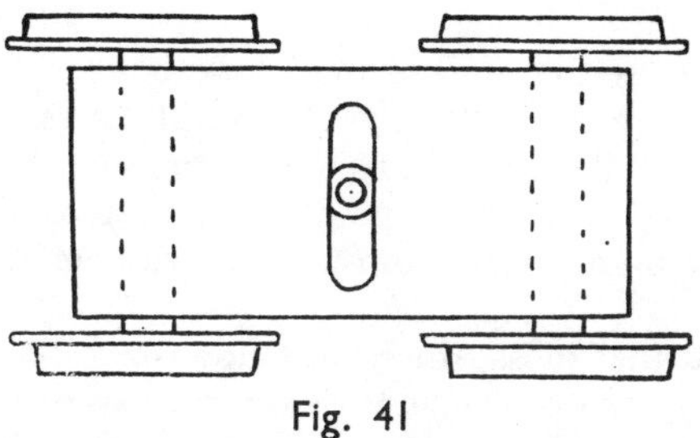

Fig. 41

bogie or truck pivot should be located. In full-size practice, the methods used to determine this are of an extremely technical and complex nature. The writer doubts if the worker in small scales will gain anything by trying to apply them. It is probably enough to know that, in all normal cases, the pivot should be located, when possible, somewhere between the flanges and axle of the nearest pair of coupled wheels to the bogie or truck. This is suggested in Fig. 36.

Some modelmakers prefer to mount the bogie on a pin located centrally in the bogie stretcher, as shown in Fig. 41, the bolster being slotted to allow side movement on curves. It is doubtful if this arrangement is very desirable as there is nothing to check the tendency of the bogie to get sideways across the track. It looks rather like a hangover from commercial tinplate practice, and the writer does not recommend it.

So far, we have made no mention of the possibility of employing the principle of compensation as an alternative to springing of axles ; but, in view of the obvious difficulties of fitting springs within a "OO" gauge bogie, it at least deserves careful consideration. The principle is that the side-frames are pivoted on the bolster at a point centrally placed between the axles, so that they can swing independently of each other through an angle of perhaps 2 or 3 degrees. The object, of course, is to allow the axles to rise and fall independently on uneven track. The movement must be severely limited or the axles would bind in their bearings ; slightly more play must be allowed than would be necessary with an uncompensated bogie. The bearings could be eased slightly with a broach, or a 48 drill could be used instead of a 49. To restrict the angular movement of the side-frames, stops of some sort must be provided.

Fig. 42 is offered purely as a tentative suggestion, not as a fully worked out design. No doubt, better arrangements of the parts could be devised to achieve the same purpose. The bogie-sides are attached by screws to a tapped central bolster, but they must not be rigidly fixed ; there must be just enough play to allow the sides to pivot freely on the screws. The stops could be arranged in various ways. In the drawing, they take the form of small rectangular pieces of sheet-metal, soldered above the bolster so as to overhang the sides. When the sides move about 2 or 3 degrees from the normal position they encounter these stops and further movement is prevented.

It must be remembered that the screws which hold the side-frames to the bolster must be secured so that they cannot work loose. They must be screwed home to the point where they allow just the right amount of freedom and no more. Most workers will, presumably, solder the shanks of the screws to the bolster on the inside, with a pencil-point iron. A possible alternative might be provided by locking-nuts and anti-friction washers of some sort, on the inside.

It may be noted that most American-made coach-bogies for " OO " and " HO " are now compensated much as described, except that the sides appear to be attached to the bolster with metal pegs instead of screws. Samples fitted to some of the writer's stock certainly hold the track better than uncompensated ones.

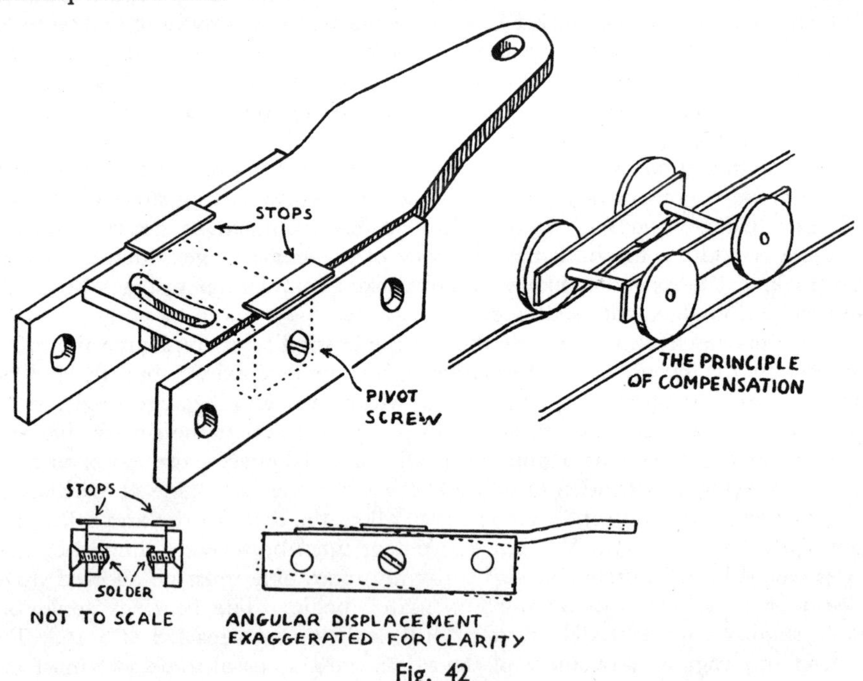

Fig. 42

CHAPTER VI

THE SUPERSTRUCTURE

HAVING covered the main points of chassis design and construction, we may next consider the superstructure. This is not much more than a shell, and does not contain any working parts. Perhaps the best way to help the beginner to visualise what is involved is to take a simple type of locomotive and to analyse it into its component parts. Fig. 43 shows side and front elevations of a typical 0-6-0 goods locomotive, and below are set out all the sheet-metal parts which are required for its construction. First, we have the running-plate, which must be cut out very carefully because it forms the foundation on which all the other parts are assembled. The centre must be cut away to accommodate the motor and wheels. Part *B* is the boiler and firebox. It can be cut from sheet-metal and rolled as shown here, or made from tube if a suitable size is available. The writer is doubtful if the advantages of tube outweigh the disadvantages. The narrow strip below the dotted line is an overlap for soldering, and must be ignored when setting out the circumference of the boiler and the positions of the holes by which the various fittings are attached. The portion on the right, marked *xx* represents the firebox ; the lower edges are not bent inwards to meet, but downwards to rest on the bed-plate as in Fig. 58. The underside of the firebox thus remains open and will be occupied by the motor. In addition, it will be necessary to cut away part of the underside of the boiler for the same purpose. It is usually better to leave this until after the boiler has been soldered up ; to roll it to a true cylindrical form if part of the underneath joint has been removed is all but impossible. Also, it may then be easier to estimate just how much must be cut away.

It will be noticed that a number of holes are to be drilled in the boiler before it is rolled, for the chimney, dome, safety-valve casing, and for the hand rail knobs and boiler feed valves. Their positions must be ascertained by measurement of the front and side elevations. Part *C* is the smokebox wrapper, with holes for the chimney and the two front handrail knobs. Parts *D*, *E* and *F* form the cab, part *F* being the roof. *G* is the smokebox front, *H* the splasher-tops, and *J* the buffer-beam. The drag-beam at the rear end will be similar, but without the holes for buffer shanks. The two small parts *I* and *K* are fitted respectively at the sides and front of the smokebox. The shape of the steps can be taken from the side elevation.

In addition to the sheet-metal parts, various small turnings are required : chimney, dome, buffers, etc. If the reader has a lathe he will probably prefer to make these (except perhaps the buffers) himself. If not he will presumably have to buy them, although wonders have been performed by chucking a piece of rod in a hand-drill fixed in a vice and turning with a file. Sundry other small parts, mostly made of wire, will be mentioned as the description proceeds.

MATERIALS

Most modelmakers are inclined to use sheet-metal which is quite unnecessarily thick for the purpose. For a " OO " gauge model, material about seven thousandths of an inch thick (about 36 or 37 gauge) is quite strong enough for most parts other than running-plates, and for " O " gauge about ten or twelve thousandths (32 or 30 gauge) is ample. A slightly thicker sheet should be used for running-plates, say 32 gauge for a " OO " gauge model, and perhaps 28 for " O " gauge. Even for the running-plate thicker material is not essential, however, as it will be stayed and reinforced by the valancing, and various other parts. For boilers the thicknesses given ought not to be exceeded, as the thicker the material the more difficult it will be to roll to a true cylinder.

Brass, nickel-silver, or tin, may be used. Brass should be avoided as much as possible as it is exasperating stuff to paint. It is also slightly more difficult to solder than nickel, since it allows heat to dissipate away more quickly from the place where it is wanted. Tin is easy to solder and takes paint well, but is liable to rust at the edges if the paint should become chipped. Objection has been made against the use of tinplate on the grounds that, being iron with a thin covering of tin, it might have some adverse effect on the permanent-magnet of the motor. Actually, the quantity used in a model locomotive is so small that it is extremely doubtful if this has any validity in fact, even if there should be some grounds for it in theory. Nickel-silver is certainly the most satisfactory material,* and has the advantage that it can be left unpainted when required as a fair representation of steel. Whether brass or nickel be used, it is advisable to obtain a soft grade, if possible. This applies particularly to boilers where the metal has to be rolled.

For small turnings, brass is usually used, but there is no reason why the modelmaker should not employ silver-steel rod. Nickel-silver, unfortunately, is difficult to obtain in rod form, but would be preferable to either. In some old locomotives the dome was left unpainted and polished ; for such it is of course essential to use brass. Some commercial fittings, such as domes and safety-valves, are cast in a white-metal alloy. Where soldering can be dispensed with, there is really no reason why duralumin rod should not be used for small turnings such as chimneys.

* The writer has recently become acquainted with monel metal. It seems to be fully equal to nickel-silver as a material for the modelmaker. It is easily worked, solders well, and has a particularly nice surface for painting.

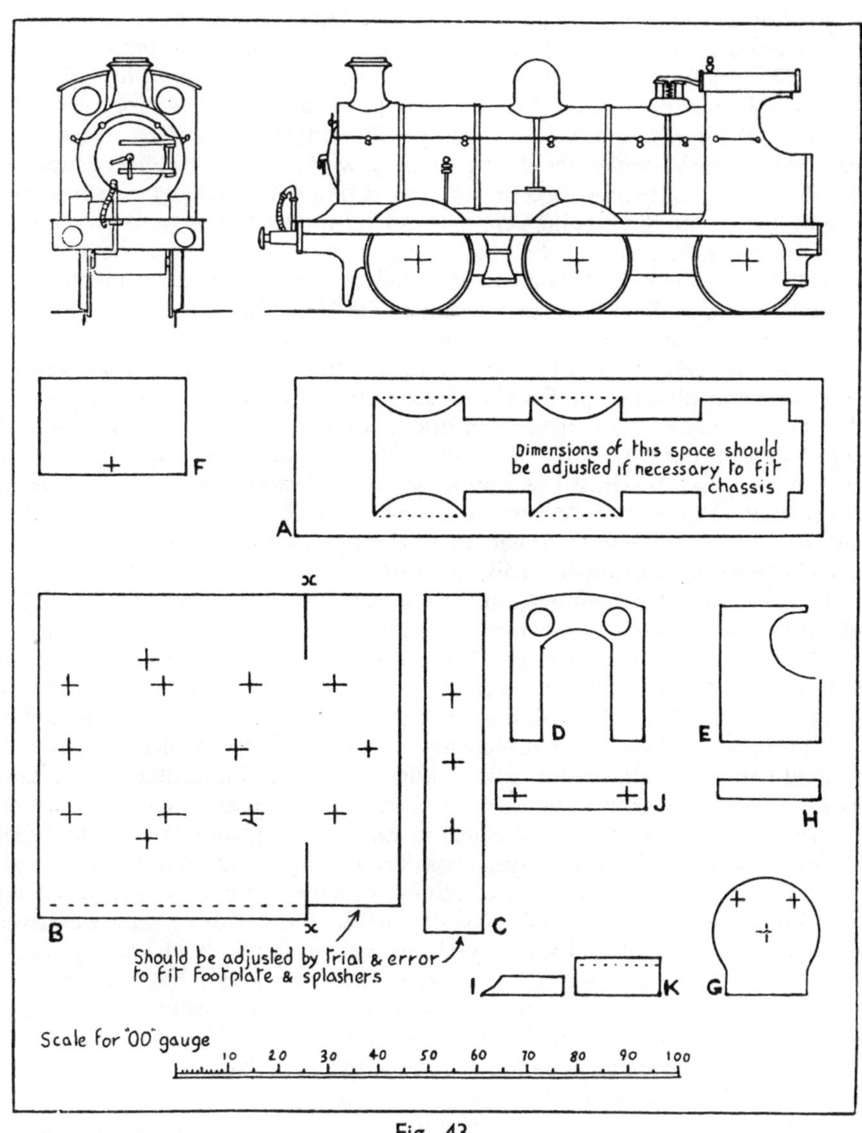

Fig. 43

THE RUNNING-PLATE

As the foundation of the superstructure, upon which the other parts are assembled, this should be made first. The shape should be set out with a scriber on a piece of metal which is quite flat. Start by making sure that one edge is dead straight and take all measurements from it. This can be verified by pressing a steel straightedge against it. It is easier to detect any error if the material and straightedge are held up to the light to see if it penetrates at any point. If necessary, the edge must be rubbed down a little with a file and emery-cloth. If the worker has acquired the knack of draw-filing, with the material held in a vice or suitably clamped, it will be much easier to obtain a true edge. Right-angles should be marked with a small engineer's square. One having a side two or three inches long is quite large enough. Mark in a longitudinal centre-line, being sure it is exactly in the middle, and on it mark the positions of the two screw holes by which the superstructure is to be mounted on the chassis. It may be difficult to obtain an accurate measurement of the distance between these holes *on the chassis* with a rule, due to the presence of various obstructions such as the motor above and the worm-wheel below. In that case, the best thing is to take the measurement as accurately as possible with a pair of dividers, preferably of the screw adjustable type, and transfer it to the bed-plate. As a precaution, the holes in the bed-plate can be drilled rather smaller than the final size ; then if it is found that a slight error has crept in they can be drifted as necessary, with a rat-tail file. Next, mark in the portion which must be cut out to clear the motor, working always from the centre-line. In the same manner, mark the parts which must be removed to clear the wheels. Personally, I like to mark in the position of the driving-axle as a transverse line extending from side to side and to use this as a check for all other dimensions. If the metal is slightly tarnished, do not clean it up until it is time to start soldering ; it is easier to see the scribed lines on a dull surface. Some people like to cover the metal with a thin coat of paint of any fairly dark colour and to mark out by scribing through the paint to the metal.

There are several ways of cutting out sheet-metal. A piercing-saw can be used with the work held in a vice, but this is rather unsatisfactory for thin sheets unless very fine blades can be obtained. Even then trouble may be experienced through the teeth catching and binding, and the mortality of blades is likely to be high until considerable experience has been gained. There are a few occasions when a piercing-saw is the best way, and there should certainly be one in the worker's tool-kit, but the writer advises that whenever possible a good pair of tinsnips be used. Make the cut about 1/64 in. " proud " of the final line, and finish with a file. When experience has been gained, it is quite possible to make the cut dead on, but the beginner should not attempt it ; it is too easy for the snips to wander. The objection to the use of tinsnips is that they are liable to distort the metal. There is little risk of this if the following precaution is observed. Cut the metal in the first place about half an inch away from the final line. Then make a second cut, removing about a quarter-of-an-inch of the remaining waste. Now make the final cut, as close to the final line as is considered advisable. Thus, when the second and final cuts are made the waste part is narrower than the part to be retained, and the narrower part, offering less resistance, will always take the distortion,

Fig. 44. This proceeding is admittedly rather wasteful, but considering the small amount of material the model-maker uses it is thoroughly justifiable.

For concave curves and internal cuts, such as the middle part of the running-plate, the simplest way is to drill a row of holes as close together and as close to the marked line as possible. The waste metal is then removed with jeweller's files and the line cleaned up with similar files, flat for straight lines and half-round for curves. Usually, a drill about $\frac{1}{8}$-in. size will be convenient for this. The work should be supported on a waste piece of wood while drilling. Do not be tempted to take the drill too close to the scribed line ; it is less trouble to do a little more filing than to start all over again. The method is illustrated in Fig. 45.

When the running-plate has been cut out it should be examined to make sure it is quite flat. If there is an *even* curve from end to end, or diagonally from corner to corner, it probably will not do any harm provided it is slight, because it will be corrected when the valances are soldered on. But if there are any kinks they must be got out now, for nothing can be done about them later. It may be possible to get rid of them by judicious persuasion with the

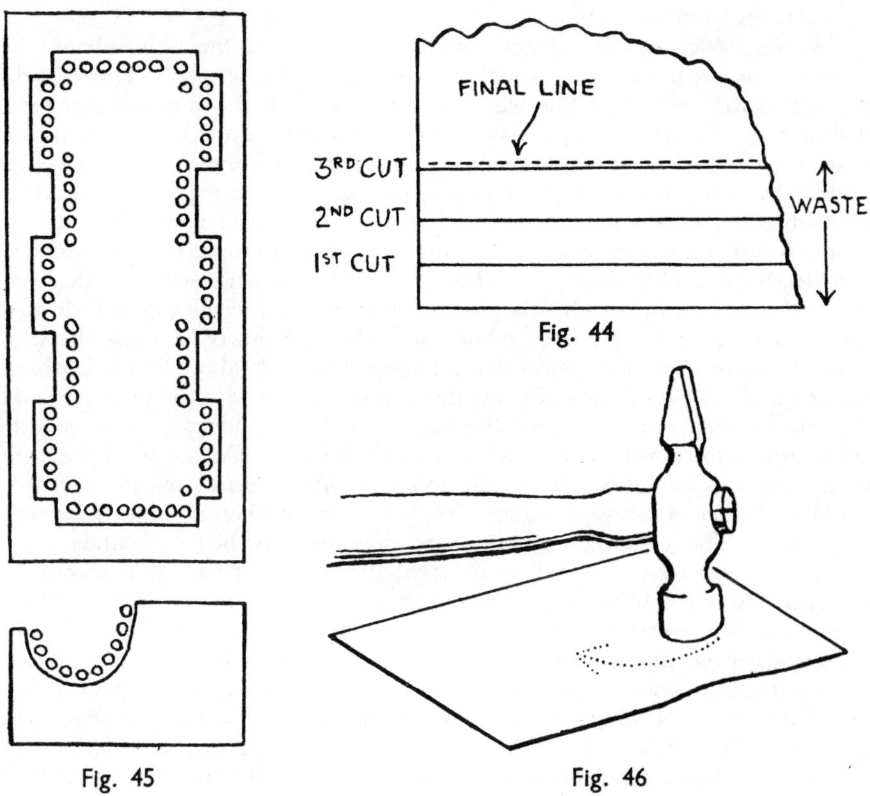

Fig. 44

Fig. 45

Fig. 46

fingers. If matters are too serious for this treatment, the work should be placed on a piece of flat iron and treated with a succession of gentle taps with a small hammer. It is recommended that a round-headed hammer be used, but the writer uses one with an ordinary flat head and with care it works quite satisfactorily. The taps should be made with what may be described as a sort of skidding motion, the hammer moving towards the worker. It is almost impossible to describe it in words and the reader should experiment on a piece of waste metal. Perhaps Fig. 46 may help. It is important that the hammer head should be smooth and clean.

The next operation is to attach the running-plate valances and buffer-beams. For valances, most workers probably use " OO " gauge rail laid flat. Alternatively, $\frac{1}{16}$-in. × $\frac{1}{16}$-in., or $\frac{1}{16}$-in. × $\frac{1}{8}$-in. brass or nickel strip may be used for " OO " gauge ; but, for a few prototypes with extra deep valances, something thicker may be necessary. Begin by cutting two pieces to the required length, usually the length of the bed-plate less the thickness of the two buffer-beams. Check for possible error by laying one of them on the running-plate with the two buffer-beams pressed against it at one end. It is advisable to cut the running-plate slightly long to allow for cleaning up after the valances have been attached.

When soldering the valances to the running-plate the latter should be secured to a flat piece of wood with two or three drawing pins. They should be pushed well in so that the heads bed down against the metal and prevent it riding up, Fig. 47. Tin the edges where the valances and buffer-beams are to be attached. Lay one of the valances on the bed-plate so that it is set back slightly from the edge. Hold it in position, either with a piece of wood or more drawing pins. Tack it to the footplate at one end with the soldering iron. Before going any farther, examine it carefully to make sure the valance is perfectly parallel to the edge. Hold it down at the point where it has been soldered to the bed-plate, with a piece of stripwood ; then slowly, a little at a time, work the iron up to the other end. Proceed slowly, holding the iron quite still on one spot for several seconds, then moving up about three-eighths of an inch and pausing again. Follow the iron up closely with the piece of wood to ensure good contact between the parts. If the valance is allowed to ride up at any point it will be difficult to correct it later. Do not work the iron backwards and forwards ; it can do no good. And do not, on any account, tack the valance at two points some distance apart and then fill in the interven-ing space. The valance, being smaller than the bed-plate, expands more when heated so that the work would probably be distorted. It is rather on the principle of the bi-metallic thermostatic control devices which are used on certain kinds of water heaters. If the iron is hot enough, and if it is kept in contact with the metal long enough to heat it thoroughly, the solder should run as freely as water, and a perfectly clean joint should result which will need little or no cleaning up. It goes without saying that the iron should be applied on the inside of the valance where the solder will not be seen.

If the soldering is blobby and irregular, it almost certainly means that

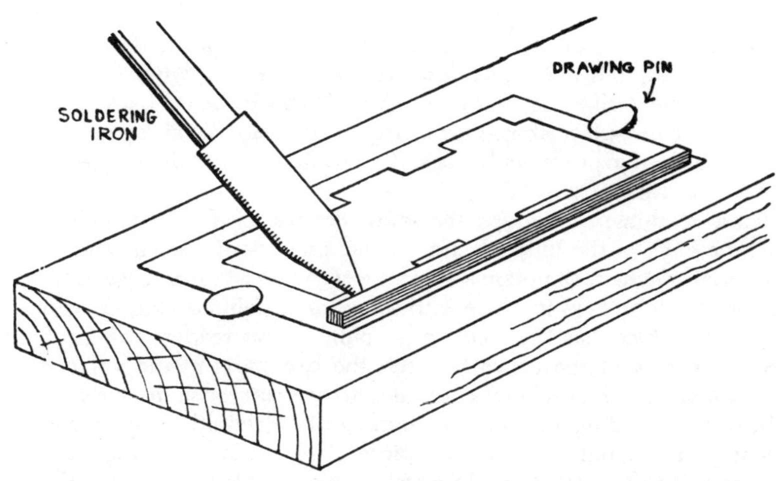

Fig. 47

not enough heat has been applied. *Practically all soldering troubles, apart from those attributable to dirt, are due either to the use of an iron which does not give enough heat or to the iron not being held in contact with the work long enough.* Any ordinary electric soldering iron, except perhaps the smallest pencil-point variety, should provide ample heat for a " OO " gauge running-plate, provided the tip is clean and well tinned. If the iron is dirty the scale will form a sort of insulating film and prevent the heat getting through to the work properly. It follows that, if trouble is experienced, the fault is probably with the worker rather than with the iron. So don't go out and buy a larger iron until the matter has been thoroughly tested. Make sure the iron is clean, and, above all things, do not move it about over the surface of the work quickly or jerkily ; you simply waste heat and nerve energy that way. Keep it quite still with the hand muscles as relaxed as possible until the solder in the immediate vicinity is quite liquid, and has the bright appearance of quicksilver ; then move on. And it is better to use too much flux rather than too little. The writer prefers the paste type, sold in a flat round tin ; but that is a matter of personal inclination. The paste type seems to be most easily removed with a small wire brush and a rag moistened with carbon tetrachloride.

Needless to say, the remarks in the last paragraph apply to most soldering jobs as well as to valances, but particularly to long edges.

After the valances, the buffer-beams should be added. For this screw a block of wood, *A*, on to another as in Fig. 48. Make sure that the angle between them is a right-angle. Do not take it on trust ; test with an engineer's square Arrange the bed-plate against the face of the smaller block as shown, making sure that it is at right-angles, and again using drawing pins to secure it. In particular, place drawing pins *BB over* the valances near the end where the new joint is to be made. This is to guard against the slight risk of the ends springing away from the bed-plate when the iron is applied. Place the buffer-beam in position and hold it against the small block, *A*, with a piece of strip-wood, *C*. If the design requires that the buffer-beam be set back slightly from the edge of the bed-plate, introduce a piece of thin card or thick paper as packing between the buffer-beam and block *A*. Apply the iron in the same way as described for valances.

There remain to be added the short sections of valance which turn over against the back of the buffer-beam. These can usually be cut and filed from the material of which the main valances were made. They are arranged as in Fig. 49 and can be held in place with some small pointed tool, or with a piece of stripwood which has been cut to a point. Most readers will probably be content to represent the curve between the two parts of the valance with a blob of solder, which is subsequently filed to the correct shape, Fig. 50.

Before proceeding further the running-plate should be examined to see that it is perfectly flat. Put it on a piece of plate-glass, or other flat surface, and see that it is in contact at all points. A good test is to press it at the corners with the finger to see if it can be made to rock. Needless to say, the flat surface should have been wiped over with a cloth first to remove any grit. If it is at all out of true a little cautious bending with the fingers should put it right.

THE CAB

The writer usually assembles the cab next. It can be made in three pieces as in Fig. 43, or the front and sides can be cut out in one piece and bent.

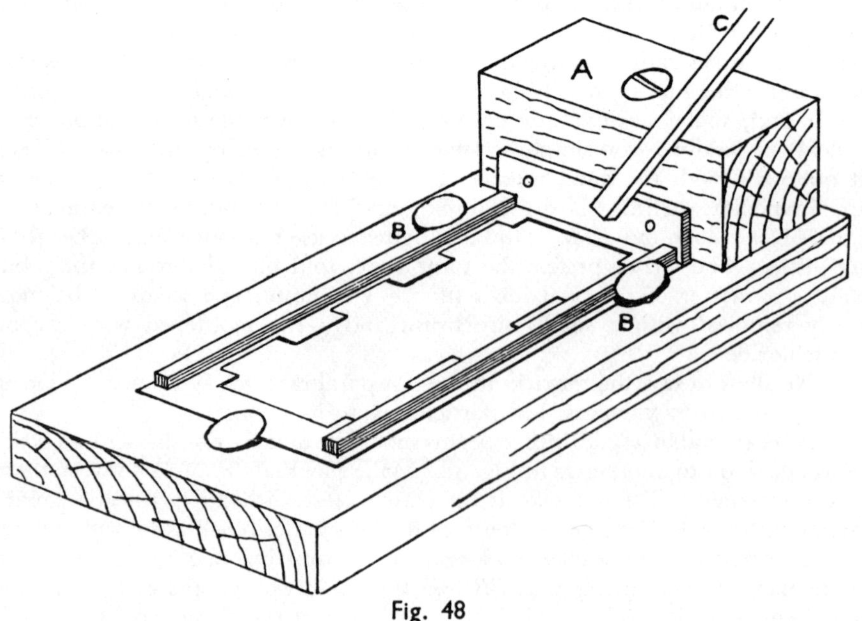

Fig. 48

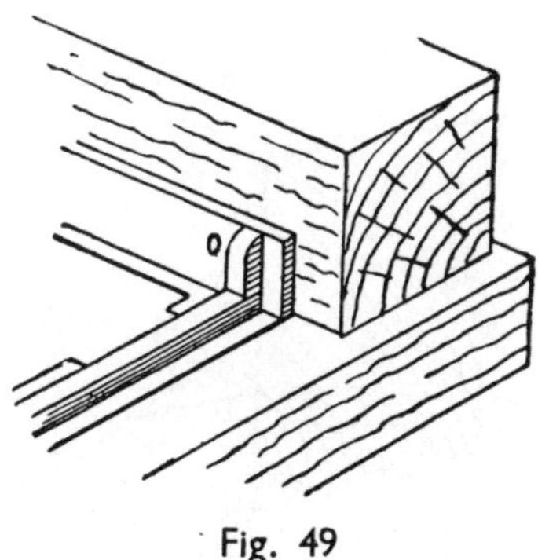

Fig. 49

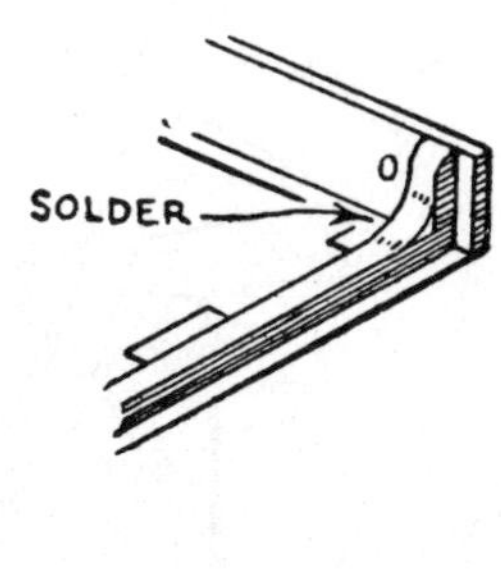

Fig. 50

The latter method cannot give quite such clean corners, but there should not be much difference if thin material is used, and the beginner will probably find the one-piece method easier. It is unwise to drill the spectacle-plate windows with a drill the final size of the hole. Large drills do not take kindly to thin metal in any case, and are liable to catch and tear when breaking through so that, in extreme cases, the surface may be distorted. It is safer to start with a smaller drill, not more than $\frac{1}{8}$ in. diameter, and to open out with a rat-tail file. For a window which is an irregular shape, two, or even three, holes may be drilled and joined with the file.

A line should have been scribed across the running-plate to mark the position of the spectacle-plate. The method of soldering the latter in position is shown in Fig. 51A. The same procedure can be adopted if the cab has been cut out in one piece. The running-plate is placed on a block of wood, narrow enough to allow the buffer-beams to overhang, and another block is attached to the first by means of a single screw, which passes through the opening which has been made in the running-plate for the motor. Again, it is of the utmost importance to be sure that the angle between the block and the running-plate is a perfect right-angle. Before the screw is drawn up quite tight the bed-plate is manoeuvred until the edge of the wood block coincides exactly with the line which marks the position of the spectacle-plate. A piece of stripwood is used to hold the spectacle-plate against the block while it is soldered.

It is not difficult to attach the cab sides (assuming that these have been cut as separate pieces) without any special arrangements, as there are now two edges to work against, that of the running-plate and that of the spectacle-plate. It is better, however, to work in the angle of a mitre block as in Fig. 51B. The cab side should be backed up with card packing, equal in thickness to the amount by which the side stands back from the edge of the running-plate. All soldering will, of course, be carried out inside the cab. The roof should be left off until the model is nearly finished.

The superstructure should be tried in place on the chassis to ascertain that the opening which has been cut in the spectacle-plate will clear the motor.

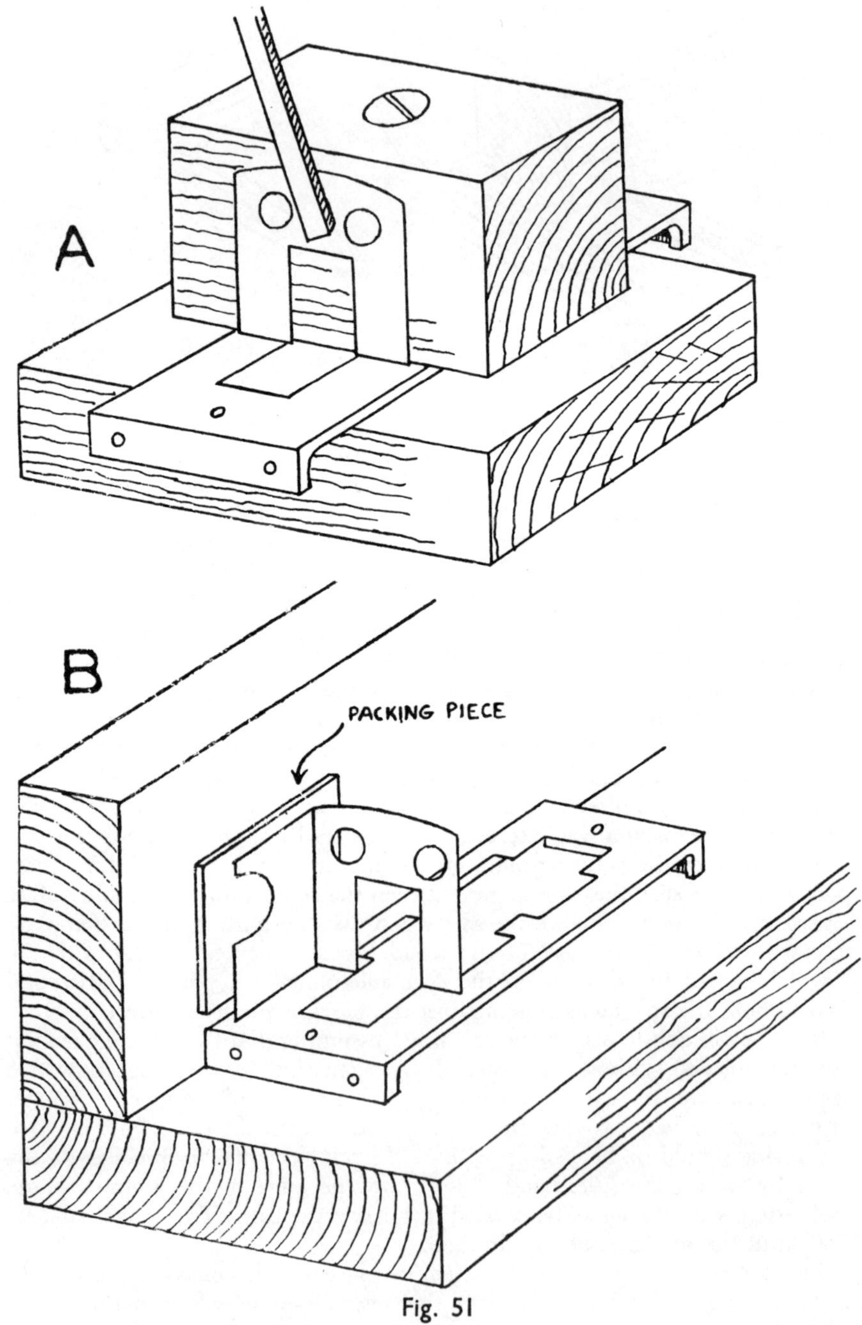

Fig. 51

SPLASHERS

Before fitting the boiler and firebox, it may be as well to build up the splashers which enclose the driving-wheels. Turning back to Fig. 43 it will be seen that the fronts of the splashers are shown integral with the running-plate, the intention being that they should be bent up at right-angles to stand vertically. I am aware that opinions will differ about this ; the more experienced worker may prefer to solder each one in place separately, but the beginner may find the method suggested easier to manage. It calls for considerable skill with the iron and a steady hand to get these tiny parts soldered in their correct positions cleanly. And few things look worse than splashers which are out of alignment. If it is attempted, the splasher should be made up first, by soldering the curved top to the front. The running-plate should be tinned where the splasher is to stand. If it does not stand upright when placed in position, the lower edges of the curved top should be filed very carefully to tip it slightly backwards or forwards as the case may be. Place the tip of the iron on the running-plate, in front of the splasher but not touching it. Keep the iron quite still and wait quietly for the film of tinning to melt, which can be seen clearly enough in a reasonably good light. It is advisable to start near one corner of the splasher and when the solder melts to move along to the other end. Remove the iron, and the part should be securely soldered in place, Fig. 52.

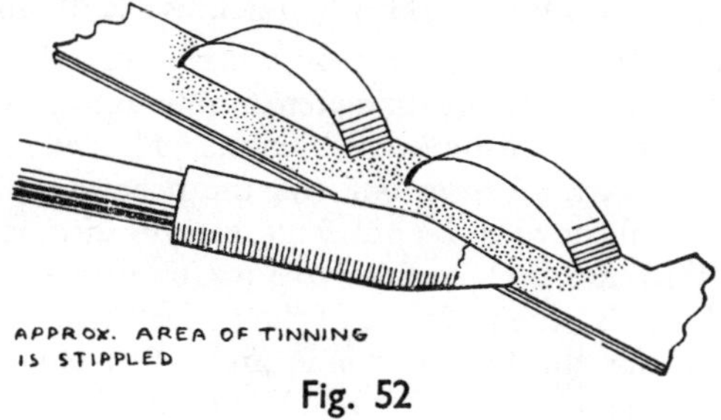

Fig. 52

May I pause here to appeal to the reader not to get " all het up " when undertaking these fiddling soldering jobs (yes, I know it isn't easy). Try to hold the iron lightly ; don't grip it as if your life depended upon it, and arrange matters so that you have something to support your wrist and forearm against. I wish I could always manage to follow my own advice !

The drawback of making the splasher fronts in one piece with the running-plate is that if a hard metal is used there is a risk that they may break off while the right-angle bend is being made. As explained earlier, there is little or no risk of this if the bend is at right-angles to the grain of the metal. There is really no objection to cutting out the running-plate accordingly, since any slight weakness thereby introduced in the longitudinal direction will be more than counteracted by the valances and other parts which are to be soldered to it. No difficulty is likely to be experienced with *soft* brass or nickel, or with tinplate.

BOILERS AND FIREBOXES

We have already mentioned the two ways of producing boilers: from sheet-metal and from tube. When the latter method is employed, thin walled (about 1/32 in. thick) tube should be obtained. Thicker stuff should be avoided because the diffusion of heat through it is so rapid that to solder cleanly and satisfactorily is very difficult. The ordinary small electric soldering-iron will be found unequal to the task, and if, by any means, enough heat is produced to fuse the solder, one joint is more than likely to come unstuck while another is being made. Tube has one advantage if the worker has the use of a lathe; it can be mounted between centres and the boiler-bands turned on it by taking a light cut from the surfaces between them. In this way one of the most delicate and fiddling jobs in the making of a model locomotive, the soldering of the boiler-bands, is avoided; and a better finish is obtained.

If sheet-metal is to be used, start by ascertaining the circumference of the boiler. To do this multiply the diameter in millimetres by 3.1416. Lay this out on the metal and mark off the overall length. The length of the smokebox is usually included. Mark off from one end the portion which represents the firebox. The metal will have to be cut for a certain distance from each side with tinsnips to allow the firebox sides to turn outwards when the boiler is rolled, Fig. 58. Mark also the positions of the boiler-bands and the top centre-line where the holes for the funnel, dome, and safety-valve, will be located. Also, mark the positions of any other holes, such as those for handrail knobs and clack-valves. These should be located by measuring as accurately as possible round the end elevation of the boiler, working from the top centre-line. It must not be forgotten that the front elevation of the locomotive probably shows the diameter of the smokebox, which is usually slightly larger than the boiler. An allowance must be made for this or the holes may be quite noticeably out of their true positions.

Another way is to measure on the front elevation the angle which the fitting subtends at the centre of the boiler with the top centre-line. That is to say: a line drawn vertically through the centre of the chimney, giving angle *acb* in Fig. 53. Suppose for the sake of illustration that this angle is found to be 50 deg., and that circumference of the boiler is 58 mm. Then the sum $\frac{58 \times 50}{360}$ will give us in millimetres the distance which must be marked off from the top centre-line; 8 millimetres as near as makes no odds.

All holes should be centre-popped and drilled before the boiler is rolled, but it is advisable to drill small pilot holes only, at this stage, and to enlarge them after the boiler has been soldered up. The reason for this is that the metal tends to bend more easily where it has been weakened by the presence of holes so that it is difficult to preserve the cylindrical form when rolling to shape. Perhaps a better way is not to drill the holes at all while the metal is flat—only to centre-pop them. After rolling to shape the boiler is mounted on a wood former (a piece of dowel-rod of suitable size) while the holes are drilled. A

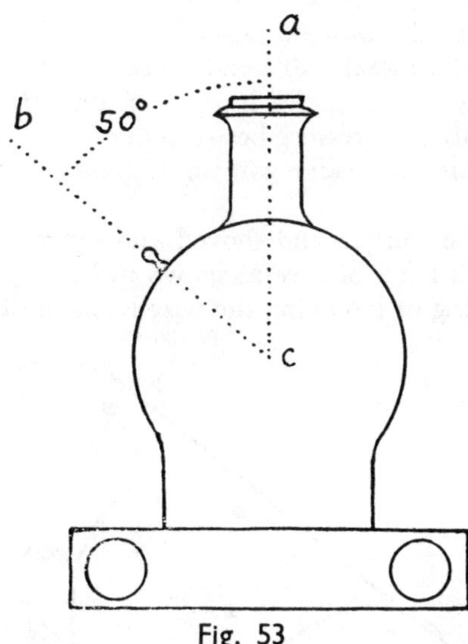

Fig. 53

strip about ⅛ in. wide should be added along one side of the boiler as an overlap for soldering, Fig. 58.

The rolling of boilers to obtain a true cylinder, free from kinks, is not easy in these small scales. Luckily, most of the distortion is likely to be underneath where it will not be seen, and much can be done to rectify matters after soldering by cautious pushing and squeezing between the fingers. Some people start the rolling process by placing the metal on a padded surface such as a pile of newspapers or a typewriter-mat, and roll with a metal rod. A steady even pressure should be applied ; it is rather like using a rolling-pin in making pastry. This certainly helps up to a point, but the writer doubts if it is a complete answer to the problem in such small sizes as 4 mm. scale. Even if a start is made with the rolling-pin method, it seems that the process must be finished by forcing the metal with the fingers round a wood or metal rod which is somewhat smaller than the required diameter. It is not difficult as regards the middle part ; the problem is to induce the outer edges to conform to the curve. Since my job here is to tell the reader what actually does happen and not what is *supposed* to happen, it had better be admitted that, in the end, it is usually a matter of bending the extreme edges inwards a bit at a time with pliers. There is no need to be discouraged by this unworkmanlike proceeding ; it is surprising how the kinks left by the pliers disappear when the seam has been well soldered and cleaned up with emery-cloth. And the seam is out of sight anyway—thank goodness. The rod used as a former should be perhaps two-thirds the diameter of the finished boiler. For the outer edges, it is worth while to see what can be done with a former of smaller diameter, and it goes without saying that the softer the metal—the better, Brass and nickel-silver can be softened by heating until bright red in a gas or blowlamp flame and plunging in cold water. It must be borne in mind all the time when rolling with the fingers that the metal will bend more easily—will be liable to kink in fact—along the lines where holes have been drilled. Therefore an effort should be made to apply the pressure between the holes. This is a little difficult to convey in words, but the reader will understand what is meant as soon as he comes to do it.

The metal must be worked and shoved and squeezed until the edges can be drawn together with loops of wire as shown in Fig. 54. The exact diameter is obtained by tightening or loosening the wire loops until the one edge exactly

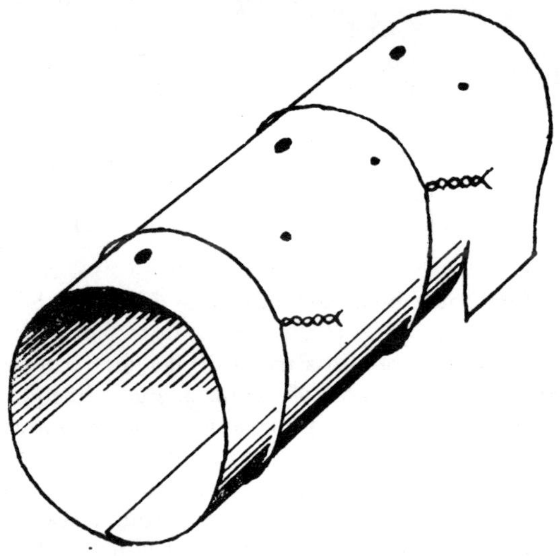

Fig. 54

coincides with the scribed line on the other. Now solder along the seam using plenty of solder to conceal the joint. Do not worry if the boiler is slightly oval ; it will be easier to deal with it after soldering. The wire loops are bound to get soldered to the boiler, but every trace of them can be quickly filed away when cleaning up.

The boiler having been soldered up, and generally made as presentable as possible, the part which must be removed to clear the motor can be taken in hand. A pair of spring dividers can be set to the width of the motor, allowing a safety margin of not less than one millimetre on each side, and the measurement transferred to the boiler. The unwanted part can be removed with a miniature hacksaw, the boiler being placed over a piece of dowel rod, slightly smaller than the internal diameter, one end of which is secured in the vice. The firebox sides should first have been bent outwards. They will need some adjustment to make the boiler stand upright on the running-plate, but that should be left until the smokebox has been fitted, Fig. 55.

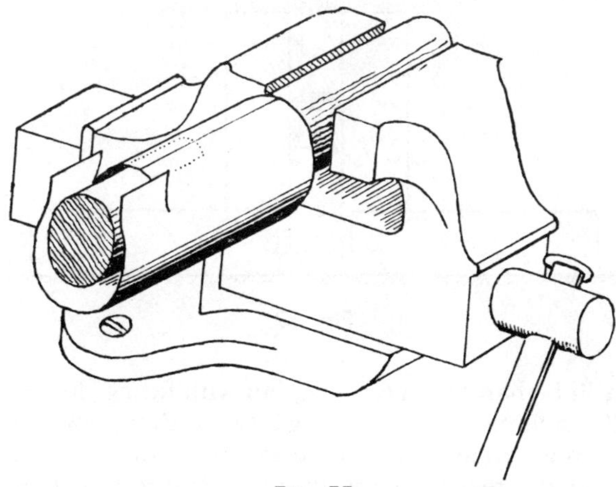

Fig. 55

THE SMOKEBOX

The smokebox is usually nothing more than a strip of metal wrapped round the boiler, with the ends bent outwards to stand on the running-plate. The length must be found by marking off small divisions, say two millimetres, on the front-end drawing with a sharp pencil. It is sufficient to measure from the top centre-line down to the running-plate on one side ; the total length will be double the figure thus obtained. This is obviously a rather rough and ready method ; it is advisable to cut the wrapper slightly longer than it appears that it should be, to allow for errors, and to file or snip a little away if it is found that the boiler stands higher on the running-plate than it should. It will be necessary also to adjust the underneath edges of the firebox so that the boiler stands perfectly horizontal. This is best judged with a height gauge, Fig. 56.

A hole must be drilled in the wrapper for the screw which secures the funnel, corresponding to the one in the boiler, and others, probably, for handrail knobs and possibly other fittings. Remember that the distance from the top centre to handrail knobs will be slightly greater on the wrapper than on the boiler to allow for the larger radius. If the handrails are high up on the boiler side

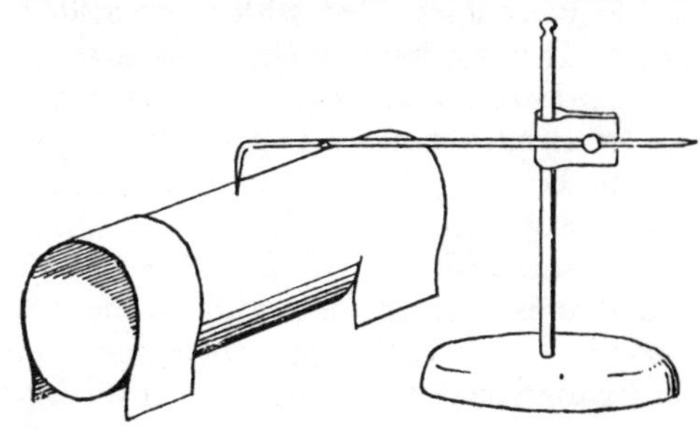

Fig. 56

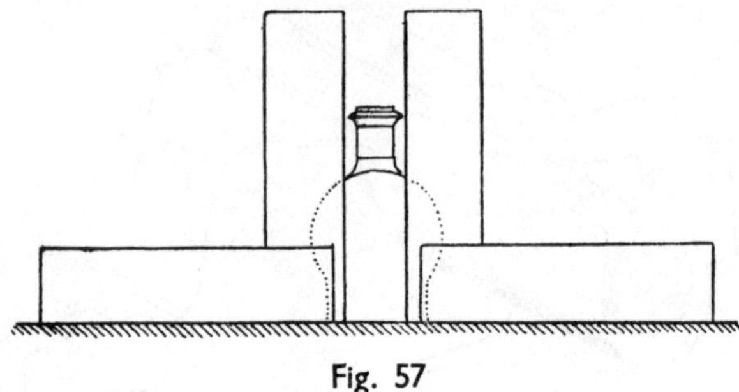

Fig. 57

the difference will be hardly appreciable, but with fittings lower down it might amount to half a millimetre in " OO " gauge. Before soldering the two parts together the chimney should be secured in place with a screw from below. It will serve to hold the two parts together and ensure that they are correctly lined up. Soldering should not present any particular difficulty. The two parts should be lightly tacked together with the iron at one or two places and a final inspection made to see that the sides of the smokebox are splayed out equally and that the boiler stands upright. Stand the assembly on a flat even surface and do not be satisfied until you are sure that the funnel is standing upright. Test with an engineer's square or, better still, two squares, one on each side, placed so that when sighted from in front the funnel is visible between them, Fig. 57. When everything is in order, finish soldering the wrapper to the boiler. Try to run blobs of solder into the angular spaces between the boiler and the wrapper to support and strengthen the flaps which form the sides of the smokebox saddle. The smokebox front should be marked out from the front-end drawing, and cut a trifle oversize to allow for trimming when in position. A pilot hole is drilled in the centre for the door handles. It should be left off until after the boiler has been mounted on the running-plate ; it is, in fact, advisable to leave it almost until the last because one may want to get inside the boiler for some unforeseen purpose. The smokebox saddle can be filled up at the back, below the boiler, with a piece of sheet-metal cut to the required shape. Another way, which helps to increase weight, is to file a piece of lead as nearly as possible to the required form. It should be soldered in place, and any gaps or crannies filled with more solder. Pewter solder is useful for such purposes. It has a lower melting point than the ordinary kind and is therefore more amenable and easier to manage in awkward corners. It is then cleaned up with an old file kept specially for work on solder and similar clogging substances.

We should now be ready to solder the boiler to the running-plate. Locate it carefully, and tack in place with the iron at one point only at the front end. Check up carefully that it is dead in the middle of the running-plate, that it is parallel with the edges, and that the top centre-line is horizontal. Repeat the test with a height gauge, shown in Fig. 56. If all is well, complete the soldering. Work inside as far as possible in order to avoid the need for cleaning up. This is usually possible at the firebox end but seldom at the front. If the firebox fits the spectacle-plate well, it is not necessary to solder all the way round the joint ; any corners which are difficult to reach with the iron can very well be ignored.

Before doing anything more, try the assembly in position on the chassis to be sure it clears the motor. If it is found to be fouling at any point, so that the superstructure cannot " sit down " evenly, we can hope to see where the trouble is through the open front of the boiler, since the smokebox front has not yet been soldered in place. If the clearances have been carefully checked at an earlier stage there is little likelihood of trouble developing now. The nuts for the attachment of the superstructure to the chassis should now be soldered in position, and the two parts temporarily joined together. It is important to make quite sure that no part of the insulated brush-gear is shorting against the side of the boiler ; once the smokebox front was on it would be next to impossible to locate a fault of that nature. It might occur without preventing the superstructure assuming its proper position on the chassis, the pressure being so slight as to pass unnoticed. It is advisable to give the model a preliminary trial on the track, or at least to try the effect of passing current through the motor. If the motor runs normally without the superstructure but not with it, there is clearly something wrong. For the benefit of those completely inexperienced in electrical matters, it is necessary to add that if a motor does not start at once when power is applied the current should be shut off immediately and the cause investigated. *Never on any account leave the current turned on for more than a few seconds when a motor fails to start* ; there is a grave risk that the armature windings may burn out. Further, if a motor does not start at once it will not start at all until the cause has been removed, so there would be no point in leaving the current on.

If the normal power supply, accumulator or convertor unit, is not available while the model is being built, enough current for a test may possibly be

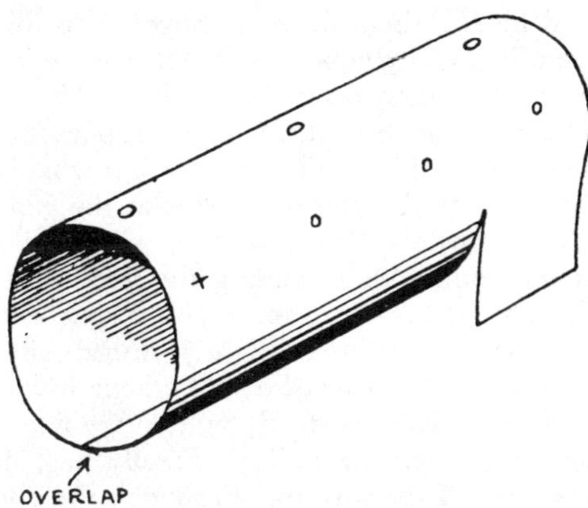

Fig. 58

obtained by joining several pocket lamp batteries in series to make up the required voltage.

If electrical shorting can be eliminated, but the motor will not run, the chances are that one of the wheels is binding against the running-plate or splasher.

For models in " O " gauge and larger sizes it may be advisable to build the smokebox in a different way. This applies particularly when the smokebox is considerably larger than the boiler. The smokebox is made up as an entirely separate unit, identical front and back plates being prepared and the wrapper soldered round them. The complete smokebox is then soldered to the front of the boiler. Any beading at the joint can be formed from wire or a narrow strip similar to a boiler-band.

BOILER - BANDS

It is probably better to fit these before the boiler is mounted on the running-plate. Thin metal strip of the correct width should be obtained if there is any possibility of doing so, for it is not easy to cut the bands from sheet without annoying and time-wasting distortion. If no suitable strip can be obtained they must be made from what is known as " shim stock," or something equivalent, not more than four thousandths of an inch thick—about the thickness of a sheet of writing paper. If cut with tinsnips, it will be found when laid out flat to be distorted into a continuous curve. It is no use while in this state, but can be straightened by gripping one end firmly and drawing it repeatedly between the thumb and finger with a firm steady pressure. The curve will gradually disappear, and it can then be laid on a flat surface and cleaned up by stroking with fine emery-cloth while one end is held down. The movement should be away from the end which is fixed.

Another method is to lay the metal sheet on a piece of hard wood or lead and to cut it with a sharp razor blade. This should give cleaner edges than tinsnips, and has the advantage that there will be less distortion. It is not very kind to the razor blade, but fortunately these are cheap.

The band should be cut about an inch longer than the circumference of the boiler, to provide a handle by which to hold it while soldering. The surplus will be removed later. Commence by tacking it to the boiler with the iron at one end, close to the seam underneath, Fig. 59. It does not matter if a rather blobby joint results here as it will be out of sight ; but what is rather important is that the band should be well secured, at least at the ends. Draw it firmly round the boiler, making sure that it corresponds with the line which has been scribed to mark its position. While holding the free end firmly underneath with one hand, tack it at two or three more points spaced round the circumference. The band should have been lightly tinned on the inside before commencing operations and the iron should be kept in contact long enough to cause the tinning to fuse. Exert a steady pull on the free end all the time to prevent it springing away from the boiler. Finally tack down the free end under the boiler, and cut off the surplus. Probably, the soldering will not be

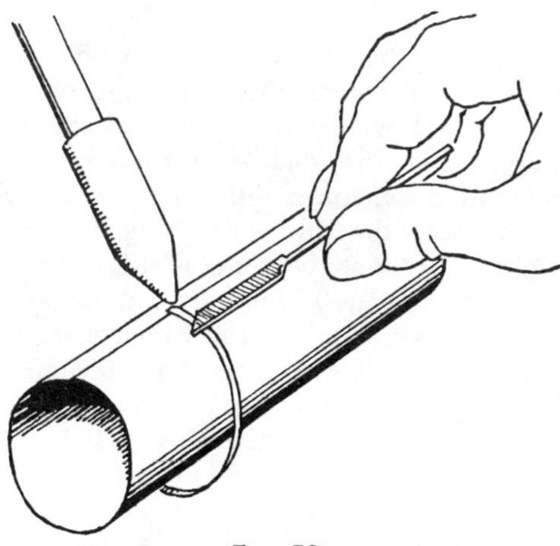

Fig. 59

very tidy at this stage, but it is not difficult to clean it up with small flat files. It is definitely necessary to put on the boiler-bands before fittings such as handrails are added ; they would be a serious obstruction to the free use of the file. A final clean up may be given with emery-cloth. To solder the band all the way round is not necessary, and this would leave an excessive amount of cleaning up to be done.

The superiority of thin sheet over brass tube for model boilers may never be more apparent than when fitting boiler-bands. With brass tube, the thickness of the metal will cause the heat to be diffused so quickly that it may be difficult to induce the tinning on the boiler-bands to fuse properly. Further, the solder on the tip of the iron is liable to come off on to the boiler in a semi-chilled mass ; its removal will be a tiresome business. If this misfortune occurs, do not remove the iron in a panic ; keep it in contact with the solder so as to heat the metal, and the solder, as much as possible. One will at least have some assurance of a firm joint that way, and if the surplus solder can be induced to become thoroughly fused by continued application of the iron it may at least be possible to spread it a little over the surface of the boiler, which will facilitate removal.

Some people prefer to make the boiler-bands of writing paper, and to apply them with tube glue after the first coat of paint is thoroughly dry. If they are bound down with at least two coats of paint and perhaps a coat of varnish they should be quite as firmly fixed as if they were of metal and soldered.

BOILER MOUNTINGS

The modelmaker will probably have to buy most of his boiler fittings if no lathe is available. It may be suggested, however, that they can be produced on quite a simple lathe, and even on one which is badly worn and unsuitable for work of a more exacting description. Some workers cut a sheet-metal template, Fig. 60, and test the progress of the work by holding it at intervals against the material in the lathe until it is found to fit. This is probably the best way for the beginner, although after a certain amount of practice it is possible and quicker to form the curves (i.e. skirt and cap of chimneys, etc.) by eye, after a few leading dimensions, such as overall length and barrel diameter have been established. It is sometimes difficult to decide whether the turning should be done with the top of the fitting or its base adjacent to the chuck-jaws. For chimneys, assuming that the shape of the skirt is to be produced by filing—the method favoured by the writer—it is usually best for the cap to be outwards, i.e. facing towards the tailstock. It should be drilled size 51 through the centre, and subsequently tapped for an 8-B.A. screw for attachment to the smokebox. It is best for the hole to pass right through ; indeed it will be obvious that it must do so if the work is set up as suggested here. The hole should be enlarged to as nearly as possible the correct internal bore for about $\frac{3}{16}$ in. or $\frac{1}{4}$ in. from the top end.

For a dome the procedure needs to be adapted to meet the particular case. If it has a sufficiently long *cylindrical* portion to permit of it being re-chucked the other way round after parting-off, it can be turned with the top outwards away from the chuck. Then, after being parted-off, it is reversed for drilling as in Fig. 61. With most modern locomotives, however, the dome is so short that there is no straight middle portion by which it can be chucked. For these we must proceed as in Fig. 62. The dome is shaped as far as possible and drilled for the fixing - screw. It is then parted-off and remounted by the skirt while the top is finished off.

When the fitting (chimney, dome, or certain types of safety-valve) has been parted-off from the rod, the base should appear approximately as shown in Figs. 63 and 64. It must be shaped to fit the boiler. It could be done partly in the lathe, but the business of setting the job up might well prove more trouble than it was worth. Begin by filing out the underside with a half-round file until it is a perfect fit on the boiler. Make sure that it stands upright. If the dome or chimney is in the least lopsided, the appearance of the model will not

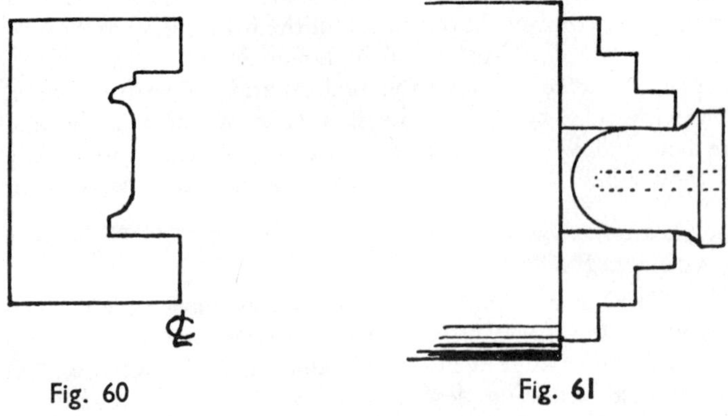

Fig. 60

Fig. 61

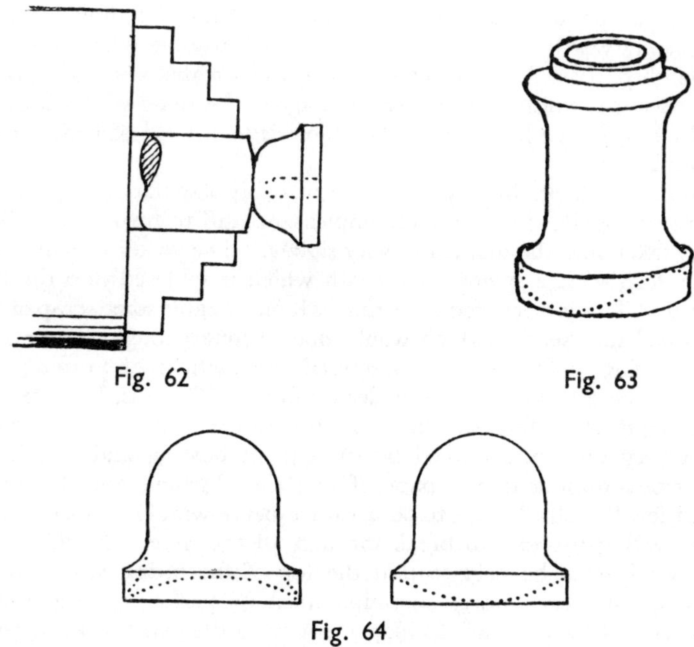

Fig. 62

Fig. 63

Fig. 64

only be spoilt but it will be slightly ridiculous. When a good fit has been secured, proceed to file away the sharp edges with the object of forming the more gentle curves at the sides, and to blend these imperceptibly into the sharper curves on the top centre-line of the boiler at back and front. Do not try to rush it, and stop frequently to consider what is happening. It will look a rather unfamiliar and hopeless job at first, but it is really not so difficult once one has got over the preliminary "stage fright." One uses small half-round files mostly, but a rat-tail may be useful here and there. *Do not work too long on one spot*; keep on turning the work round so that all parts progress towards the final shape concurrently. It will be easier to visualise the ultimate form if it is done that way, and to know when to stop, than it would be if deep cuts were taken on the sides, almost down to the final line, and the "transition curves" were worked in to meet them afterwards. When it is thought that the final shape has been reached, the work should be cleaned up with emery-cloth, finishing with the finest grade. And now comes the acid test—if, that is, the worker is prepared to face the labour necessary to obtain a really first-class finish. Examine the fitting to see if the reflections of surrounding objects run true on the polished surface from whatever angle the fitting is viewed. It is quite possible that the reflections instead of running in smooth sweeping lines will show kinks in places where the skirt flares out. If this should be the case—well, it is up to the worker to decide whether he feels inclined to put any more work into it or not. It is not very important if the fitting is to be painted, especially if a matt or semi-matt finish is favoured, but it is really worth while to take a little extra trouble when modelling the highly polished brass domes of certain old-time locomotives. If it is decided to try for a better finish any further work should be done with various grades of emery-cloth, remembering that the object is to get rid of high spots ; files should not be used.

Chimneys with bright copper caps are probably best made of copper throughout. Unfortunately, it is extremely unpleasant stuff to turn. Only light cuts should be taken and the tool fed in very slowly. The writer usually makes the cap separately, with a spigot underneath which is soldered into the barrel of the chimney. This is worth remembering as it may enable some scrap of material to be pressed into service which would not be long enough for the complete funnel. So far, we have only considered the method of forming the skirt when it is to be shaped to fit the boiler by filing. There is, however, another way of doing it which finds favour with some people. By this method the skirt is turned very thin, and shaped by subsequent beating and bending. The skirt must be almost as thin as paper if for " OO " gauge, and the turning off of the last few " thous " is apt to be a rather nerve-wracking operation ; one is half expecting the tool to break through all the time. It will be obvious that the work must be held so that the top of the fitting faces towards the chuck jaws, since the boring operation must be performed inside the skirt. The worker will have to use his judgement as to the exact form to which the skirt should be turned ; it will be a compromise between the minimum height on the centre-line of the boiler and the maximum height at the sides, remembering that while it is fairly easy to force it down for the sides it is a little risky to force it up too much for the middle of the saddle. While boring out, Fig. 65, the remaining thickness should be tested frequently with a small pair of outside calipers.

To shape the skirt, after parting-off, the fitting is held upright on a piece of rod of the same diameter as the boiler, held in the vice; a piece of waste wood is held on top to protect the metal from damage, and tapped lightly and repeatedly with a small hammer, Fig. 66. It must not be allowed to turn in relation to the rod during this operation ; it is advisable to make a mark on the fitting, to coincide with the top centre-line of the boiler. With repeated tapping the skirt will begin to assume the curve of the boiler, and the process should be carried as far as it will go. It is important to hold the job upright all the time. It is, however, unlikely that it will be possible to finish the skirt by this means alone. Probably the skirt will refuse to assume quite the desired shape at the sides, and will have to be assisted by a little gentle persuasion with a small pair of pliers. These, needless to say, should have smooth and not serrated jaws. It may now be necessary to finish up with fine emery-cloth if the skirt has become dented or kinked during the shaping process. Now screw the fitting temporarily in place on the smokebox and see if it stands upright. It may lean to one side as in Fig. 67, and if it does a little filing is indicated to tip it over until it comes upright. In many cases the

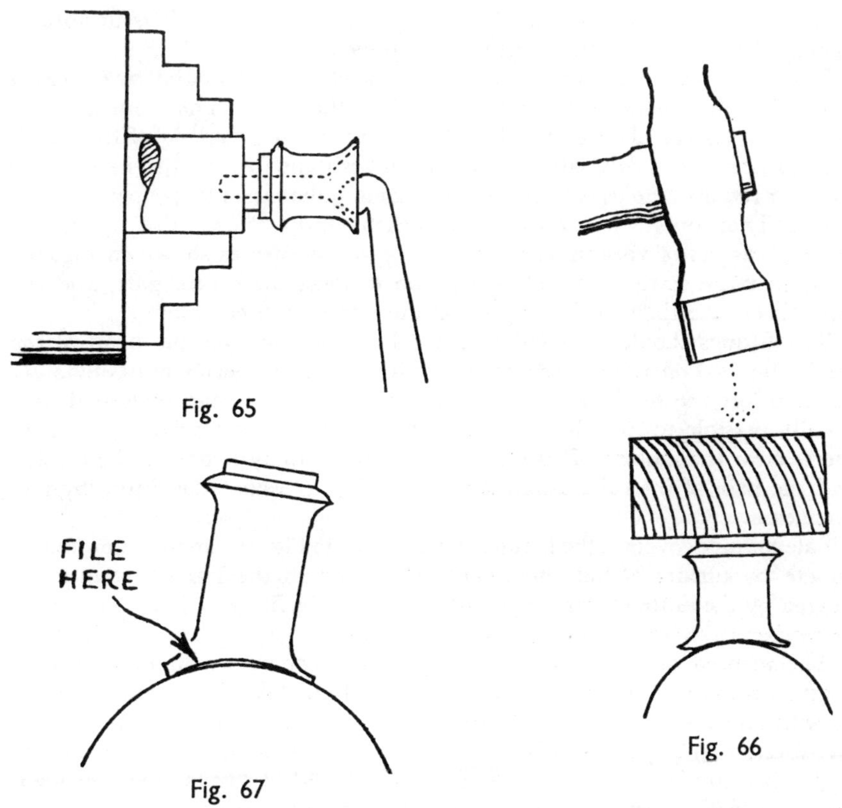

Fig. 65

Fig. 66

Fig. 67

desired result can be obtained by "drifting" the screw hole in the boiler to one side with a small round file, Fig. 71.

There is yet another very excellent way of forming the skirts of funnels and domes, for which the writer is indebted to Mr. M. D. Thornburgh. The fitting is turned minus the skirt; it is drilled for the fixing-screw and the underside is filed to a curve to fit the boiler. Cut a disc of sheet-metal a shade larger than the maximum diameter of the skirt (to allow for the slight loss occasioned by bending); drill a centre hole for the fixing-screw, and then bend it carefully to match the curve of the boiler. The two parts are screwed together and a fillet of solder is applied all round to form the skirt, Fig. 68. Provided the iron is hot enough, very little filing should be necessary to produce a perfect curve. Probably a little of the skirt may have to be filed away back and front on the top centre-line, to reproduce the exact shape of the original, but this filing is better left until the skirt has been formed and the effect can be judged with the fitting in position on the boiler. This method should produce just as good a finish as any other, and is more suitable for beginners or those who have no lathe. Unfortunately, and for obvious reasons, it is unsuitable for polished brass domes on old-time locomotives.

Very successful boiler fittings can be produced without a lathe, by chucking the material in a hand-drill which is held in the vice. The " turning " is done with a variety of files of different shapes while the handle of the hand-drill is turned. It is advisable to obtain an assistant to turn the handle, for the worker requires the use of both hands to manipulate the files properly.

Mr. Thornburgh has produced excellent fittings for " O " gauge by soldering washers of various sizes one on top of another as shown in Fig. 69. Usually, a piece of tube or rod is required to form the centre part, and the sharp corners are then filed away to produce the required shape.

The fittings should be fixed in place by soldering over the head of the screw inside the boiler. In the case of the chimney, this soldering must obviously be done before the smokebox front is put on. For domes and safety-valves it is usually possible to introduce the iron through the opening which has been made to clear the motor. It is much better not to apply solder on the outside round the base of the skirt unless it is impossible to secure the fitting by any other means.

Safety-valve covers of the familiar form shown in Fig. 70 cannot be produced complete by turning ; but they can be turned in the lathe to the shape indicated by the dotted lines, and must be finished by filing away the unwanted parts.

The method of dealing with fittings of the type shown in Fig. 72 must depend to some extent on the worker's skill. Probably, the simplest way to deal with the horizontal levers is to file them from sheet-metal, preferably nickel-silver, and to solder them into slots, cut with a fine piercing-saw, in the open bell top of the dome. The free ends should be bent round, as shown in the plan view, to surround the ends of the upright rods, which in the prototype incorporate the springs, in order to provide a larger surface of contact for soldering. These rods are of course the most difficult part of the assembly in small scales. If a watchmaker's lathe were available they might be turned from brass wire ; but they would be very delicate and easily damaged if anywhere near to scale size. The writer gets over the difficulty quite successfully by soldering a piece of brass tube, $\frac{1}{16}$-in. outside diameter, over a steel domestic pin. The result will be rather in excess of scale size as regards the diameter of the tube part for " OO " gauge, but this does not seem to be very noticeable. It can be brought nearer to the scale dimension by rubbing between the thumb and finger with emery-cloth, or by mounting in the lathe and turning very cautiously with a fine file and emery-cloth. For " O " gauge it will be approximately correct as it is. The vertical rods are soldered to the horizontal arms at the top end, and into holes drilled in the boiler at the lower end. Any adjustment to bring them exactly vertical, and parallel to each other must be effected by cautious bending.

Safety-valves of the type shown in Fig. 73 are produced by soldering two pieces of wire into holes drilled in the base-casing. The holes should be

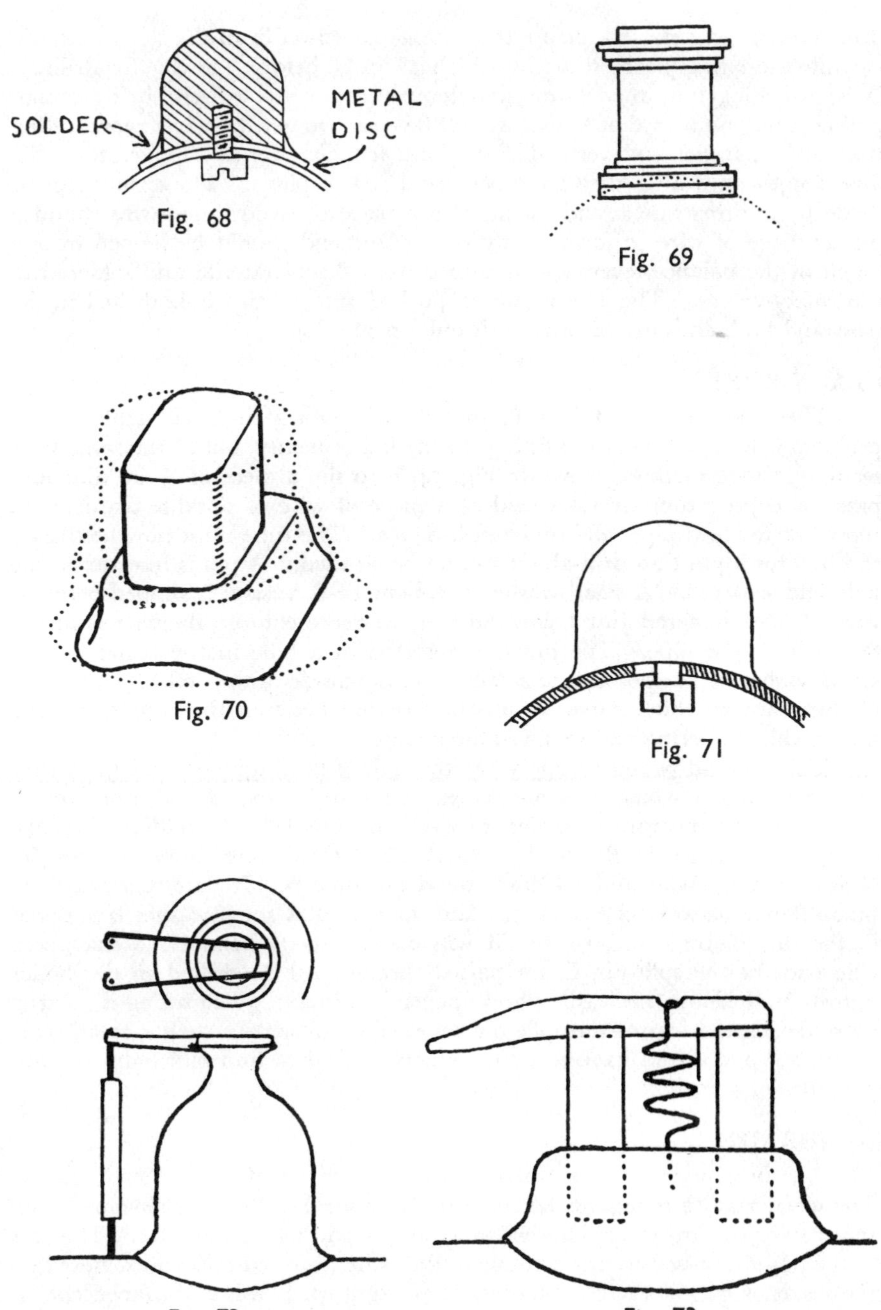

Fig. 68

Fig. 69

Fig. 70

Fig. 71

Fig. 72

Fig. 73

drilled, or at least started, before the base is parted-off from the stock material —while there is still something by which it can be held in the vice for drilling. It is surprising how much time and temper can be saved simply by anticipating little points of that kind. It will be easier to get the wires representing the valves parallel and vertical if they are left considerably longer than the final length until after they have been soldered in place. The spring can be made by twisting one strand taken from a piece of electric flex wire round a pin or piece of wire to form a tiny coil. One end should be looped over a notch in the balance lever, which is filed from sheet material and soldered to the safety-valves. The lower end is pushed into a third hole drilled in the base and both ends are secured with touches of solder.

CLACK-BOXES

These are difficult things to model satisfactorily in small scales. The problem is how to attach the fittings to the boiler neatly, but at the same time securely. One method, shown in Fig. 74, is to slip a piece of $\frac{1}{16}$-in. diameter brass or copper tube over the end of a piece of wire of suitable diameter to represent the feed-pipe, and soldered in place. The tube must now be drilled through for a pin *C*, a drill about size 68 being used. A pin is inserted in the hole and soldered. A small washer *D* (about 16-B.A. size) is slipped over the wire *B*, and soldered just below tube *A*, to represent the flange where the fitting joins the pipe. The pin *C* is inserted in a hole in the boiler with a small washer *E* interposed, and soldered on the inside of the boiler. A washer of thin card or thick paper should be inserted between the fitting and the boiler while soldering and removed afterwards.

This method would certainly tax the skill of the beginner, and the writer has used another which does not represent the prototype so well, but is quite satisfactory in appearance. A piece of $\frac{1}{16}$-in. diameter tube *A* is soldered over the end of a piece of wire *B*, Fig. 75, exactly as in the former case. A split-pin, *C*, is bent from wire and soldered round the pipe *B*. It thus represents the union flange between the clack-box and the pipe. A small washer is soldered to the side of the boiler so that it will come directly behind the clack-box. The ends of the split-pin *C* are passed through a hole drilled in the boiler immediately below the washer, and opened out inside. The fitting is secured by soldering the legs of the split pin inside the boiler. In such a small scale as 4-mm., one would have to be extremely critical to find fault with the appearance of the result.

HANDRAILS

Are best nade of nickel-silver wire, size 26 or 28 for " OO " gauge. The usual way to represent the supports is by means of small split-pins which the worker can make for himself, preferably from half-round wire. The legs of the pin are passed through a hole in the boiler, opened out, and soldered on the inside, Fig. 76. While soldering, a piece of card with a V-shaped cut, as in Fig. 76B, should be inserted under the handrail to hold it at a proper dis-

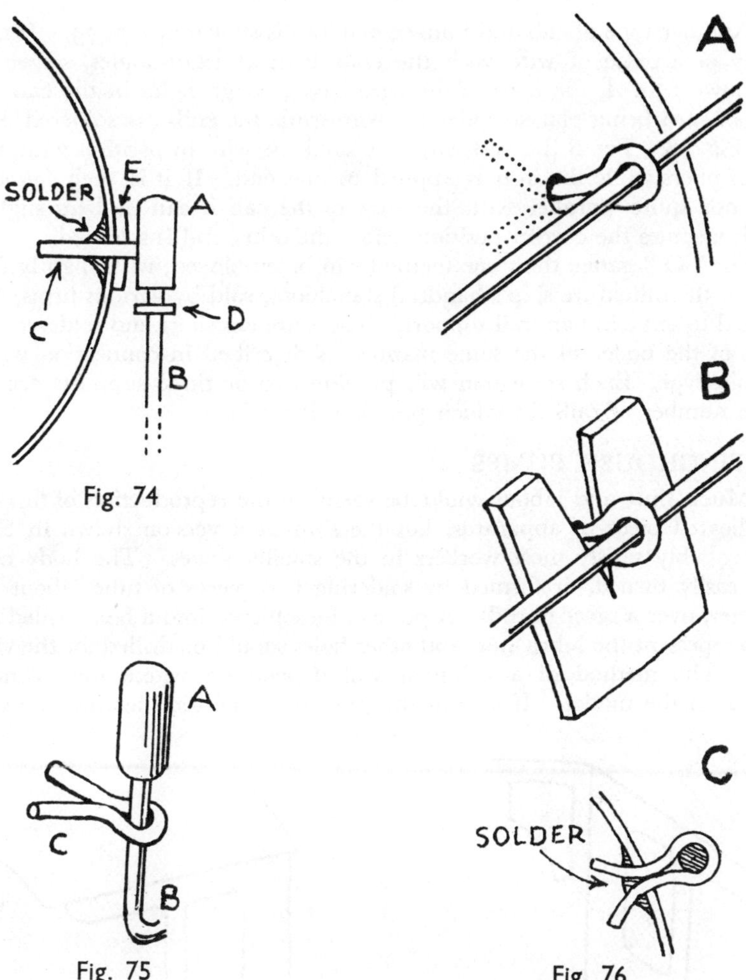

Fig. 74

Fig. 75

Fig. 76

tance from the boiler. Since it is usually impossible to solder some of the supports inside the boiler after the smokebox front is on, they should be fitted at an earlier stage with the handrail temporarily in position ; then the handrail can be withdrawn while construction proceeds, and again threaded through the eyes of the split-pins when the work has reached a more advanced stage.

For the short handrails at the sides of the cab a similar method can be employed. Fig. 78 shows a piece of wire (an ordinary pin will serve) and two split-pins, similar to those used for boiler mounting, soldered on the inside of the cab. It is advisable to fit handrails before the cab roof is put on, particularly in the case of tank locomotives. Substantially the same remarks apply to Fig. 77.

Another type of cab and bunker handrail is shown in Fig. 79. It consists simply of a piece of wire with the ends bent at right-angles. Two forms are shown : in *A*, the ends of the wire pass through holes in the cab side, a piece of card being placed under the wire while the ends are soldered, exactly as in Fig. 78. For *B* the best way is to hold the wire in position with a small pair of pliers while the iron is applied to one end. If it is then found that it is not quite parallel with the edge of the cab it can be bent slightly so that it assumes the correct position before the other end is soldered.

For " O " gauge the same method can be employed, with slightly thicker wire, or the miniature ship's handrail stanchions, sold by various firms, can be adapted to serve as handrail supports. These are cut short and soldered on the inside of the boiler in the same manner as described in connection with the split-pin type. Each stanchion will provide two or three supports according to the number of rails for which provision is made.

WESTINGHOUSE PUMPS

Much time and labour could be spent on the reproduction of this rather complicated piece of apparatus, but the simplified version shown in Fig. 80 will probably satisfy most workers in the smaller scales. The body can be quite easily turned, or formed by soldering two pieces of tube, about $\frac{3}{16}$-in. diameter, over a piece of rod. A pin can be soldered into a hole drilled in the top to represent the lubricator, and other holes should be drilled for the various pipes. The method of attachment will depend on where the cylinder is located on the model. If it is in the most usual position against the side of

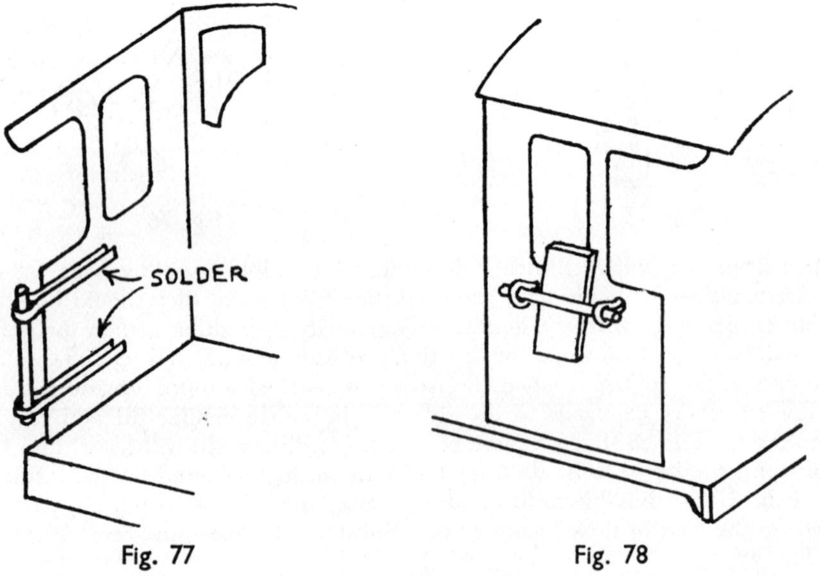

Fig. 77 Fig. 78

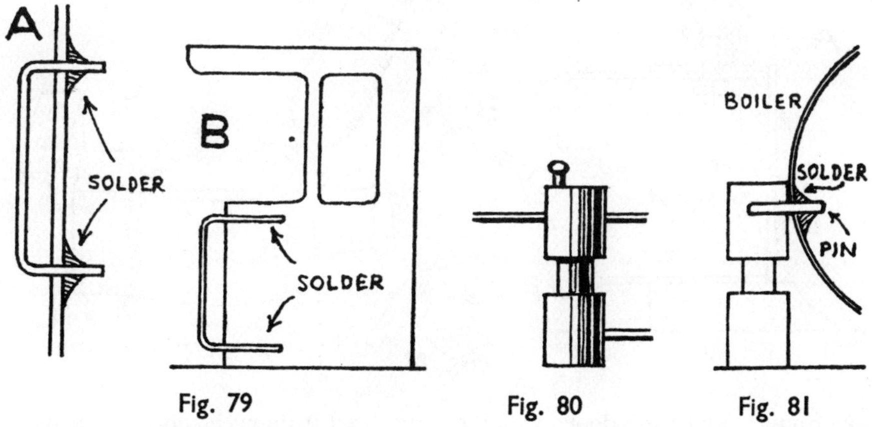

Fig. 79 Fig. 80 Fig. 81

the boiler, it would be advisable to provide a pin, Fig. 81, which would pass through a hole in the boiler side and would be soldered inside. A better way would be to drill and tap the cylinder for an 8- or 10-B.A. screw.

It is very necessary to make sure that small parts, such as these, are securely attached. Few things are more exasperating than to have one come loose after the model has been painted.

SMOKEBOX DOORS

These can be bought for " OO " gauge in the form of white-metal castings, complete with hinges and other embossed detail.

The writer has used large brass drawing pins quite successfully for the actual door. If a lathe is available, they are easily turned from rod, and a short spigot can be left on the back to be passed through a hole in the smokebox front, which is a very convenient method of fixing, Fig. 82A. For the lock-handles, a hole should be drilled through the centre of the door. It is not very easy to model the handles so that they are both satisfactory in appearance and strong enough to withstand ordinary handling, but the method shown in Fig. 82B is at least reasonably robust and looks quite well if carefully carried out. A piece of thin wire is simply looped round a pin under the head and soldered. The wire should be cut considerably longer than the final length, to provide a hold while fixing in place, and the surplus cut off when the job is finished. The pin is soldered at the back of the door.

It is usually safer not to solder the door to the smokebox front until the latter is in place on the model. This is because the front will require slight trimming round the edges after fitting (unless it is very carefully made and fitted). If the door were already in place, it might be found, after trimming up, that it was slightly out of centre. To attach the door, commence by lightly tinning the smokebox front. The model should be fixed in the vice, with strips of card or cloth to prevent damage by the jaws, with the front

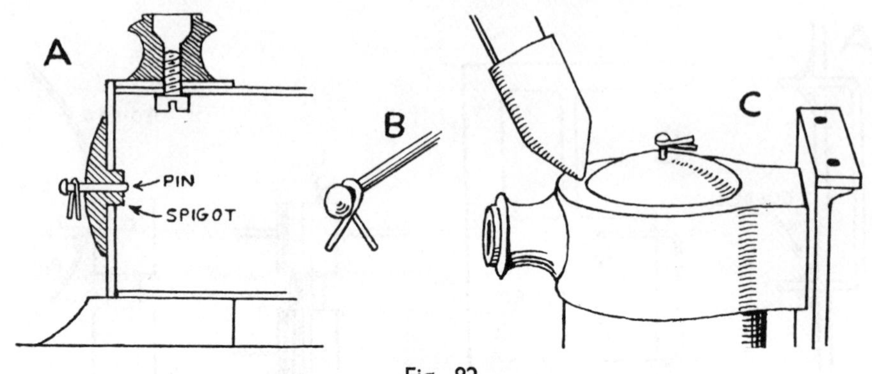

Fig. 82

uppermost. Place the door in position and hold it down firmly with a piece of stripwood or a small file. If necessary, the hole for the spigot—assuming there is one—should be enlarged slightly by filing with a rat-tail file to enable the door to be located exactly in the centre. Rub the tip of the iron on an odd piece of metal which has been smeared with flux, to remove surplus solder. Hold the iron against the smokebox front, and wait for the tinning to fuse, Fig. 32C, then, as soon as this is seen to happen, move the iron round a little and wait for the new area to become heated. Proceed all round in this way.

The hinges are the most difficult and fiddling part. It is, perhaps, better to leave them until the door has been fixed in place, but the model must be well secured against movement, in the vice or by other means. The writer cuts little strips of shim metal, about a millimetre wide and three or four " thous " thick. They are bent round a pin from which the head and point have been removed, and soldered as in Fig. 83B. The rest depends very much upon a steady hand and an iron which gives adequate heat. The backs of the hinges should have been well tinned, and it is advisable for the part of the door where they will be located to be tinned also. But there should be no surplus solder on the tip of the iron or the result will be a mess which will be difficult to clean up.

Place the hinges on the door and work them into the correct position with some sharp pointed instrument. Hold one of them down with the point, or a pair of tweezers may be used to hold both at once, a shown in Fig. 83A. Hold the tip of the iron in contact with the door as close to the hinge as possible ; keep it still and wait for the tinning to fuse. If any part of the hinge has sprung up away from the door, gently press it back with the point and apply the iron again. When the solder melts it will be felt to give slightly under the pressure of the pointed instrument ; the iron should be removed at once for if it remains in contact longer than necessary there is a chance that some other part of the hinge may come unsoldered. When both hinges have been soldered the job is finished by tacking the pin to the smokebox front somewhere about its middle. If, in spite of every precaution, unwanted solder

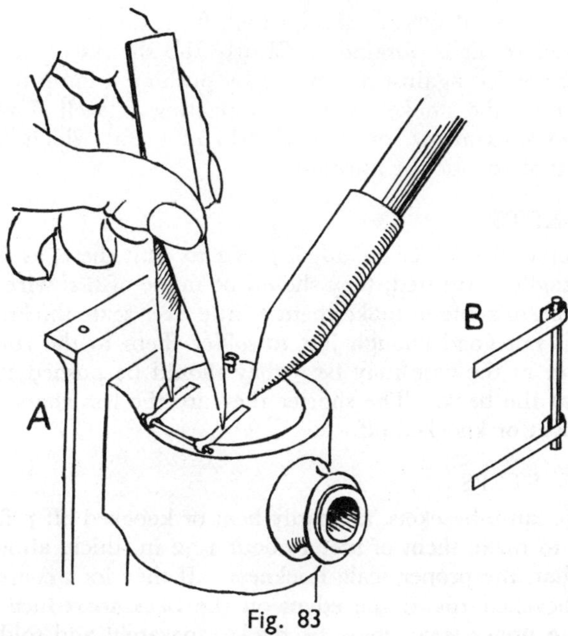

Fig. 83

has got on to the smokebox front, there is nothing for it but to clean up laboriously with small files and scrapers.

Before leaving the subject of smokebox fronts it may be as well to revert for a moment to handrails. Since the handrails on both sides of the boiler usually form one continuous length, which turns at right-angles in front and rises in a curve over the smokebox door (in American locomotives often below it), obviously it cannot be fitted until after the smokebox front has been added. On the other hand, some of the handrail supports must be fitted while it is still possible to obtain access to the boiler through the front. The solution was suggested in the section on handrails : fit the supports at an earlier stage of construction, with the handrails temporarily in place. Then remove them until the front is on and the model nearly complete. They can then be threaded through the supports a second time, and soldered to them if it is thought necessary to do so. It may be sufficient to solder them to one support on each side ; then, if, in time, they become bent out of shape, they can easily be removed and straightened or replaced.

The last paragraph refers mainly to handrail supports on the sides of the smokebox. If there is also one of these fittings on the smokebox front, on the centre line above the door, this method obviously will not work. The only way of dealing with this situation, as far as the writer can see, is to pass the shanks of the support through the hole which has been made for them when the handrail is being finally mounted. When everything is in, insert a spacer of card under the rail, as in Fig. 76B and open the shanks as much as possible by inserting a small screwdriver, or similar tool, from the inside and just fiddling until the desired result is obtained. Clearly the shanks cannot be soldered, but they can be sealed against movement by pushing a lump of Loy metal, or plastic wood, into the smokebox and compacting it well down with some suitably shaped instrument, or with a strip of metal which has been bent to a convenient shape for the purpose.

LAMP-BRACKETS

Many people, the writer included, prefer to omit these, as they are necessarily rather fragile. If fitted, they should be made of *steel* wire ; and it may be considered permissible to make them a little over scale thickness for greater strength. It is not good enough just to solder them to the running-plate or smokebox front, as the case may be ; they should be pushed through a hole and soldered at the back. The shorter they are the less chance there is that they will get bent or knocked off.

FOOTPLATE STEPS

These, like lamp-brackets, are easily bent or knocked off ; for this reason, it is advisable to make them of metal about 1/32 in. thick, although this is of course more than the proper scale thickness. If they look coarse and clumsy they can be bevelled round the edges on the back to reduce the apparent thickness. The upper tread must be made separately and soldered in place as in Fig. 84A and B, and for this, thinner material can be used. The upper tread is better soldered to the larger part before the latter is soldered to the model. The solder should be used liberally in the space between the upper and lower treads to hide the edge of the turned over portion by which the former is attached, Fig. 84B.

The unit is soldered below the running-plate, usually to the valance, by the upper tab, which is bent over at right-angles. It is rather difficult to rig

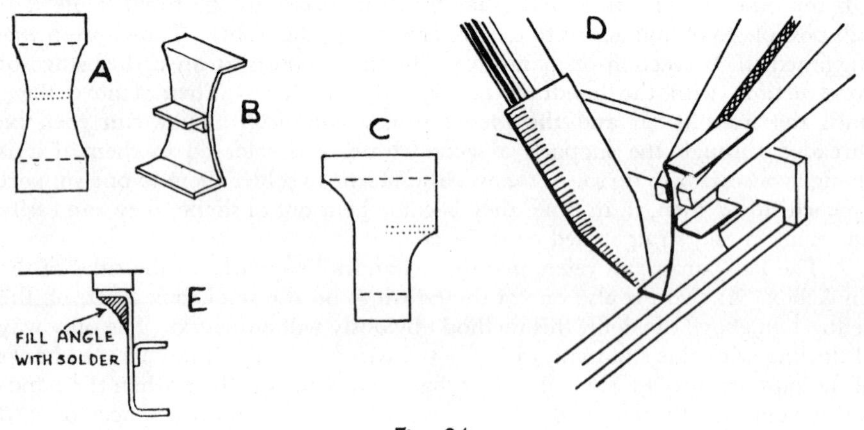

Fig. 84

up any sort of clamp to hold the step in position while soldering, but the model can be held upside down, either between the jaws of a vice or propped up with sundry heavy objects. The step must be held in position with thin-nosed pliers, Fig. 84D. There is a slight risk that the upper tread might become detached if the iron were held in contact too long. To obviate this the iron should be in contact with the running-plate of the model rather than with the step itself. As a further precaution, the pliers can be located so as to grip the tab by which the upper tread is soldered, so that it will not shift if the solder should begin to melt. However, if the iron is hot enough, and is used deftly, there is not likely to be any trouble. Naturally, one of the surfaces, either the running-plate or the fixing tab on the step, should be tinned. For greater strength the angle between the running-plate and the step should be filled with a good fillet of solder, Fig. 84E. Another type is shown in Fig. 84C.

BUFFERS

Most constructors will buy these ready-made, so there is little which need be said about them. The holes in the buffer beams for the reception of the shanks should be a good tight fit so that the buffers will stay put and not slip out of alignment while being soldered. The holes may be drilled a shade smaller than the shanks, and opened slightly with a brooch until the shank can be forced in. This little bit of extra trouble is well worth while, because, if the hole is a sloppy fit, it is a fiddling business to hold the buffer square while the solder is applied.

For a few old-time locomotives the buffers may have to be fitted to a wood buffer-beam. The best way to secure them is to solder a small washer over the shank where it projects through the back of the beam.

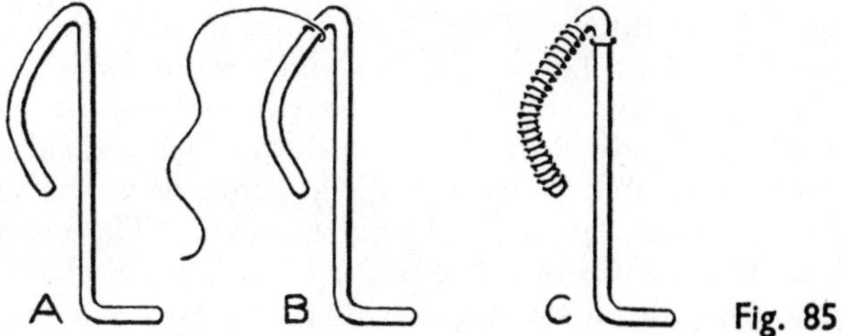

Fig. 85

VACUUM AND AIR PIPES

The usual method of making these is explained in Fig. 85. A piece of hard wire, about 22- or 24-gauge for 4-mm. scale, is bent to the shape of the pipe and hose-connection, as shown in Fig. 85A. To form the sharp bend at the top it may be advisable to bend the wire while almost red hot. It can be held in a gas or spirit flame and manipulated with two small pairs of pliers. If necessary the bend can be formed by successive stages, the wire being re-heated two or three times. There will be no risk of fracture if this method is adopted. Remove the insulation from a piece of lighting flex, about 4 in. long. Take

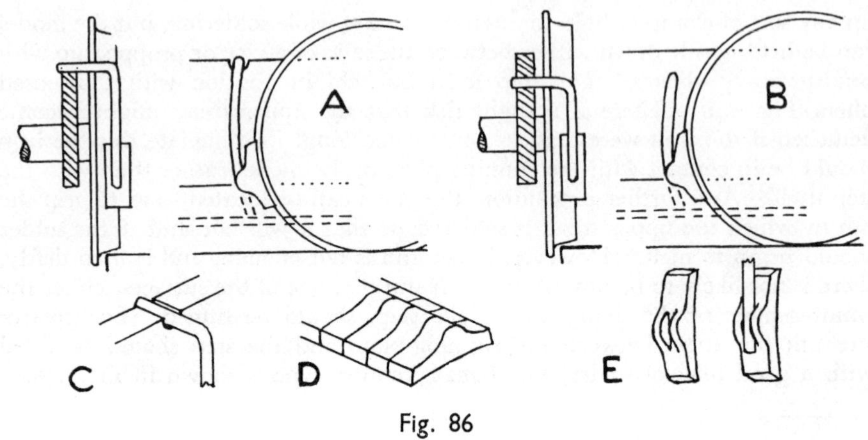

Fig. 86

one strand of wire and solder it in place, as shown in *B*. Wind the strand of flex round the thicker piece of wire in a tight close spiral, as *C*. Run the soldering-iron along the spiral, to secure it permanently in place, then snip off any loose ends. A washer made of one turn of wire soldered round the upright part of the fitting, as shown in *C*, will give a better finished appearance. The completed fitting is soldered to the buffer beam.

BRAKES

If brakes are fitted, care must be taken that they do not foul the wheels, rods, or other working parts. Usually, it is better to attach them to the chassis rather than the superstructure, but there may be exceptions. The brake operating-rods are rather delicate fittings and should be made of a hard metal —steel, nickel or hard brass. Fig. 86A and B shows two ways of attaching the hangers to the chassis. In *A*, the hanger is soldered into a notch, as shown more clearly in *C*. In *B*, it is soldered into a hole drilled in the side-frame. This is more applicable to chassis made at home, when the holes can be drilled while the side-frames are still soldered together. The brake-rods are shown by broken lines in these two diagrams ; many people who fit the hangers and shoes omit the rods on the grounds that they are too easily bent or broken. If the three-rail system is in use, one must take care that they cannot foul the third rail or collector shoes.

A simple and comparatively quick way to make brake-rods, and similar parts, is to use 18 or 20 gauge wire, preferably nickel or steel, and to file it on opposite sides until it becomes practically a flat strip. Hold it flat on the bench and work with a fairly large file. Only the side which will be outwards need be finished with fine emery cloth. The rods, being non-working, can be attached to the hangers with solder.

Brake blocks can be " mass produced " as shown at *D*. A piece of strip metal, preferably nickel, is sawed and filed to the outline of the block ; slices are cut off with a small saw. Finally, a saw-cut is made across the thickened portion at the back, as at *E*, and the hanger is soldered into this slot.

Many modelmakers consider that brakes are too delicate for a working model and omit them altogether. It is better to do so than to produce a clumsy and over-scale job.

CAB WINDOWS

If it is proposed to fit celluloid or slips of thin glass in the cab windows the method shown in Fig. 87 is suggested. Slips of thin sheet-metal are bent to form a rebate and soldered above and below the window opening. The glazing material need not be inserted until after the model has been painted. Celluloid can be simply sprung into the rebates, but for glass the clips must be sent back and closed when the glass is in place. With tank engines it may be impossible to insert the glazing after the cab roof has been fitted.

BOLT AND RIVET HEADS

It is difficult to reproduce these really well in " OO " gauge. The usual method is to mark the line on which the rivets are to be impressed with a scriber or pencil on the back of the part. It is then placed, reverse side up, on a piece of lead or hard wood ; then with a gramophone needle held in a pin chuck tap it sharply with a small hammer, to form each rivet. The writer prefers to mark the guide-line with a pencil rather than with a scriber, since the latter tends to weaken the metal, however slightly, just where this is least to be desired. The trouble is that the metal tends to assume a pronounced bend along the line of the rivets, and this is difficult to correct entirely without eliminating the rivet heads also. The more closely they are spaced the more pronounced the trouble becomes ; but when they are very closely spaced, the number can be reduced considerably without the fact being noticeable, except

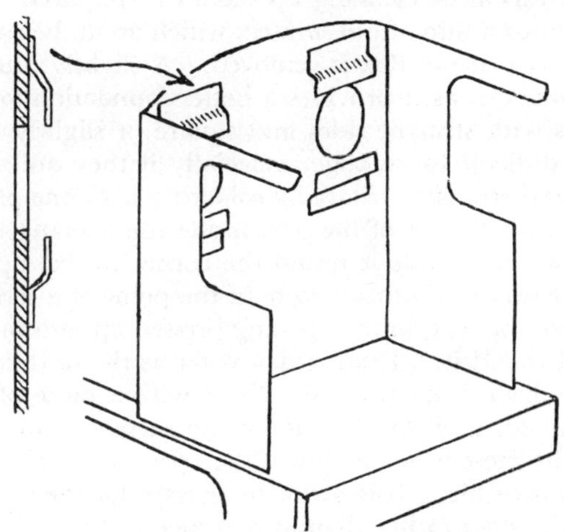

Fig. 87

perhaps to an ultra-critical eye. The thinner the metal the easier it is to obtain sharp, clean impressions, free from distortion. The gramophone needle should be sharpened on a grinder, or replaced frequently.

Some workers emboss the rivets on pieces of shim stock, about three " thous " thick. These are tinned on the back and soldered so as to cover the thicker metal completely. Such a proceeding cannot be recommended for beginners ; it requires more than ordinary skill to avoid bubbles of solder underneath and to induce the thin metal to lie evenly.

CAB BEADINGS

It is a tricky business to apply the beadings on the edges of cab side-plates and windows neatly and accurately, and some workers prefer to omit them. It is much better to do so than to apply them clumsily and out of truth ; but there is no doubt that they put the finishing touch to a model, if well executed. The first step is to tin any surfaces where beading is to be applied. Special half-round wire may be used for beadings if available, or copper wire of about 28- or 30-gauge. It must be clean and perfectly straight. Copper wire can be straightened by gripping one end in a vice and drawing the other with a pair of pliers until the wire stretches slightly.

Suppose a beading is to be applied to the side of a cab shaped more or less as shown in Fig. 88. Start by laying the wire on the side as shown, and hold it in place with a piece of stripwood or some small tool. Tack the wire in place at the top corner with the soldering iron, as shown in *A*. Now start working the wire round to follow the curve of the cab side as shown in Fig. 88B, and solder it at one or two more points. One more illustration, *C*, should suffice. When the wire has been tacked at several points and there is little risk of it moving, we can run the iron along the intermediate spaces. If the iron has been confined to the *edge* of the cab side, and has not been allowed to touch the surface, very little cleaning up should be required. It is not necessary to remove surplus tinning from surfaces which are to be painted, provided, of course, that every trace of flux is removed. A slightly rough surface may, in fact, be an advantage, as it provides a better foundation for the paint.

Cab windows with straight sides and square or slightly rounded corners are a little more difficult to manage, especially if they are very small. See that the wire is dead straight. Start by soldering it to one of the sides of the opening, working with the tip of the iron inside the opening, and holding the wire as in Fig. 84A. Pursuade it round the corner to line up with next side. Perhaps the easiest way to do this is to hold the point of a scriber, or a panel-pin, or something of the sort, in the opening pressed up into the corner, so that the wire can bend round it. Then solder as far as the next corner, and so on until all four sides have been covered. Start with a piece of wire somewhat longer than is wanted, and do not cut off the surplus until the last side has been reached. The most delicate part of the operation is to join the two ends so that the joint is invisible. It is better to arrange for the join to come in the middle of one of the sides rather than at a corner.

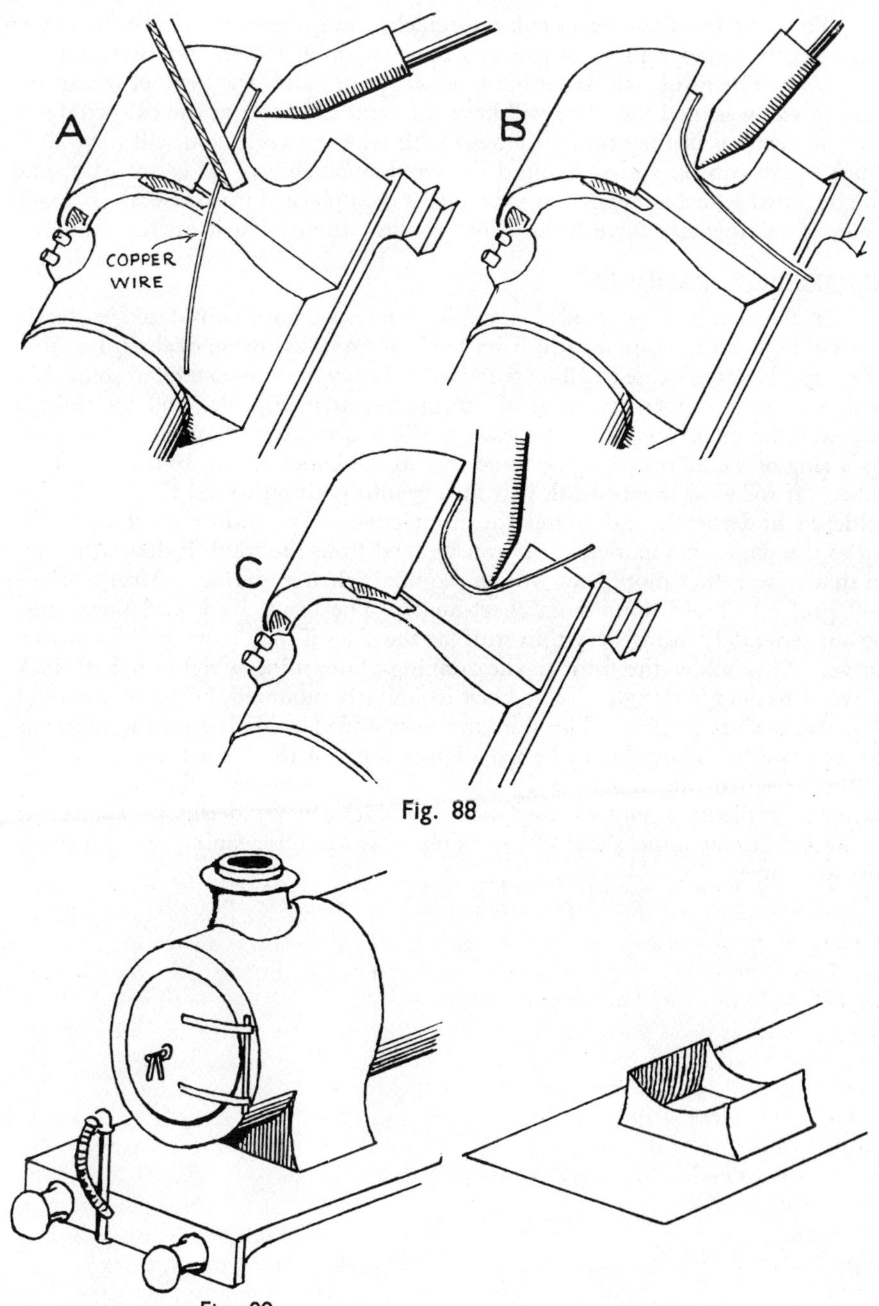

Fig. 88

Fig. 89

Fig. 90

To make beadings for circular spectacle plate windows, wind a length of wire tightly round a piece of rod of somewhat smaller diameter than the cab window. The result will resemble a spiral spring, and if a piece of rod of the correct size was used the turns will have the same diameter as the cab windows. Cut off sections of the required length with wire cutters ; you will have little rings which can be soldered round the window openings. It is not easy, and the beginner is recommended to experiment on a piece of waste metal, in which holes of suitable size have been drilled, before attempting it on the model.

SMOKEBOX SADDLES

In the simple 0-6-0 goods locomotive which we have considered in detail, the saddle has the same length, from back to front, as the smokebox, but this, of course, is not the case in all locomotives. Many have an extended smokebox which projects forward in front of the saddle, as in Fig. 89, and for these a rather different procedure is necessary. The smokebox may be represented by a ring of metal, rolled in the same way as the boiler or cut from thin-walled tube. If rolled in sheet-metal, it is sprung into position round the boiler, and soldered underneath and round the front edge. The saddle must be made up as a separate component. It can be filed from the solid, if desired ; but, in that case, rather more heat will be required when soldering. Most workers will prefer to build it up from sheet-metal. The front, back and sides must be cut separately, using very thin stuff for the sides if they have to be bent to a curve. First solder the front to the running-plate, using a right-angled block of wood to hold it upright. The back is similarly mounted, being very careful that the two are in line. The sides are next added, soldering on the inside as far as possible. They should be left slightly long on the top edge to allow for trimming when the smokebox is fitted. The appearance will now be as in Fig. 90. If plenty of solder is used along the sides when soldering the smokebox to the saddle, the joints should be invisible after careful cleaning up with small files and emery.

CHAPTER VII

OUTSIDE CYLINDERS, RODS, AND VALVE-GEAR

IN the preceding chapters we confined our attention to the various parts of one of the simplest types of locomotive : a 0-6-0 goods engine with inside cylinders. This has served our purpose of describing the general procedure in building a model locomotive, but we must now consider various features which appear in more complicated types.

Of these, the first to engage our attention may be outside cylinders. There are several ways of making them : they can be cut and filed from the solid or cast in brass, bronze, or some form of white-metal alloy, but most constructors will probably prefer to build them up from sheet material. The general method for this is shown in Fig. 91. The walls should be made from the thinnest material available, not more than about six " thous " thick, but the ends should be of slightly thicker stuff. The ends are filed to shape, and the wall takes the form of a sort of wrapper soldered round them. It will be appreciated that care and skill are required to solder the assembly together truly and squarely, and the job will be facilitated if some method is devised of holding the ends in their correct relation to each other while the wall is soldered to them. One way to accomplish this is to pin, or clamp the ends to a block of wood of a length equal to the internal length from back to front of the cylinders. The ends must of course be carefully lined up, and then the wall is soldered round, starting at the bottom and gradually forcing it into position with a piece of wood as the work proceeds. The result will be rather untidy as the presence of the wood block will render it necessary to work outside. The surplus solder is quite easily removed, however, as there are no obstructions to hinder the free use of files and emery cloth. The wood block can be removed or left in place and drilled for the piston- and valve-rods.

Another, and perhaps better, method is shown in Fig. 92. In this case, the cylinder ends are held in line and the proper distance apart by two long screws (possibly 10-B.A.) and nuts placed inside and outside as shown. The wall is wrapped round and soldered as described above.

The cylinder and valve-chest covers can be sliced off a piece of rod or parted off on a lathe. They are tinned on the back and soldered in place. If made on the lathe, it is an excellent idea to leave a short spigot on the back which can be pressed into a hole in the cylinder-block and will hold the cover securely in place for soldering, Fig. 91 and Fig. 93. Those at the rear end must, of course, be drilled through for the piston- and valve-rods, and the cylinder cover must, in addition, be drilled for the crosshead guides. The latter can be represented quite adequately in 4-mm. scale by ordinary pins. A better representation will be obtained if steel wire is carefully filed flat on one side and polished with fine emery. They are mounted so that the flattened side faces outwards and soldered in the holes provided for them.

There is usually a gland cover at the rear end of the cylinder through which the rod emerges. If the cover is a turning this is easily represented. If not, perhaps the simplest way is to make it from a piece of $\frac{1}{16}$-in. tube, soldered into the hole in the cylinder cover as shown in Fig. 93.

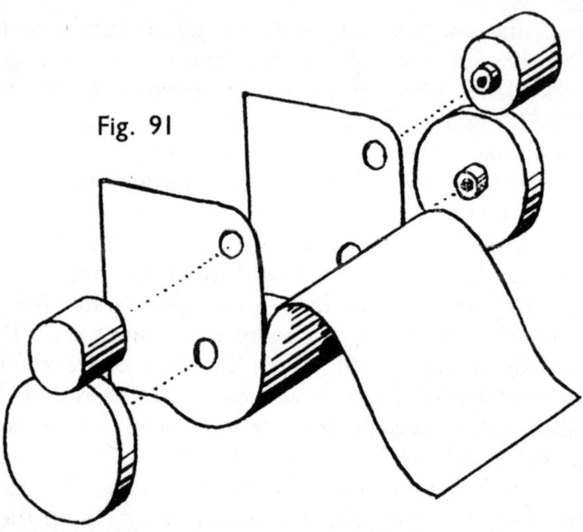
Fig. 91

It is not easy to represent bolt-heads in cylinder covers, and it is much better to omit them rather than to do the job badly. Perhaps the only really satisfactory way is to drill holes round the cylinder cover with a drill about size 66 or 68. Then, when the cover has been soldered in place, little pieces of wire are tinned and inserted in the holes. The solder is raised to fusing point by the application of the iron to the edge of the cover, the latter being held down to prevent it moving. The wires should now be securely soldered in place, and can be filed down until almost flush with the surface of the cylinder cover.

How the cylinders can be best attached to the side-frames depends on how they are made. If they are built up from sheet-metal it is quite easily done by soldering. It should be noted that since the side-frame is made of much thicker material than the cylinder, and since the latter is a rather delicate soldered assembly, heat should be applied to the frame rather than to the cylinder. This is important because, if the tip of the iron were applied to the cylinder, the chances are that the cylinder would begin to fall to pieces before the frame became sufficiently heated. The frame should, of course, be tinned.

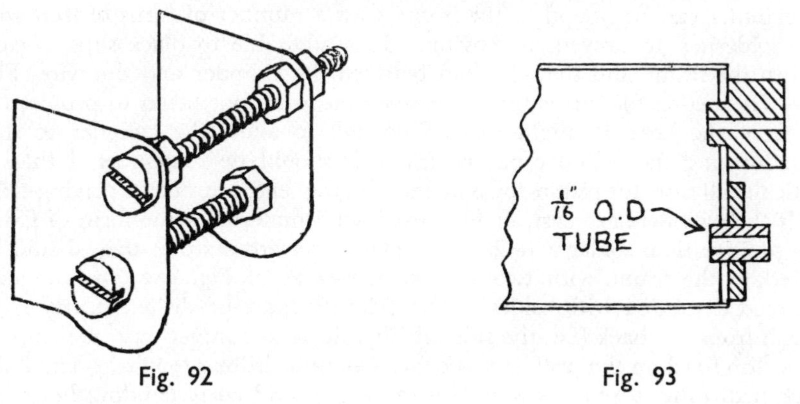

Fig. 92

Fig. 93

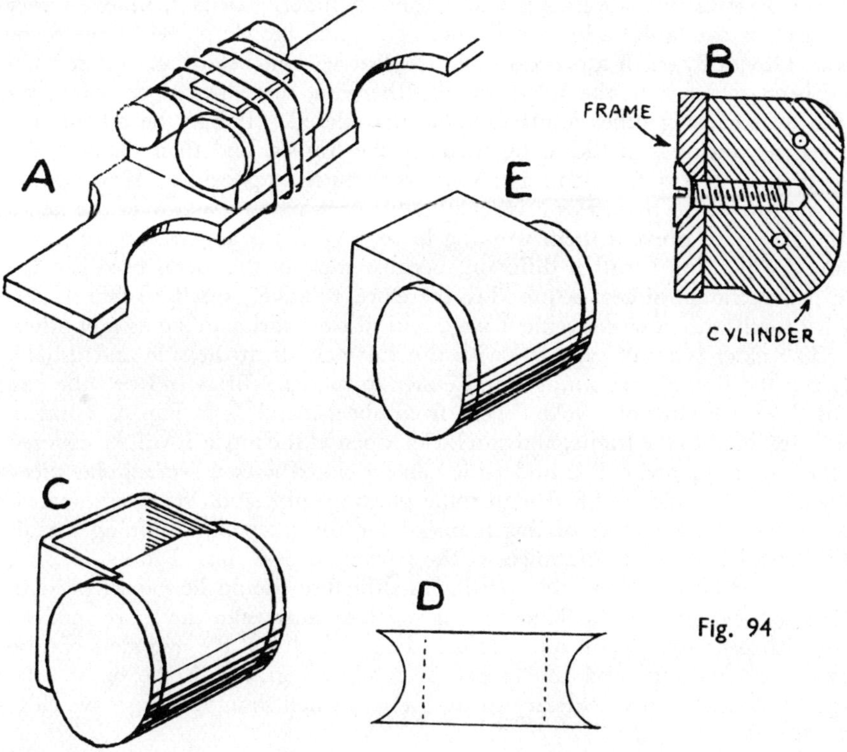

Fig. 94

The cylinder can be bound to the frame with a number of turns of thin wire while soldering, to prevent it moving. It is advisable to place slips of card between the frame and the wire and between the cylinder and the wire, Fig. 94A. The reason for this is that, if precautions were not taken to protect the wire from the heat, it might expand enough to allow the cylinder to slip. When locating the cylinder on the frame it should be remembered that in practically all cases the piston-rod is in line with the centre-line of the driving-axle.

If the cylinders are cast, or filed from solid material, some form of fixing more positive than solder is desirable. The writer advises that they should be screwed to the frame with two 10-B.A. screws as in Fig. 94B, and the joint reinforced if desired with solder. The cylinder must be drilled nearly right through from the back (i.e. the side which will be in contact with the frame), with a stop fixed on the drill as a safeguard against drilling too far. The holes are tapped, using a plug as well as a taper tap, and corresponding holes are drilled in the side-frame. It will be seen that the cylinder must be attached to the frame before the latter is assembled, since once the two side-frames are permanently joined by the crossmembers it is impossible to get a screwdriver between them. It is also desirable because, if solder is to be used in addition to the screws, considerable heat will be required to unite such comparatively massive parts as the side-frames and a solid cylinder. In fact, unless a very large iron is available, a bunsen burner or a small blowlamp will have to be used. Obviously, such a process should be carried out before any other parts have been soldered to the side-frame; otherwise, there would be some risk of the heat causing other joints to come unsoldered. It may be added that due to the thickness of the metal used for the frames, and their capacity for absorbing heat, it is better to rely on screws as much as possible. If two pieces of metal are joined by screws it is really only necessary to solder over the heads of the screws to prevent them working loose. With the superstructure of the model the position is rather different, because most of the metal used is quite thin; the amount of heat required is, therefore, relatively small, so that soldering is usually the most convenient way, and just as workmanlike as any other.

The older types of cylinder, with the valve-chests at the side and usually between the frames, are simpler and easier to model. Brass rod or tube can be used with a kind of "yoke" bent from sheet-metal as in Fig. 94C and D. This is soldered to the frame, and can be left open at the top as it will be covered by the running-plate. The underside can be closed with a rectangular piece of metal, or it could be filled with some plastic composition such as so-called cold solder. The virtues of this material for the purpose of joining metals may depend on the circumstances of the particular case, but of its utility as a filler there is no question. No particular difficulty should be experienced in soldering a cylinder of this kind as it is much smaller than the more modern types with piston-valves on top. It may be noted that if the cylinders can be turned from rod, the end covers can be made integral with the body. To suggest them, it is only necessary to turn a very small shoulder or groove close to each end.

Another method is shown in Fig. 94E. In this case the cylinder is filed complete from a suitable piece of thick metal. The end covers would be separate metal discs, attached by sweating. This cylinder could be joined to the side-frame with screws, as described above.

It will be understood that when solid cylinders are used they must be drilled almost right through, from back to front, for the piston-rod. This is not a very difficult operation if a lathe, or sensitive drilling machine, is available, but if it must be performed with a hand-drill, care and considerable patience will be required. For this reason many workers will prefer to use tube, or to build their cylinders up from sheet.

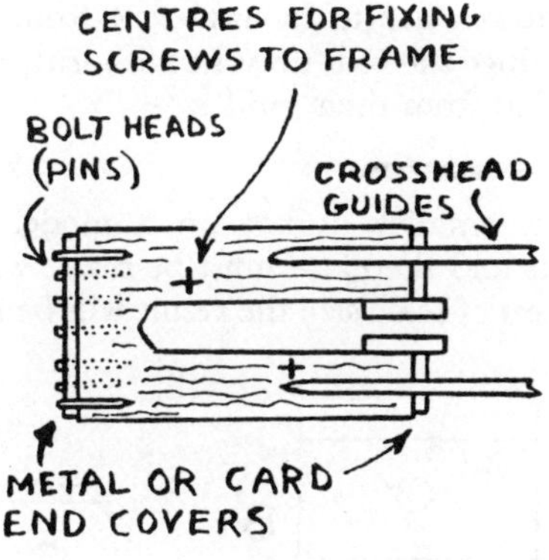

Fig. 95

On more than one occasion, the writer has produced perfectly satisfactory cylinders from hard, close-grained wood. There is quite a lot to be said in favour of wood cylinders ; when painted they are indistinguishable from metal. The covers can be discs of card, glued on, or metal with spigots forced into the wood. Bolt-heads in cylinder covers are very easily represented as it is only necessary to drive the smallest fretwork pins into the wood through holes drilled or punched in the cylinder covers, and cut off to length, Fig. 95. As the pins are inserted in the end grain there is very little risk of the wood splitting. It will be seen from the illustration that the crosshead guides are driven into the wood in the same way ; the gland can be represented by a short piece of $\frac{1}{16}$-in. tube. One or two coats of shellac varnish should be applied to the wood before painting. Such cylinders can be fixed to the side-frame with two $\frac{1}{4}$-in. No. 0 or 00 countersunk wood-screws. After the holes for them have been drilled in the frame, the cylinder should be held against the frame in its correct position and pricks made through the holes in the frame to mark their position on the cylinder. Corresponding pilot-holes should be drilled in the wood as a safeguard against splitting. These holes must, of course, be very small ; they should not be large enough to prevent the screws getting a good grip. They should be staggered in relation to the grain of the wood, as shown in the drawing, where one is above and the other below the hole drilled for the piston-rod. To make cylinders of wood will, no doubt, sound rather unorthodox, or even heretical, to some readers, but it is not unlikely that beginners will obtain a better finish—and possibly a more solid job—this way than with metal construction.

Small details such as cylinder drain-cocks are usually contrived with wire and pins. If they are to be fitted it is better for the cylinders to be built up from sheet, due to the difficulty of soldering neatly to solid ones.

One sometimes sees models which have the cylinders mounted on the superstructure instead of on the chassis. This cannot be a very satisfactory arrangement and the reader is advised to keep clear of it. Difficulties must arise every time the chassis has to be removed from the superstructure for servicing or lubrication since the rods must be withdrawn from the cylinders and the crossheads unthreaded from their guides.

CROSSHEADS

Unlike most of the smaller fittings on a model locomotive, these are essentially working parts and therefore must be made within fairly close limits. If they are much in excess of scale size the result will be rather crude, especially

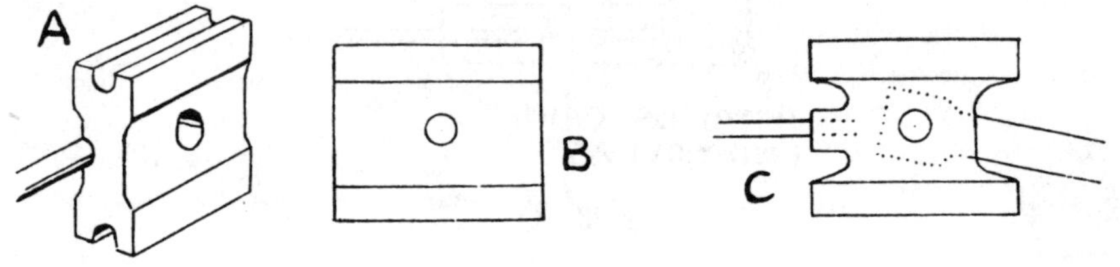

Fig. 96

in a photograph. The first step is to establish as accurately as possible the distance between the crosshead guides ; if these are found to be not exactly parallel they must be bent gently, close to the cylinder, until they are correctly lined up.

There are several ways of making crossheads ; the best and most workmanlike is shown in Fig. 96A, B, and C. In these diagrams the part is filed from one piece of metal. The material should be about $\frac{1}{16}$-in. thick for 4-mm. scale. Nickel-silver should be used if possible. The channels or grooves at top and bottom for the guides to run in may look rather " watchmakerish," but in fact they are quite easily formed, provided suitable tools are available. These are a couple of the smallest jeweller's files, one half-round and the other rat-tail, and a piercing saw. The work is held in a vice, and the channels started by filing a notch at the end nearest to the worker with the half-round file. The notch is extended to the full length with the saw, and cut in, to what is estimated to be the required depth. When both channels have been cut, they are enlarged with the rat-tail file until the crosshead runs freely between the guides but without unnecessary play. The crosshead should be " offered

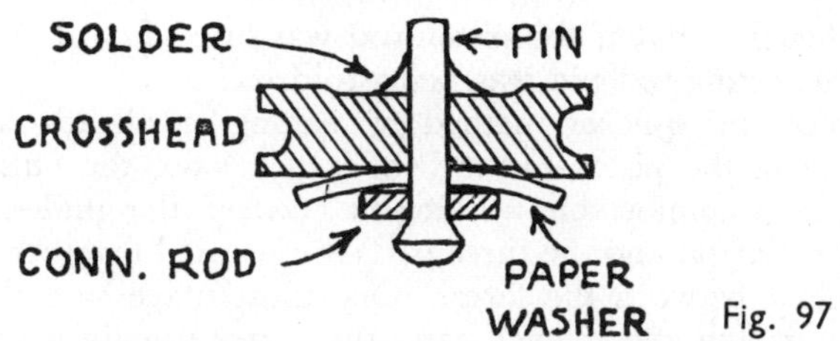

Fig. 97

up" at intervals as the filing proceeds; it should not be carried further than is necessary, but on the other hand there must be no suspicion of binding anywhere. If the crosshead runs freely at one point but not at another, this suggests that the guides and not the crosshead are at fault. They must be out of alignment either vertically or horizontally.

The finishing of the crosshead, once the guide channels have been formed, is a straightforward filing job. The exact shape will, of course, follow that of the prototype as closely as the small size permits. A hole must be drilled for the pin which forms the pivot for the connecting rod, and a notch can be filed, as in Fig. 96A, into which is soldered the pin or wire which serves for the piston-rod. This will provide a larger surface for the soldered joint, and will make for a better finish. The piston-rod can be "joggled" with small pliers to bring it in line with the centre-line of the crosshead, and it may have to be bent slightly, by trial and error, until it runs without binding in the cylinder. There is, of course, no reason why the hole through the cylinder should not be quite a sloppy fit to facilitate matters; the assembly must work with perfect freedom or some part of the power of the motor will be absorbed, and starting may be uncertain when the cranks are in certain positions.

Of the connecting-rods more will be said later, but the method of pivoting them to the crossheads may be mentioned here. The parts are arranged as shown in section in Fig. 97. A pin is passed first through the connecting-rod, next through a thin paper washer, which gives the necessary clearance and is torn away when the job is finished, and finally through the crosshead. The shank is soldered over and cut off as nearly flush as possible. It is advisable to attach the connecting-rod before the piston-rod, since the former can hardly become unsoldered, while the second joint is being made, if the work is laid

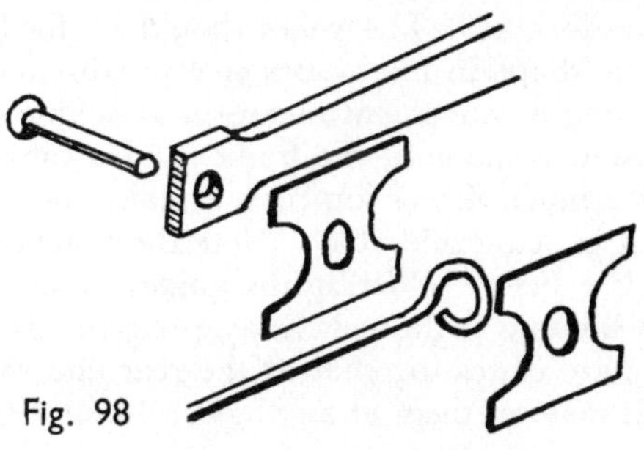
Fig. 98

flat on the bench. But if the piston-rod was fitted first it could easily move while the connecting-rod pin was being soldered over.

A simpler and quicker method of making crossheads is shown in Fig. 98. The end of the piston-rod is bent into a loop, the outside diameter of which must be a comfortable working fit between the guides. The faces are filed from sheet-metal and the three parts are sweated together with the piston-rod sandwiched between the faces. One must make sure that the holes in the faces are in line and in such cases the writer usually inserts a stiff bristle out of a brush or broom. It cannot get soldered up, and holds the parts in their correct positions. This method is not quite equal to the one described above from the point of view of appearance and finish, but it should function equally well.

An improvement is shown in Fig. 99. In this case, the three parts of the sandwich are filed from sheet-metal, the stuff used for the middle part being thick enough to provide clearance for the guides. The parts are tinned and sweated together with the piston-rod inserted in the slot cut for it in the middle portion. The parts are laid on the bench and held together while the iron is applied with a pointed instrument, or a small pair of tweezers. After soldering, the guide channels will be more or less choked up with solder and must be cleared with a fine saw or rat-tail file.

For Walschaerts valve-gear, the front face can have an extension in one piece with it, as shown by the dotted line, to represent the drop-link, Fig. 99. If preferred, of course, this part can be made separately and soldered on, but the one-piece method will be found simpler and will probably give a better finish.

The type of crosshead fitted to L.N.E.R. Pacifics, S.R. Lord Nelsons, and other engines, where both guide-rods are above the crosshead, is not easy to reproduce to scale in " OO " gauge. The arrangement shown in Fig. 100, which gives a perspective sketch and a sectional diagram, is suggested. A pin is soldered through a hole in the crosshead and slides between the guides which, by this method, can be practically the scale distance apart.

The cylinder assembly is completed by the crosshead guide yoke. It is an unfortunate fact that drawings of locomotives, whether specially prepared for the use of modelmakers or otherwise, usually fail to show the shape of this part. It has to be admitted that the Americans do that sort of thing very much better than we do here. The yokes should be filed from sheet metal, preferably nickel ; the shape in most cases is approximately as shown in Fig. 101, and in this drawing a convenient means of attachment to the side-frame is suggested. A saw-cut is made in the frame, and a tongue on the yoke fits into it. This makes a much firmer job than a plain butt-joint, and holds the yoke securely while it is being soldered. Note the notches which receive the ends of the guide-rods. Before soldering the guides to the yoke, the crosshead should be tested for binding ; the yoke may press the guides slightly out of parallel, so that they are closer together at the rear end than at the front, or if not quite upright it may set them at an angle. In either case the yoke must

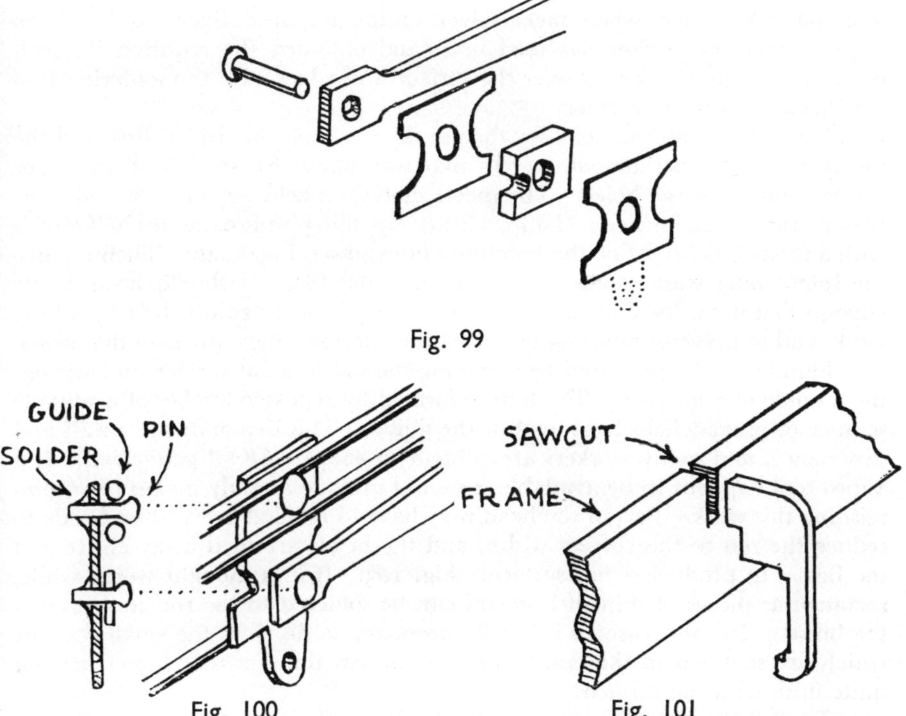

Fig. 99

Fig. 100

Fig. 101

be filed, or adjusted for position, until the crosshead runs quite freely between the guides. It may be pointed out that if the guide rods are securely attached to the yoke it is not essential that they should be soldered to the cylinders. They can be a push fit in holes drilled in the cylinders and the yokes will prevent movement. This is a convenience with solid cylinders where neat soldering may present difficulties.

In some cases it may be more convenient, and avoid a certain amount of rather fiddling adjustment, to make the yokes in one piece which passes across the top of the chassis. This method is certainly stronger, and has the advantage that the distance from the guides on one side of the engine to those on the other can be adjusted with certainty.

RODS AND VALVE-GEAR

Coupling- and connecting-rods are best made from nickel-silver sheet or strip, 1/32-in. thick for " OO " gauge or $\frac{1}{16}$-in. thick for " O " gauge. If strip is used it should be slightly wider than the maximum width of the finished rod to allow for the shaping of the crankpin bosses and any slight errors in the location of the holes. Strip $\frac{1}{8}$-in. wide is convenient for " OO " gauge, but it is more than likely that the worker will have to cut his rods from sheet material. At times, when nickel-silver of the required thickness has been unprocurable, the writer has used brass and obtained the required " steel " colour by lightly tinning all over the surface and edges with the soldering iron and finishing with fine emery.

Needless to say, the holes for the crankpins should be drilled first and the metal filed to shape afterwards. In that way one is free to adjust any error in the centring of the holes. The metal should be held for filing in a vice or, better still, a toolmaker's clamp. Start by filing approximate half-circles with a rat-tail file to define the positions of the bosses, Fig. 102B. Then remove the intervening waste portions with a small flat file. It should have a safe edge so that it can be guided by means of a finger held against the edge of the work, and to prevent it cutting into the little curves at the corners of the bosses.

Fluting can be produced by clamping the rod to a flat surface and arranging a guide of some sort. The flute is formed by repeated strokes of a suitable scraper or graver, held hard against the guide. This demands some skill and experience, and many workers are content to adapt " OO " gauge rail. If a Vibro tool happens to be available it should provide a ready means of accomplishing this work. Part of the head may have to be filed away at each side to reduce the rod to the correct width, and the heads are filed away enitrely at the bosses to produce a flat surface. Fig. 103. If it is thought worth while, rectangular pieces of thin sheet-metal can be soldered to the rod to represent the bosses. In most cases it is hardly necessary to do so as the small washers which are soldered to the crankpins will conceal the fact that bosses are not quite flush with the surface of the rod.

To drill the holes for the various pins in motion and valve-gear rods, the modelmaker should provide himself with one of the miniature centre-punches which are sold for fine work. The ordinary engineer's centre-punch is much too clumsy a tool. If one is not available a serviceable substitute can be made quite easily by filing or turning a piece of silver-steel to a point, the angle being about 55 degrees, as in Fig. 104, and tempering it to a dark straw colour.

For valve-gear joints, ordinary domestic pins can be used, and for these a drill size 70 or 72 will be about correct. For crankpins a somewhat thicker pin should be used, if the wheels are not already fitted with these when purchased. Small drills are very easily broken, and to reduce the risk to a minimum they should be fixed in the chuck so that only about one-eighth of an inch projects beyond the jaws. A sensitive-feed bench-drill is a great convenience when small holes have to be drilled, and, next to a lathe and grinder, is the most useful tool which can be installed in the amateur workshop. The difficulty with an ordinary hand-drill is that it cannot be worked at a sufficiently high speed for very small drills, and if no alternative is available the handle must be turned as fast as may be possible consistent with holding the tool steady, and avoiding excessive pressure.

The usual method of securing coupling- and connecting-rods to crankpins is shown in Fig. 105. With some wheels, it is advisable to start with a thin

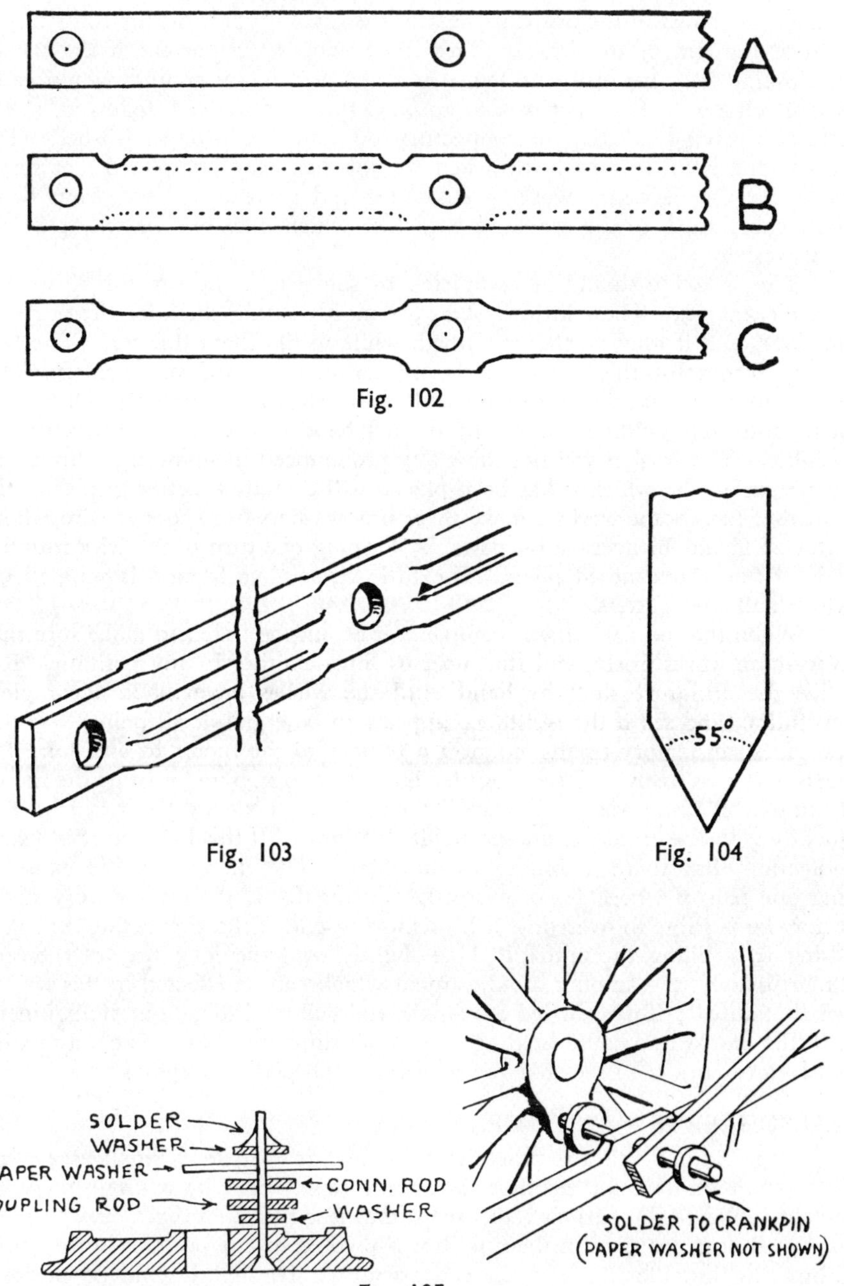

Fig. 102

Fig. 103

Fig. 104

Fig. 105

washer, as shown in the drawing, next to the crank to prevent the rod rubbing against the rim of the wheel. This is particularly important if the wheels are insulated for two-rail working, when such accidental contact would cause a short circuit. The next part to go on is the coupling-rod, followed, in the case of a driving axle, by the connecting-rod, and then a paper washer. The last-named is to be torn away when the job has been completed ; it serves to ensure the necessary working clearance and protects the rod from being immovably stuck to the crankpin by solder which may find its way past the final washer.

The assembly should be completed by soldering a 14- or 16-B.A. washer to the crankpin. These little washers are mostly rather thick for the purpose, however, and it may be thought worth while to file them thinner. The best way to accomplish this is to place the washer on a piece of coarse emery cloth, or an old coarse flat file, then file evenly and deliberately with a small smooth or medium file, guiding the end by the left hand to keep it as nearly level as possible. The washer will not show any pronounced inclination to slip as the coarse surface on which it has been placed will exercise a better grip than the smoother file. Some workers make these tiny washers from copper wire, about 24 or 26 gauge for average purposes, by forming one turn of the wire round a pair of fine round-nosed pliers. The little circle thus formed is snipped off with small wire cutters.

When the rod assembly is complete, it should be tested to make sure that everything works freely, and that no part fouls another in any position. Revolve the armature shaft by hand until the wheels have made a complete revolution, and see if the resistance appears to be equal at all points. If this test gives satisfactory results, connect a battery to the motor to ascertain if it starts and runs freely. A good test for binding is to stop and re-start the motor a number of times and to observe if there is any tendency for it to stop frequently with the cranks in one particular position. If this happens it is a sure indication that there is binding somewhere. The most probable cause is that one pair of wheels is not correctly quartered. If the error is very slight it may be possible to overcome it by removing one of the connecting-rods and easing it by filing the crankpin hole slightly oval the long way of the rod Unfortunately, the amount of adjustment which can be effected in this way is strictly limited ; if it is carried too far the rod will tend to get out of alignment with the cranks and cause binding of a rather different kind. The only really satisfactory cure is to see that the wheels are properly quartered.

WALSCHAERTS VALVE-GEAR

Some simplification is practically essential in a scale as small as 4-mm. The expansion-link, for example, is usually represented by a single piece of metal, similar to the various rods except that it is filed to a slight curve. The valve-rod does not slide in the link, but is pivoted in one position in the same manner as the other joints in the rod assembly. The link is similarly pivoted to the hanger.

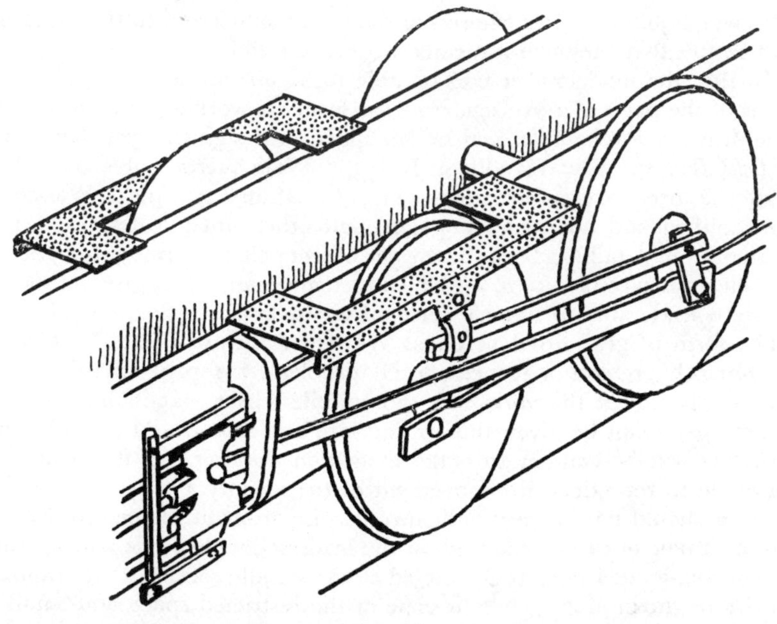

Fig. 106

The expansion-link is suspended from a sort of bracket which must be built out from the side-frame, somewhat as in Fig. 106, which shows part of the chassis with the superstructure removed. It is suggested that the bracket, which should be formed from sheet material, should be soldered into a shallow recess filed in the top of the side-frame. It should, of course, be suspended from the underside of the running-plate, but this is out of the question in an electrically-driven model as it would necessitate disconnecting the expansion-link every time the superstructure had to be removed from the chassis. It must be shaped so that it *appears* to be suspended from the running-plate when the superstructure is in place.

The reversing-lever and lifting-arm will, of course, be built on to the superstructure, and in reality will have no physical connection with the other parts of the valve-gear. Since these are not working parts they can be soldered together, or even filed from one piece of metal. Fig. 107 shows a simplified arrangement of the lever and lifting-arm, which may be considered sufficiently detailed for " OO " and " HO " gauges.

The drop-link can be in one piece with the crosshead, as in Fig. 108A, or made separately and soldered to it, as in Fig. 108B. The return-crank should be soldered to the crankpin, and will take the place of the final washer shown in Fig. 105. It should be remembered that in certain positions the eccentric-rod will be set across the connecting-rod, so there must be adequate clearance between them. Special attention should be paid to the shanks of the pins which join the eccentric-rod to the return-crank and to the expansion-link, to ensure that they will not catch against the rod.

Usually, the modelmaker will be able to obtain the lengths and relative positions of the parts of a Walschaerts gear from his working drawings. If no reliable drawing is available, and he is obliged to design the gear for himself, *The Model Railway News* Handbook No. 3, " Walschaerts Valve-Gear," will give all the necessary information. Fig. 109 shows a typical Walschaerts gear, simplified and adapted for 4 mm. and other small scales. The minimum amount of detail has been shown, the object being to present the essentials in the clearest possible form. The constructor can, of course, refine and elaborate considerably to suit his personal inclinations.

The form of gear fitted to Great Western Railway " Stars," " Castles " and " Kings," presents a rather special problem. Hardly anything of the gear is visible except the valve-rod and spindle-rocker. It is difficult to see how these parts can be given the appropriate movement, and probably most constructors will be content to make them non-working. If it is considered worth while to reproduce the movement of the prototype when the model is running, it should not be very difficult to devise an arrangement consisting of a cam, or a pair of cams, mounted on the leading coupled axle and operating against spring-loaded tappets connected to the spindle rockers. Alternatively, eccentrics might be used ; but in view of the restricted space and small size of the parts, cams would probably be simpler and more satisfactory.

Stephenson motion is usually located between the frames and, being practically invisible, is usually omitted in small-scale models. In the case of a few old locomotives with small, rather high-pitched boilers, it may be worth while to make a dummy representation of as much of the gear as can be seen. This is quite easily done with strip nickel, or even wire beaten or filed flat, provided that no part of the motor or gearing gets in the way.

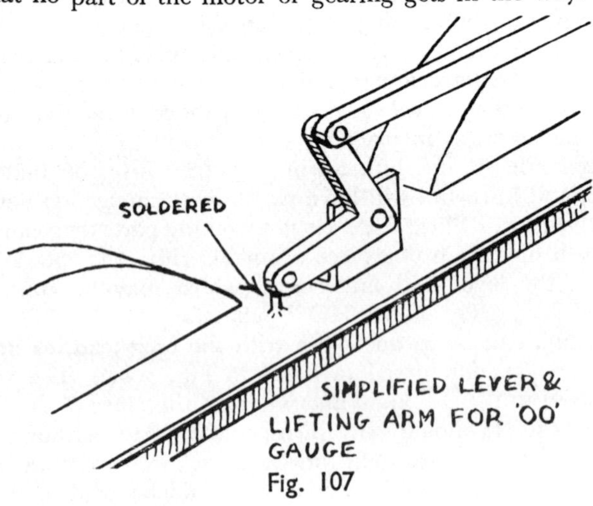

Fig. 107

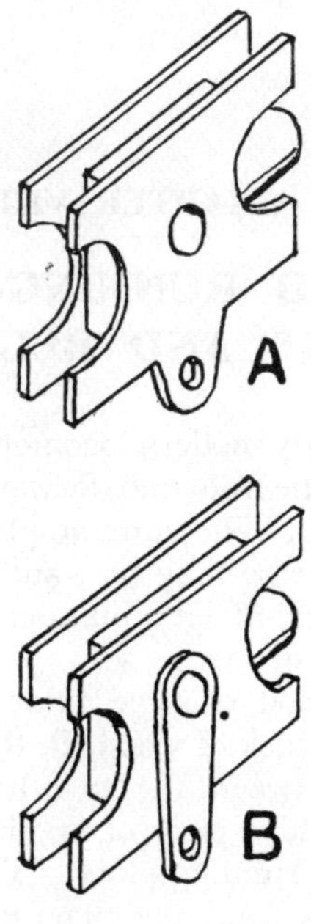

Fig. 108

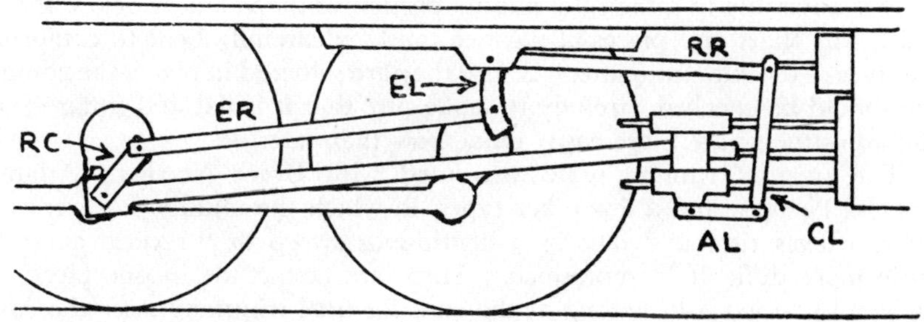

AL ANCHOR LINK
CL COMBINATION LEVER
EL EXPANSION LINK
ER ECCENTRIC ROD
RC RETURN CRANK
RR RADIUS ROD

Fig. 109

CHAPTER VIII

CURVED RUNNING-PLATES, TAPERED BOILERS, AND BELPAIRE FIREBOXES

MOST modern and fairly modern locomotives have running-plates which are downswept at the front end, forward of the smokebox, and usually under the cab also. The running-plate should be made of two or three separate pieces, as the case may be ; and they must be assembled with great care, since any errors will affect a number of other parts. The following method of assembly is recommended.

Select a flat piece of wood to serve as an assembly bed, *A* in Fig. 110. To it nail or screw another block of wood, *B*, the thickness of which is exactly the difference in height between the two levels of the running-plate, as shown at *B* in Fig. 110. A third piece of wood, *C*, is attached to *A* as a guide for lining up the parts of the running-plate. The method of using this simple soldering-jig will be obvious from the diagram. The main portion of the running-plate is firmly secured upside down to block *A* with drawing-pins, or by any other convenient means. The curved portion is laid on block *B*, also upside down, and may be held in place with drawing-pins also. Both parts are pressed firmly against the guide, *C*. The joint is now made with the soldering iron, a good fillet of solder being formed right across, except near the edges where it would be in the way of the valances. If there is a downswept portion at the rear end also, the running-plate can be reversed in the jig.

It is advisable to attach the middle portion of the valances before the end parts. The short end pieces of valance must be carefully bent to conform to the curves of the running-plate. Before they are soldered in place, the running-plate should be checked carefully to make sure that it is flat and square ; any small adjustments are more easily made now than later on.

The type of running-plate associated with Great Northern Atlantics, L.N.E.R. Pacifics, and a few other types, in which the middle part above the driving wheels rises and falls in a continuous sweep or " reverse curve," is a little more difficult to reproduce. These are best made in one piece, and they should be left a little long at the ends for final trimming after the curves have been formed. It should be remembered that, in some cases—the Great Northern Atlantics, for example—the front portion under the smokebox and the rear portion under the cab are not at the same level. The difference is not great, possibly about five or six inches, but quite enough to spoil the appearance of the model if it were overlooked.

The curves must, of course, be formed before valances or any other parts

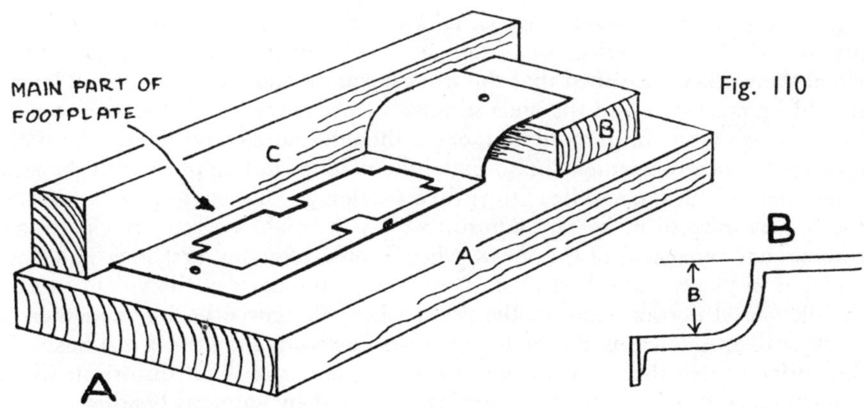

are added. They can be formed partly by rolling over a metal rod of slightly smaller radius than the required curve, and partly by coaxing and " wangling " with the fingers. When it is thought that the desired shape has been obtained, the work should be tested on a flat surface as in Fig. 111A. Note the card or thin wood packing to allow for the difference in height between the front and rear ends. It is most important that the middle and the front and rear portions should all be absolutely parallel ; the end parts must be in contact with the flat surface at all points, for nothing looks worse than a running-plate of which part is going down hill. With the running-plate as in Fig. 111A, measure the height of the raised part at several points ; the measurement should be the

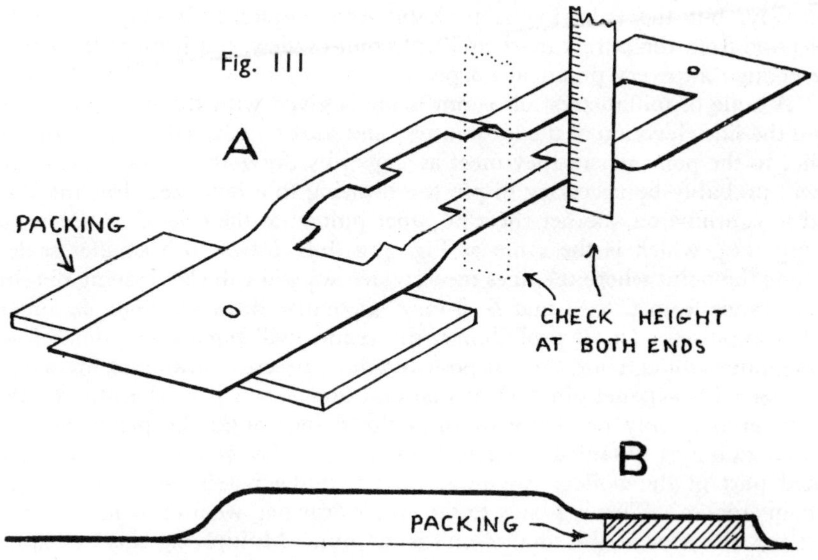

same everywhere. *Do not forget to test both sides.* A slight error in the bending would have the effect of lifting one side higher than the other. Only when the worker is satisfied that the work is square and true, the overall length should be measured and the ends trimmed if necessary. The valances can be made in one piece, or in more than one if thought more convenient. Actually, the safest proceeding might be to make the valance in two parts with the joint somewhere about the middle of the raised portion. This would give the worker the opportunity to make any adjustment which might be rendered necessary by unequal expansion of the metal when heated after the first part had been soldered in place. It is best to start by tacking the parts of the valance to the middle raised portion close to the point where the curve begins, and then to work outwards towards the ends. A final check-up should be made on the flat surface when the valances are in position, and any slight distortion which may have crept in during the soldering corrected by cautious bending.

A particularly awkward problem is presented by the L.N.E.R. Pacifics, where, as shown in Fig. 111B, there are four distinct levels. The short front section should, of course, be made separately, and for the rest the method described above can be followed.

CONED BOILERS AND BELPAIRE FIREBOXES

Fig. 112 is a side elevation of the type of coned boiler favoured by the Great Western Railway about the beginning of the century. The front part, including the smokebox, is cylindrical, and can be rolled or made from tube as described in an earlier chapter. But how may we best deal with the coned portion? How are we to lay the shape out on the metal so that, when rolled and soldered up, it will assume the correct coned form? There is more than one way, but the following is probably the simplest; it may be open to objection from the purely mathematical point of view, but is more than accurate enough for every practical purpose.

A scale of millimetres for 4-mm. scale is given with the drawing. Work from the side elevation of the locomotive, and start by projecting the lines of the boiler to the point where they meet as shown by the dotted lines. To do this, it will probably be necessary to pin the drawing to a fair sized drawing-board and to continue on another sheet of paper pinned at the side of it. Now turn to Fig. 113, which is the same as Fig. 112, but drawn to a smaller scale to include the point where the lines meet, which we will call *C*. Having obtained the distance from *C* to *A* and *B*, from *C* as centre, draw the lines *Aa* and *Bb*, with compasses. In all probability, the reader will not have a pair of com passes large enough for the purpose but he can use a trammel, or a piece of string with a panel-pin tied at one end and a pencil at the other. With the latter it is only necessary to wind the string round the pencil until the desired radius is obtained. These lines, *Aa* and *Bb*, give us the ends of the coned part of the boiler; we must now find the maximum and minimum circumferences. Turning back to the larger drawing, we find by measurement that the diameter at the smaller end is 22 mm. Multiplying this by 22/7, or

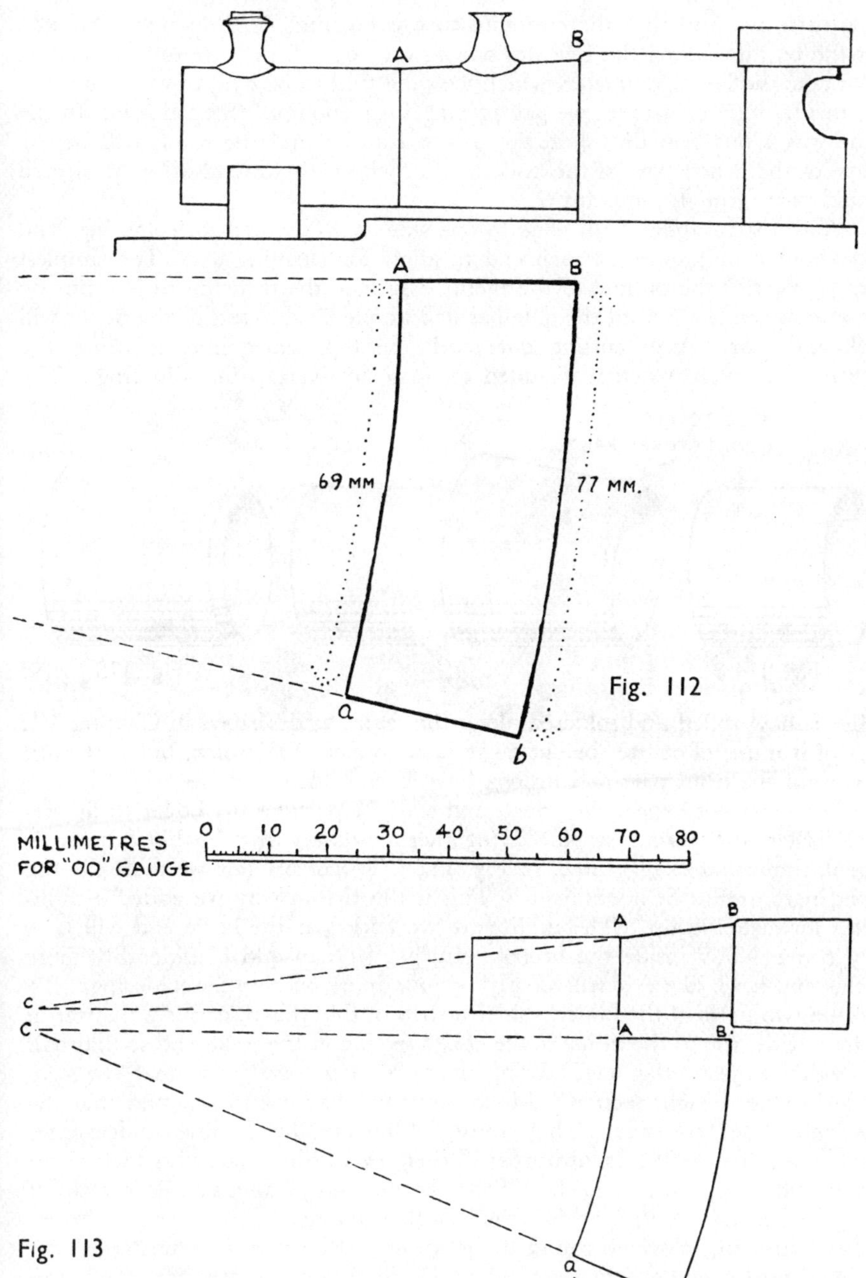

Fig. 112

Fig. 113

by 3.1416, we find that the circumference is 69 mm. near enough. So step out the 69 mm. along the line *Aa*, ticking off steps of, say, 10 mm. at a time. Now take the larger diameter, which we shall find to be 24.5 mm. Multiplying this by 22/7 or 3.1416, we get 77 mm. near enough. Step this out in the same way along line *Bb*. Join the points *a* and *b* and the result will be the shape of the coned part of the boiler. As a check the line *ab* when projected should pass through the point *C*.

Add a strip about $\frac{1}{8}$ in. wide to one side as an overlap for soldering, and add about a millimetre at each end to allow for cleaning up. The simplest way to transfer the outline to the metal is to glue the drawing to it. But do not attempt to cut it until the glue has had ample time to set, or the paper will ruck and tear. After cutting out mark the top centre line, ignoring the eighth of an inch which was added to form an overlap for soldering. The

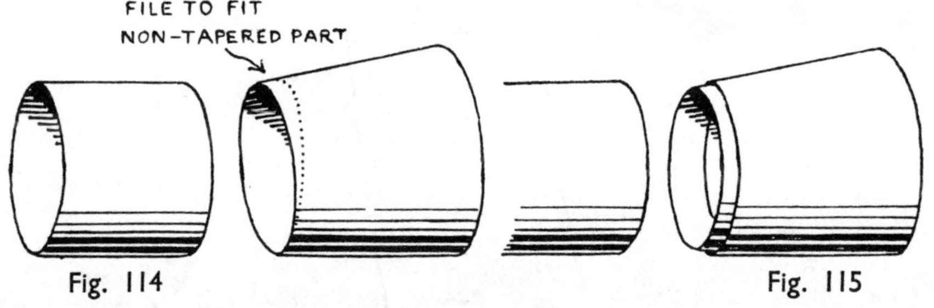

Fig. 114 Fig. 115

boiler is now rolled and soldered along the seam, as described in Chapter VI. Part of it must, of course, be cut away later to clear the motor, but that must wait until the front part and firebox have been added.

We must not expect the coned and straight parts of the boiler to fit perfectly when they are first placed together ; what will probably happen is shown, somewhat exaggerated, in Fig. 114. To correct this we must file the coned part until a fit is obtained. This is the reason why we added a millimetre for cleaning up. The millimetre we added at the large end will tuck very conveniently inside the firebox. In fact we can add considerably more at this end if we like ; it will simply provide more overlap for soldering. To join the two parts of the boiler, solder a strip of thin metal, about a quarter of an inch wide, round the inside of the coned section at the small end so that half the width projects, Fig. 115. Bring the two parts together so that the strip fits inside the straight section. Make sure that they are in line and that the top centre lines coincide. They must, of course, be in line underneath, because all the coning is upwards. When everything is ready, tack them together at one point, somewhere near the top centre line, say. Now check up again for alignment, for this is the last chance to correct any error. When you are satisfied, solder all round the joint, and clean with files and emery.

Fig. 116A shows another method, and it eliminates the need for calculation and setting out. A piece of metal tube of a size equal to the diameter of the boiler at the front end is used. Slit it longitudinally with a small hacksaw, and force it open with the fingers until the required diameter is obtained for the firebox end. Do not cut it quite for the full length if it will give sufficiently without ; try to leave about a quarter-inch joined at the front end. Do not hurry the job of opening it out ; it is better to go slowly and to check frequently with a slide-gauge. Solder a strip of metal over the V-shaped slot thus formed, to prevent the tube getting out of shape, and proceed as described for the other method. At a later stage, it will be necessary to cut part of the strip away to

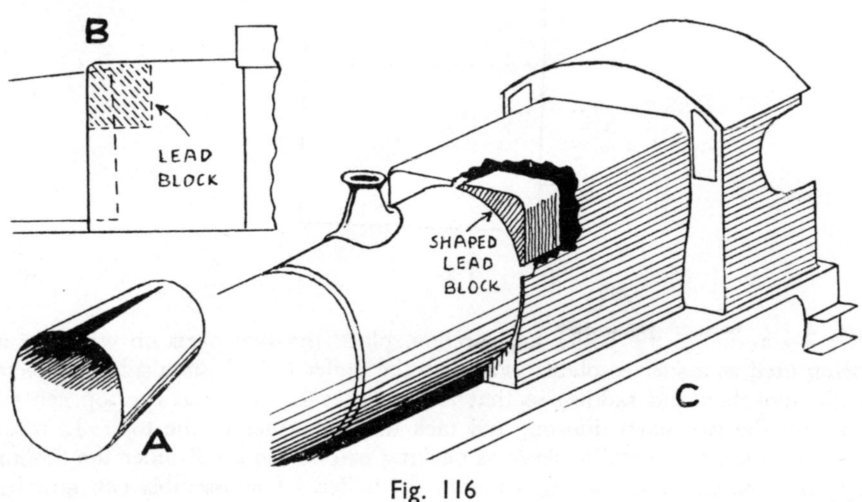

Fig. 116

clear the motor, but when the boiler and firebox assembly has been soldered up this will not matter. As an additional precaution a strip of thin metal, about an eighth to a quarter of an inch wide, can be soldered round the boiler on the inside to check any possible tendency of the tube to revert to its original shape.

The shape of a Belpaire firebox must be found, to a certain extent, by trial and error. It is a rather subtle thing and repays careful work. Take the dimensions as accurately as possible from the front and side working drawings, remembering that the top corners are gentle curves and not sharp bends ; they should be formed round a rod, perhaps $\frac{1}{16}$-in. to $\frac{1}{8}$-in. diameter for 4-mm. scale, according to the prototype. Most Belpaire fireboxes incline downwards slightly towards the cab end, the angle from horizontal being one or two degrees. This is most important to the appearance of the model, and must be allowed for in setting out. The shape, therefore, will be approximately as shown in Fig. 117. The sides should be cut a little deeper than is thought to be necessary to allow for trimming if the firebox is found to stand too high above the running-plate.

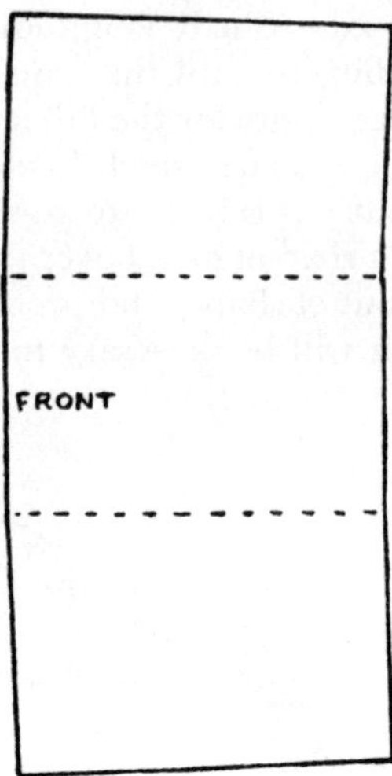

Fig. 117

To assemble the boiler and firebox, place the two parts on whatever is being used as a surface-plate. Pack up the boiler (which should be complete with smokebox and saddle) so that it stands level. See that the top centre-lines on the two parts line up, and tack them together at the top. In mose designs, a strip of metal to serve as packing will be required under the firebox top, because this is a little higher than the boiler. The assembly can now be tried in position on the running-plate, and generally tested for squareness. When everything is in order, the boiler-smokebox unit can be mounted by soldering the saddle to the running-plate and the firebox to the cab. It remains to fill in the top corners and sides of the firebox which, at this stage, are still open. We can file pieces of sheet-metal to conform to the shape of the boiler and solder them in place. Note that rather thick material must be used, about $\frac{1}{16}$ in in 4-mm. scale, because the rounded front corners of the firebox must be formed by filing and this could not be done with thinner stuff without destroying the soldered joint. A suitable allowance must be made for the thickness of the front wall of the firebox when setting out the top and sides.

Another way is to file pieces of lead to fit the corner spaces as accurately as possible, Fig. 116B and C, and to solder over on the outside, taking care to fill any chinks where the lead may not fit perfectly. The lower corners can be filled in the same way.

CHAPTER IX

TANK ENGINES

FOR side-tanks, the usual order of assembly is first to mount the front spectacle-plate and boiler on the running-plate, then the tanks, which in most designs can be in one piece with the cab side-plates and, in certain cases, may include the sides of the bunker as well. The fronts of the tanks can usually be in one piece with the sides and bent as shown by the dotted line in Fig. 118A. The curved inside edge of the tank front should be filed to fit the boiler when the prototype requires this. It is advisable to solder a soffit, which may be a piece of $\frac{1}{8}$-in. by $\frac{1}{16}$-in. strip, or a length of " OO " gauge rail, along the top inside edge of the tank, *A* in Fig. 118B. It will serve as a support for the tank top and help to keep the side straight. In many designs, it is a very sound idea to solder similar strips along the top inside edges of the cab side-plates. Lengths of strip metal should also be soldered along the edges of the running-plate, as at *B* in Fig. 118C, as stops to keep the lower edge of the tank sides correctly lined up while being soldered. Unfortunately, one must usually solder the tank to the running-plate on the outside so that careful work is necessary to keep subsequent cleaning up to a minimum, and to avoid destroying rivet detail if present. It cannot be emphasised too often that the secret of clean soldering is an iron which gives adequate heat.

One advantage of side-tank locomotives over others, from the modelmaker's point of view, is that, if necessary, the sides of the boiler can be cut away entirely behind the tanks. It is thereby possible to accommodate wide motors which could not be used in any other type ; or, for low-boilered locomotives, the motor could be turned on its side if there was not sufficient headroom for it to stand upright. The writer adopted this method for an 11-mm. gauge tank-engine described in Chapter XVI.

In some types, the width of the cab is less than that over the tanks. This does not introduce any particular complication ; the tanks will be mounted on the running-plate first ; then the cab sides, which are short pieces extending down only as far as the tank tops, are added in the ordinary way.

It should be noted that the cab side can be made in two parts, if it is thought more convenient to do so, the division being at the point marked *X* in Fig. 118A. If the cab side is made in one piece it is advisable, in fact almost essential, to solder temporarily a strip of metal or a piece of stiff wire across the door near the lower edge to prevent the part getting out of shape. This is unsoldered after the side has been mounted on the running-plate.

The soldering of the tank tops should be carried out from the inside as far as may be practicable. It is usually possible to introduce the bit of a small iron if the greater part of the boiler sides, where concealed by the cab, have been cut away.

If side-tanks provide more room for the motor at the sides, saddle-tanks allow additional head-room for it above the boiler. In extreme cases, practically the whole of the boiler below the tank can be cut away.

The first step, after mounting the boiler and cab-front on the running-plate, is to file the front of the tank to shape ; and it is as well to note that the contour of such tanks is seldom a simple curve of uniform radius. Mr.

Superstructure for a tank locomotive showing lead ballast in boiler and firebox

Maskelyne's article in *The Model Railway News* for July, 1938, provides an illuminating example, for in the particular case there cited, it was found that no fewer than nine different radii went to make up the contour of the tank. The simplest way to arrive at a reasonably accurate reproduction is to take a tracing from the working drawing and to glue it to the metal. The inside curve must be adjusted by trial and error until it fits the boiler perfectly. This part is soldered to the boiler ; and, to ensure that it is upright, a small right-angled block of wood can be used as a guide. The appearance of the job will then be something like Fig. 119A. Solder the tank front to the boiler at one point, just enough to hold it securely in place and, before completing the joint, examine it carefully to be sure it is not leaning over to one side. The tank front should have been marked with a centre-line when setting out which is lined up with the centre-line on the boiler, as in Fig. 119A. If the worker thinks it will make matters easier, he can solder

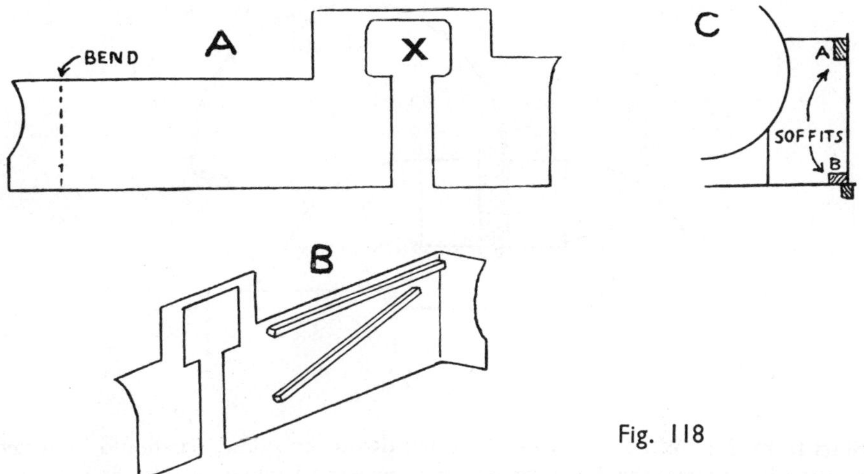

Fig. 118

an identical end-plate at the cab end—to the cab spectacle plate in fact—to ensure that the tank is level and that its contour is the same at both ends.

We now have a guide by means of which the principal part of the tank can be shaped. The overall width can be obtained by bending a strip of paper, about $\frac{3}{8}$ in. wide, round the front. Make a mark where it touches the boiler on one side ; hold it firmly at this point with one hand and draw it over the top of the tank front and down the other side until it again touches the boiler. Without allowing it to slip, make a mark at this point with the finger-nail, or ask someone to mark it with a pencil while you hold the paper in place. When opened out this will give the overall width, but a margin of about a millimetre should be allowed for possible errors. The tank must be rolled to shape in much the same way as a boiler, but as the radius is larger the task will be easier.

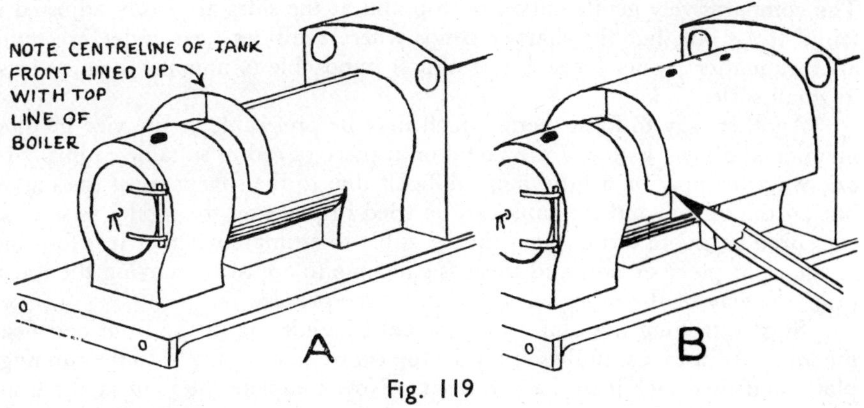

Fig. 119

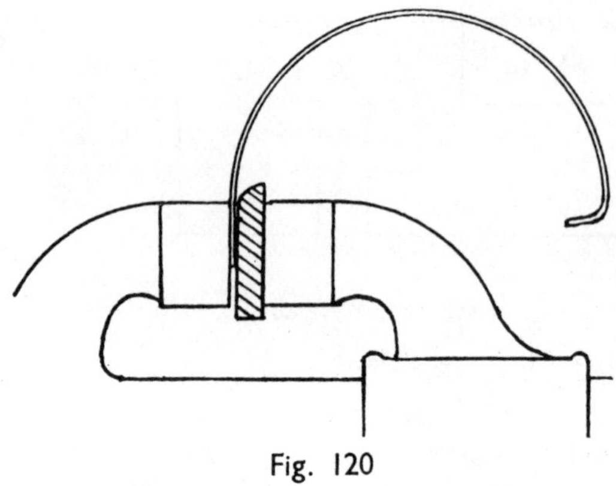

Fig. 120

Start from the middle and work outwards down the sides. It should be tested frequently against the front as one proceeds, and when a good fit has been obtained, mark the points where the sharper bends commence, where the sides turn under to meet the boiler. A pencil can be used for this, as shown in Fig. 119B. The writer may be unduly cautious, but he thinks it better not to use a scriber in a case like this. If a scribed line is sufficiently clearly marked to be seen it must weaken the metal to a certain extent just where this is least desirable. This would not be of any importance with thicker material, but we should use the thinnest sheet available, not more than six " thous " thick, for this part, even if it should be necessary to reinforce by soldering pieces of strip brass or rail to the underside.

The bend can be made in a vice, clamping the work so that the marked line is level with the edge of the jaws. Since the bend is nearly always a curve and not a sharp edge, it should be made against a piece of packing, clamped alongside it in the vice, with its edge filed approximately to the required curve, as shown in Fig. 120. Considerable discretion is required in shaping the tank. The comparatively gentle curves on top and at the sides are easily adjusted if found to be out, but the sharper bends where the sides turn under are quite another matter ; once formed, it is almost impossible to unmake them, at least in small scales.

Another way to form them, which may be preferable to the vice method mentioned above, is to roll the metal on a piece of rod of suitable radius. In one way this may be a little more difficult due to the sharpness of the curve, but on the other hand the tank can be tried in place on the model as soon as the curve begins to form. It is thus possible to estimate whether it is forming in the right place or not, and there is still time to adjust by moving the rod a little one way or the other when resuming the process.

Start attaching the tank to the model by soldering at the front end near the top. Adjust it carefully so that the top centre-line is parallel to the running-plate, and then tack it to the cab front. Now complete the joint at the front end, using a piece of wood or cloth to force it into contact with the edge of the tank front. Soldering at the cab end is quite simple, but the worker should be on guard against the tank springing away from the correct curve, which might produce a slightly lopsided appearance. The pressure applied at the forward end while soldering might cause this to happen.

If there are handrails, fillers, or other fittings on the tank they should be fitted before it is mounted on the boiler ; it will be impossible to solder them from inside afterwards.

The pannier tank locomotive, a speciality of the Great Western Railway, requires rather different methods. There are several classes in service, presenting minor variations as regards external appearance, but in all of them the boiler and smokebox are almost completely concealed by the tanks. Hence for small electrically-driven models it is not necessary to model the boiler in the accepted sense, and the obvious alternative is illustrated in Fig. 121. The tanks, plus as much of the boiler as is visible below them, can be bent to shape from one piece of sheet-metal. If the reader has any misgivings about his ability to shape this tank-cum-boiler unit accurately, he can bend and solder it round an upright template, cut to the outline of the front less an appropriate allowance for the thickness of the metal which is to be wrapped round it. The small portion of the boiler which is visible above the tanks can be filed from a piece of strip-metal, which, for " OO " gauge, should be about $\frac{1}{16}$ in. thick by $\frac{1}{2}$ in. or $\frac{5}{8}$ in. wide. One side of this is filed to a segment of a circle as will be clear from the drawing. A piece of sheet-metal bent to fit closely over this will represent as much of the smokebox as can be seen. This false boiler top, as we may call it, can be bolted in place by the screws which secure the chimney and dome, and which should be inserted from inside the tank unit. Similarly the top of the firebox can be represented by a piece of thick sheet-metal, left flat, but with the edges rounded off because these loco-

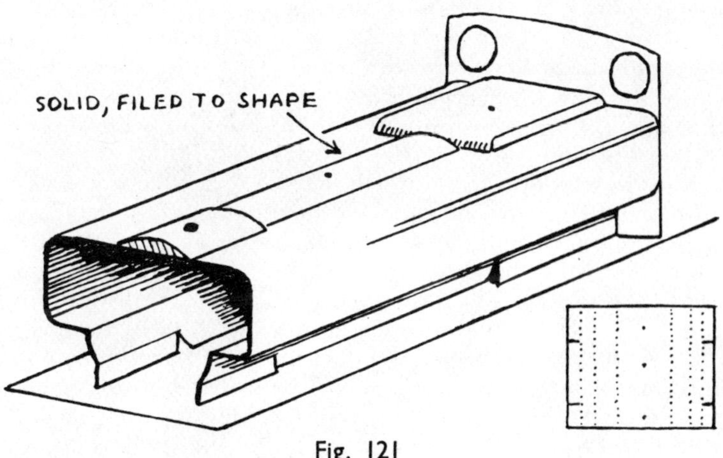

Fig. 121

motives have Belpaire type fireboxes. The smokebox front, which includes the fronts of the tanks, is cut to shape and soldered in place in the usual manner.

TANK FILLERS

These fittings are very easily made on a lathe, but in the absence of turning facilities they can be produced by soldering a disc of metal to a slightly smaller but thicker disc or washer. In certain cases, the lid might be well represented by a small brass drawing pin. The hinges, when of the strap type, must be fitted in much the same manner as that described in connection with smokebox doors. The various forms of fastening in use can usually be represented with pins and scraps of wire.

CHAPTER X

TENDERS

BUILDING a tender should not present much difficulty to anyone who has produced a locomotive. The running-plate should be made first and will be something like the corresponding part of a locomotive, with valances and buffer-beams. If large-size wheels are to be used it will be necessary to cut slots to allow the flanges to project through into the inside of the body ; whether this will be necessary is easily ascertained from the working drawing.

If the frames are to be soldered to the running-plate—so that the wheels will be irremovably locked in place—it is probably best to build up the body first and add the frames afterwards. But if, on the other hand, the wheels are mounted in some way which renders it possible to remove them temporarily, the reverse order might be more convenient.

The body is usually quite straightforward ; the sides and back can be made separately, or in one piece and bent to shape. The latter method simplifies assembly, but cannot give quite such clean sharp corners. The sides should be soldered to the running-plate against a block of wood, to ensure that they are upright and parallel to the edge of the running-plate, Fig. 122. The method has been described in connection with certain locomotive parts. Note that a piece of card packing is inserted, equal in thickness to the amount by which the side is set back from the edge. Typical interior arrangements are shown in Fig. 123 ; but it is hardly worth while to reproduce more than the tank top, as the rest is concealed by the coal. For this the writer shapes a block of soft wood to fit the interior. The top is rounded with a knife and a coarse rasp to suggest piled coal. In shaping the block it should be remembered that towards the front the coal would be slipping down towards the door in the front plate. The wood is brushed over with Indian ink or black water-colour, and when this has had time to dry it is covered with tube adhesive or office gum. A piece of coal is held over it and rubbed briskly with a rasp, so that a shower of coal-dust falls on the wet adhesive, and this is continued until the block is completely covered.

Tool-boxes can be made up in sheet-metal and soldered to the tender-sides ; or they may be made from wood, in which case, it may be more convenient to attach them to the coal block than to the tender itself. In place of wood, the coal could be moulded in some plastic material such as Pyruma, the finish being exactly as described above.

The setting out of old-fashioned tenders with flared tops may appear

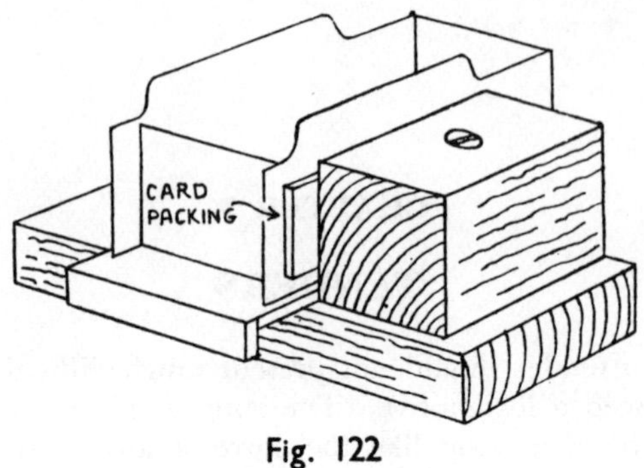

Fig. 122

slightly formidable but is really quite simple if approached in the right way. In Fig. 124, the end elevation is represented by *A*, while *B* is part of the side. *C* shows the actual shape of the corner as set out on the metal. To form the corner correctly, it is only necessary to remember that the dimension *a* in diagrams *A* and *B* will be equal to dimension *a* in diagram *C*. The flared tops are bent outwards while clamped in a vice and, provided they are bent to the correct angle, the corners will be found to match up. It will be obvious from the above description that, for a tender of this type, the back and sides must be made separately and not in one piece.

The type of side-plate shown in Fig. 125, typical of Great Western tenders, is more difficult to manage, due to the double bend. It is better not to attempt to produce it in one piece ; divide as shown in *B* and solder the parts together. Start soldering at one end and, before proceeding, make sure that the two parts are correctly lined up.

Coal-rails are most easily produced by the method shown in Fig. 126. The upright supports, which may be ordinary plated pins, are soldered to the tender body first. Then strips of card or thin wood, equal in thickness to the distance between adjacent rails, are laid across the top of the tender,

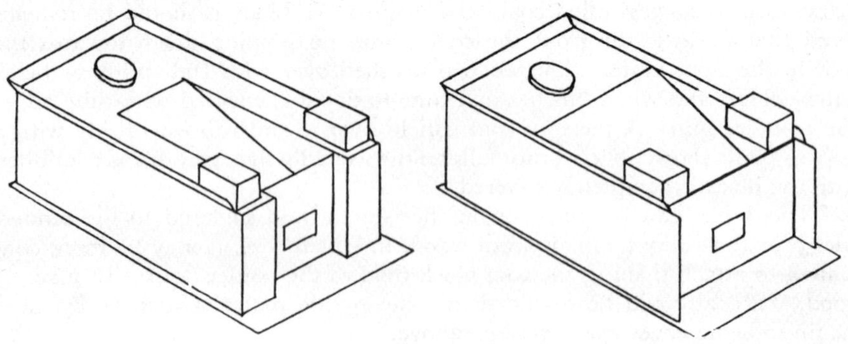

Fig. 123

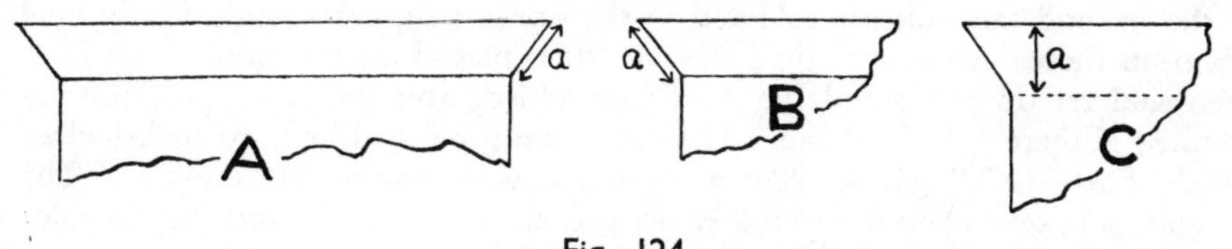

Fig. 124

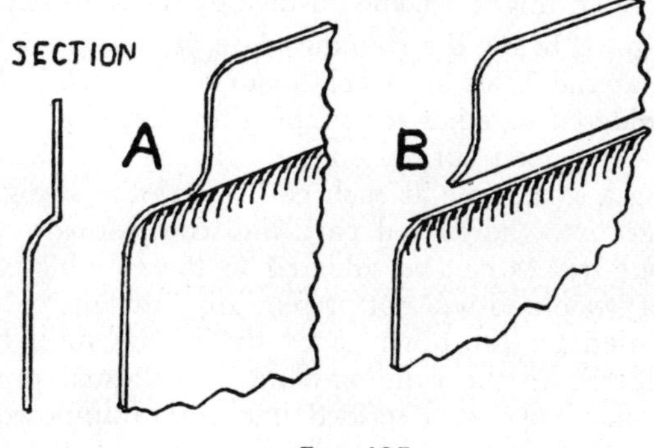

Fig. 125

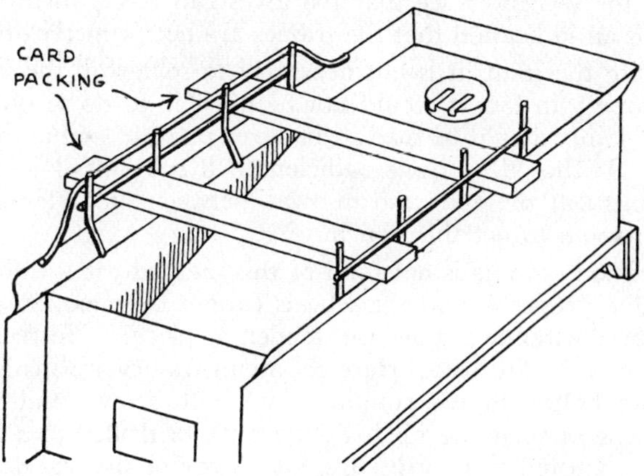

Fig. 126

as shown, and the rails are soldered to the upright supports while firmly held down on these. More spacing-pieces are then placed on the rails which have been soldered in place and the next pair added, and the same procedure is adopted if there is a third rail. The rails should be steel or hard nickel-silver wire. For "OO" gauge, 22- or 24-gauge will usually be suitable. The upright supports should be rather longer than required, and the surplus snipped off when the rails have been added.

Joints of this kind, in wire, are necessarily rather delicate if executed in soft solder. It is better, if possible, to form them with Easy-flo silver-solder, using a fine, almost pin-point, flame from a small blow pipe such as jewellers use. In this case it would be safer to attach the coal rails to the tender sides before the latter are assembled on the running plate to avoid any risk that other joints, in soft-solder, might become unstuck by the high temperature.

Turning to the parts below the running-plate, it is suggested that, for the main frames, strip material, brass or nickel, about 1/32 in. thick be used. The two pieces can be soldered together for shaping and drilling, as described for locomotive frames. The open cut-out spaces between the axleguards should be formed by drilling a small hole at each end, where the straight lower edge of the opening merges into the curved part, and completing with a piercing-saw. One of the side-frames can be soldered to the running-plate against a right-angled block of wood and will not present any difficulty ; but a different procedure must be used for the other, since the wheels must be in position before it can be soldered to the running-plate. The usual procedure seems to be to hold it in place against a scribed line with thin-nosed pliers, as in Fig. 127, while the tip of the iron is introduced between the wheels. After securing it at one point, make sure that it is upright and parallel to the other frame. If it is found to be slightly out of true, the soldered joint may be strained sufficiently to correct the error. If it is too much out for this treatment, the only thing to do is to unsolder and try again. Before completing the joint, spin the wheels to see that the axles run freely in the bearings. If they do not it is an indication that the frames are not properly lined up.

To complete the joint, it is not necessary to solder all the way along the edge of the frame ; in fact it would not be possible to do so on the *inside* — where soldered joints should be made whenever possible — due to the presence of the wheels. It should be quite sufficient if a substantial joint is made at about four points : at the ends and midway between the axles where there is usually enough room to get the iron in.

The writer confesses he is not fond of this method ; it is difficult to locate the second frame properly, and the wheels cannot be removed, if this should ever be necessary, without pulling the tender to pieces. He recommends the modification shown in Fig. 128. Here the main frames are made from angle-section, and are bolted to the running-plate with screws and nuts. If the screw holes in one of them are filed slightly oval, or drilled to a larger size, its position can be adjusted if the axles are out of true or the wheels refuse to run freely. This method is so simple and excellent that it is surprising it is not used

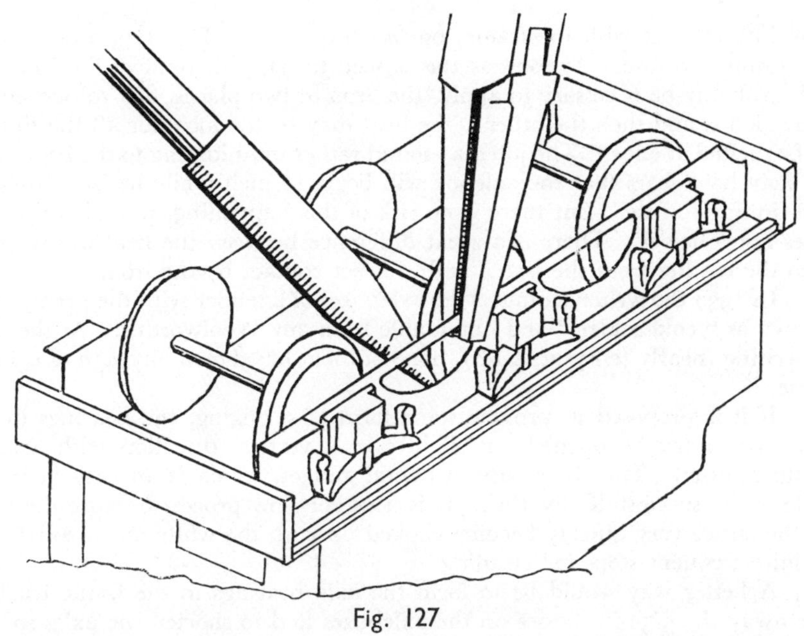

Fig. 127

more extensively. If the internal fittings of the tender are fully built up it would be necessary to solder the nuts to the upper side of the running-plate, but if a removable wood or plastic coal block is substituted, so that the interior is accessible, even this is unnecessary.

Opinions may differ as to whether the axleboxes should be soldered to the main frames before these are assembled on the running-plate or afterwards. If the frames are screwed to the running-plate as suggested in the previous paragraph, the point does not, of course, arise. The writer thinks it is probably better to mount the axleguards first, *but care must be exercised during the subsequent operations not to touch them with the iron* ; they are cast in a white-metal alloy with a melting-point little higher than that of soft solder, and would melt at once. It will be found that most kinds have a boss cast on the back which is obviously intended to fit a 5/32-in. hole in the frame. This is an excellent arrangement, as it disposes of any possibility of the axlebox slipping during the soldering. The worker should satisfy himself that the bearing in the axlebox is quite clean by inserting a $\frac{1}{16}$-in. drill and giving it a twist with the fingers to dislodge any foreign matter and to remove any roughness. The portions of the frames where the axleboxes will be located should be tinned. It does not matter in the least if the tinning is allowed to spread over a considerably larger area as it will be concealed when the tender is painted. Lay the frame on the bench and place an axlebox in position with the boss resting in the hole which has been drilled for it. Hold it down with a small file or strip of wood to ensure firm contact. Bring the tip of the iron into contact with the frame, but *not* the axlebox, Fig. 129, and wait for the tinning to fuse. As soon as this is seen to happen, remove the iron. It will probably be necessary to apply the iron in two places, first to one side of the axlebox and then the other ; the heat may be too local for all the tinning to be melted at once. The job may sound rather intimidating to the beginner ; he may have fears that the axlebox will begin to melt while he is waiting for the tinning to fuse. But there is no risk of this happening, provided the iron does not touch it. There is a great difference between the heat diffusing up into the casting from the frame and a direct contact by the iron.

In 1937 the writer mounted the axleboxes of a tender with the preparation known as " cold solder " and obtainable from any Woolworth's. At the time of writing (nearly ten years later), none of them has shown any sign of coming loose.

If it is proposed to provide some form of springing, the bearings in the axleboxes must be opened out slightly in a vertical direction with a small milling-cutter. The writer uses a dental gadget, which is an easy fit in the hole, quite successfully for this. It is a rather slow process because the teeth of the cutter very quickly become choked up with the white-metal swarf, and require frequent stops for cleaning.

A better way would be to form the axle bearings in the frame itself, to file away the 5/32-in. bosses on the axleboxes and to shorten the axles so that they run entirely in elongated holes in the frames and do not enter the axleboxes at all. Washers should be placed on the axles, between the wheels and the frames, to restrict side-play to the minimum necessary for free running. For two-rail the washers should, of course, be of fibre or other insulating material, unless the wheels are of the popular plastic type. The axleboxes would thus serve no purpose except to enhance appearance. The frames should be $\frac{1}{16}$ in. thick, to provide an adequate bearing surface.

But perhaps the best solution of the springing problem is that shown in Fig. 130. The outside frames and axleboxes are dummies ; the axles actually run in an inside frame, which can be built up from strip or made of $\frac{1}{2}$-in. brass channel section, very much like a locomotive frame. The axle bearings are filed oval vertically to allow the necessary up and down movement of the wheels. Any excessive side-play can be taken up by washers, but these are not shown in the drawing, for the sake of clarity. It may be mentioned here that in any rigid-wheelbase six-wheeled vehicle it is advisable to allow rather more side-play to the middle axle than to the others to ease the pressure on the flanges on sharp curves. The ends of the axles should be cut off practically flush with the faces of the wheels. The sub-frame is attached to the running-plate with a couple of nuts and bolts, and can be removed in a few moments for adjustment of springs or any other purpose. The only disadvantage of this method is that the presence of the inner frames is hardly likely to improve the end view of the tender. However, if they are cut away immediately behind the trailing axle their presence will not be very noticeable.

With eight-wheeled tenders, the mounting of the bogies is much the same

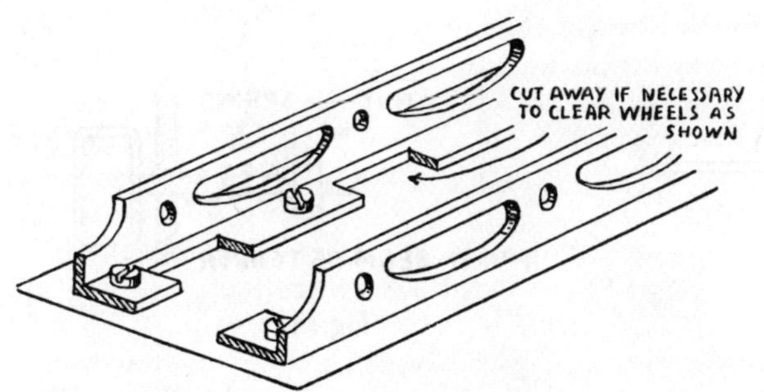

Fig. 128

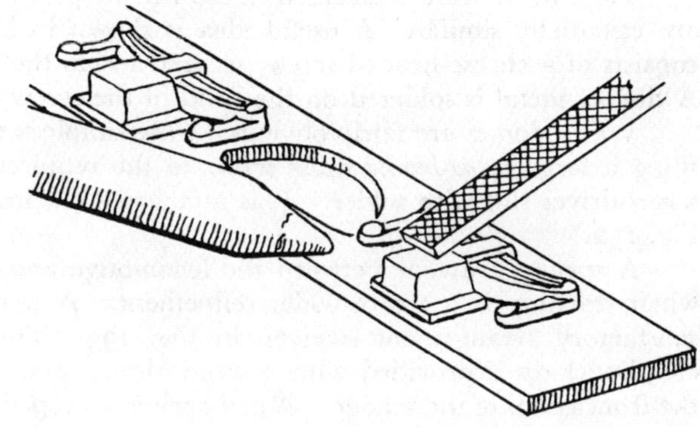

Fig. 129

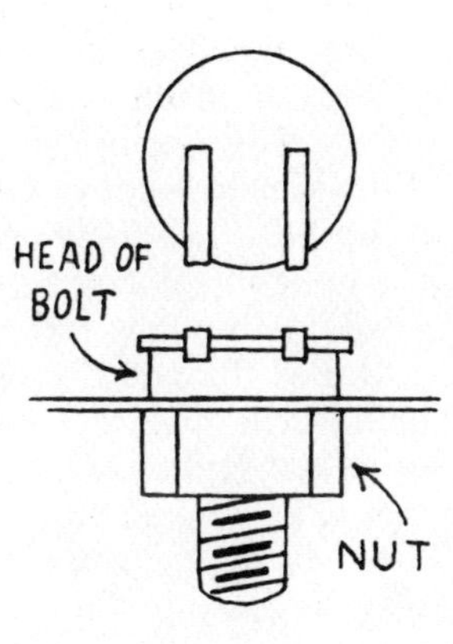

Fig. 131

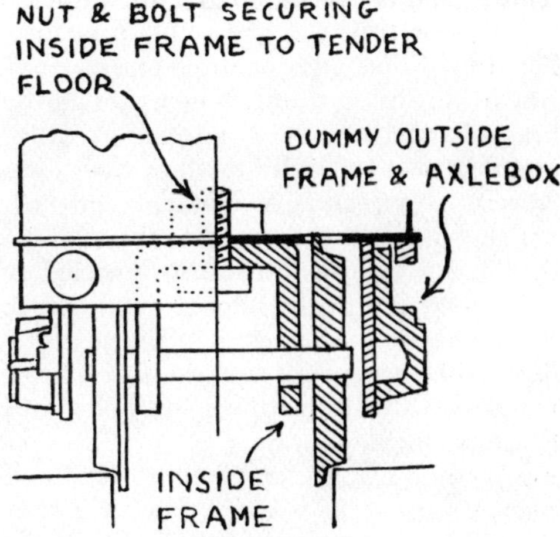

Fig. 130

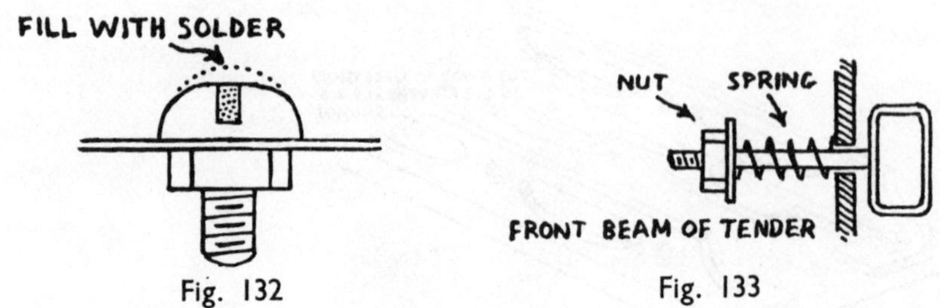

Fig. 132

Fig. 133

as for passenger and freight stock. A pair of nuts can be soldered to the running-plate and the king-pins screwed into them.

Tank fillers were considered in the last chapter and those fitted to tenders are essentially similar. A useful idea is shown in Fig. 131 ; here the filler consists of a cheese-headed screw, secured inside the tank by means of a nut. A disc of metal is soldered on the head of the screw to represent the lid.

Water domes are fairly obvious. One simple way to produce them is by filing a large *round-headed* brass screw to the required shape, after filling the screw-driver slot with solder. It is attached from inside the tank with a nut, Fig. 132.

A sprung drawbar between the locomotive and tender, to ease the load when starting, is a worth-while refinement. A plan view of a simple but satisfactory arrangement is given in Fig. 133. The shank attached to the coupling loop is provided with a screw thread and passes through a hole in the front beam of the tender. A coil-spring is slipped over it and secured with a washer and nut. It might be necessary to solder the nut in place after the correct adjustment of the spring had been found, to prevent it working loose. This should not be required if an anti-friction washer is provided.

CHAPTER XI

OUTSIDE FRAME LOCOMOTIVES

LOCOMOTIVES with outside frames make particularly attractive and interesting models, and workers who have produced several of the more usual inside-frame type should find one an acceptable and stimulating change. There appears to be no particular reason why a model chassis should not follow the prototype in having outside frames in place of the usual internal ones, but the writer thinks that most workers will probably prefer to start with a chassis on normal lines, and to add dummy outside frames which reproduce the appearance of the prototype, but do not perform any structural or mechanical function. This chapter is written on that assumption, and details the methods which the writer has used on several models. There is, of course, ample precedent for a model with both outside and inside frames ; many early locomotives were so built.

For a model in the smaller scales the outside frames can form part either of the chassis or of the superstructure ; the former produces a more businesslike job and is usually preferable, but the latter may *look* simpler though it is apt to prove rather fiddling in practice and is hardly worth while except in special cases. For an inside-cylinder single-driver, which has no external cranks, it is quite suitable, but hardly so in other cases.

The writer's method is shown in Fig. 134A. The foundation is a perfectly ordinary mechanism, either bought or quite easily made at home ; diecast mechanisms are quite suitable for this treatment. The external side-frames can be made of 1/32-in. brass or nickel, and secured with 10-B.A. screws by means of holes tapped in the frame, with the addition of drilled spacing-blocks which hold the outside frames at the appropriate distance to clear the faces of the wheels. It will be seen from the drawing that the slots which take the place of the horn-guides are open at the bottom so that the dummy frames can be removed if required by simply releasing the screws. It is sufficient if the outside frame is secured by two screws, one near the front and the other at the rear, but an extra spacer might be added somewhere near the middle in the case of a long chassis to guard against the outside frame becoming bent inwards so as to foul the wheels. This additional spacer need not be attached to the chassis in any way ; it would be sufficient to solder it to the outside frame so that it pressed against the inner one.

The outside frames can, of course, be drilled and filed while soldered together, as described in an earlier chapter. The upper photo on page 131 shows the chassis of a Lynton & Barnstaple locomotive made as in Fig. 134A. The cylinders are, of course, soldered to the outside frames, but the buffer beams and their cowcatchers form part of the main chassis. The lower photo on page 137 shows a 4-mm. scale model of a Great Western Dean single-wheeler in which the outside frames are soldered to the running-plate of the superstructure, and take the place of the usual valance. The mechanism is a specially made pre-war Reidmere.

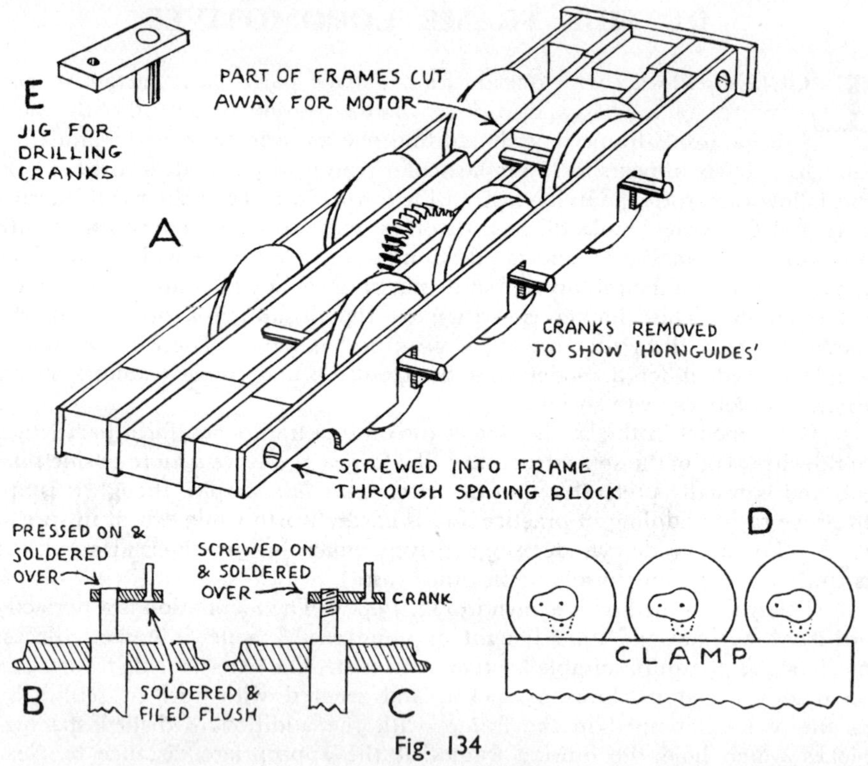

Fig. 134

It will be clear from the foregoing that the outside frames themselves do not present much difficulty, but the extended cranks, in the case of a four- or six-coupled engine, require some care and ingenuity. If the mechanism is obtained complete from a manufacturer, extended axles and cranks should be specified when placing the order. If it is built at home, the constructor will have to provide new axles for the driving wheels, extended to enable the cranks to be fitted. The question naturally arises how driving wheels with squared centres of the type now usually supplied can be adapted. Two courses seem to be open : the manufacturer can be asked to supply special axles with the threaded ends extended to allow the fitting of the cranks, or the wheel centres can be drilled out to provide an ordinary force-fit on the axles. In

Outside frame chassis by the author for a model of the Lynton & Barnstaple *Exe*. See Fig. 134

Great Western 2-2-2 outside frame locomotive with the outside frames forming part of the superstructure

the latter case it might be necessary to plug the wheel centres and re-drill on a lathe to obtain a hole of the required size.

The cranks should be made from flat stock, preferably nickel or steel, about 1/32 in. thick. It is advisable to drill them with a simple jig to ensure that they all have the same throw. This may consist of a piece of metal with a pin, which is a close fit in the crank centre, inserted and a small hole which serves as a guide when drilling for the crankpin, Fig. 134E. Start by centre-popping for the extension of the axle, and scribe the outline of the centre boss with dividers ; drill for the axle and then insert the jig and drill for the crankpin. Lastly file to shape. The cranks can be a force-fit on the ends of the axles and secured with solder, Fig. 134B, but it is more satisfactory—and simpler when it comes to quartering—to cut screw threads, say 10- or 12-B.A., on the ends of the axles and to tap similar threads in the cranks, Fig. 134C. They can then be adjusted with much greater ease and precision, and finally soldered over. If it should be discovered that an error has been made so that one of the cranks is not accurately quartered it is easy to make adjustments with small pliers while holding a soldering iron against it to keep the solder in the molten state.

The crankpins can be ordinary steel pins or panel-pins for " OO " and " HO " gauges. They should be a good press-fit, the holes being drilled slightly small and opened with a fine broach. Solder over on the back of the crank and file the heads of the pins off practically flush to prevent them rubbing against the outside frames.

The writer's method of quartering is shown at *D*. Cranks are mounted on one wheel of each axle, and the wheels are gripped in a vice, toolmaker's clamp, or, best of all, a simple clamp made for the purpose. This may consist of two pieces of wood or metal bolted together by a couple of screws. All the cranks should be dead in line. It is now a fairly simple matter to adjust the cranks on the opposite side at right-angles, as indicated by the dotted lines.

CHAPTER XII

MULTIPLE GEAR TRANSMISSIONS

SO far, we have considered only one form of gearing : that which consists of a worm, usually of steel, on the armature shaft of the motor, and a worm-wheel, of brass or bronze, on the driving axle. Such an arrangement is very convenient and compact, but has the disadvantage that, when designed to provide the high ratios of thirty or forty to one, which are necessary for the good behaviour of locomotives in the smaller scales, the frictional losses are rather high. Some model locomotives have been fitted with spur-gears as an alternative to the worm and worm-wheel, the Essar mechanism being an example of this arrangement. Quite a number, perhaps the majority, of " O " gauge mechanisms employ this system, but apart from the Essar it has not had much popularity in the smaller scales.

Generally speaking, the overall efficiency of spur-gears should be higher than that of worm gearing, but spur-gears are more difficult to accommodate in the restricted space offered by the chassis and boiler. A further difficulty is that either the armature shaft must be placed across the frame, instead of lengthwise, which involves re-designing the motor entirely, or a pair of bevel-gears must be introduced to effect the necessary change in the direction of rotation. On the other hand, the use of spur gears and a transverse motor shaft facilitate the use of an armature of larger diameter which is desirable.

Perhaps the best compromise is a combination of spur-gear and worm-and worm-wheel. The worm-wheel and a suitable spur-gear are mounted together on a jack shaft which has bearings in the side frames, the worm being on the armature shaft exactly as usual. The spur-gear engages another rather larger one on the driving axle and thus a further reduction of speed is obtained. Suppose, for example, that the worm-wheel gives a reduction of 20-to-1, and that the spur-gears have 10 and 20 teeth respectively : then the total reduction would be 40-to-1. If the spur-gears had 10 and 18 teeth, with the same worm and wheel, the total reduction would be 36-to-1. The simple rules for calculating the final reduction resulting from any combination of gears will be found in " Workshop Facts and Figures " published by Percival Marshall & Co. Ltd.

Since two-stage gear-trains enable higher reductions to be obtained, they also permit the use of worm-gears giving somewhat lower reductions, which tends to higher efficiency. This aspect of the matter may have little attraction for the modelmaker, unless he is in a position to cut his own worms and wheels, since his choice will be restricted to what the trade can supply. In many cases, however, the use of two-stage gear-trains may be commended for other good reasons. The motion of a locomotive which can be run really slowly *and remain under control* is much more satisfactory than that of one which cannot ; it is rather disconcerting when a locomotive which is being backed on to a train either bucks into it with the pugnacity of a young ram or else stops dead half-an-inch short of its target. Then again, the worm-wheels supplied for " OO " gauge are usually about half-an-inch or five-eighths in diameter. Now, it may be desired to model a locomotive with exceptionally small wheels : say 12-mm. diameter ; obviously, the worm-wheel being the same diameter as the driving wheels, or slightly larger, it would, if mounted on the axle, foul the track at points and crossings, and also uncoupling ramps if in use. The only way out of this difficulty is to mount the wormwheel on a jack-shaft and to transmit the drive through a pair of pinions, the one on the axle being small enough to clear the track by a comfortable margin.

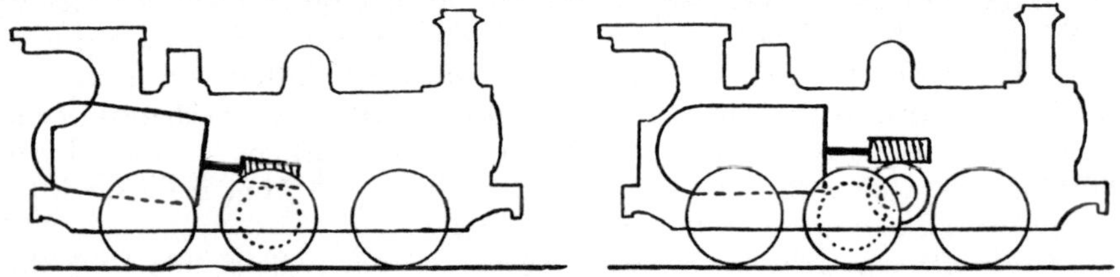

Fig. 135

Yet another consideration in favour of two-stage gear-trains may be mentioned. In the restricted space allowed by many small locomotives it may be very difficult to locate the motor so that the worm can engage with a worm-wheel on one of the axles. It may be found, for example, that the motor would have to project out of the cab in an unsightly manner, or make a nuisance of itself in some other way. In such cases, it is usually possible to overcome the difficulty by mounting the worm-wheel on a jack-shaft which is located forward of the driving axle, thereby enabling the motor to be brought forward also. This is shown in Fig. 135, where the drawing on the left shows what might happen with a simple worm-and-wheel drive, while that on the right shows the improvement effected by the introduction of a pair of pinions. It will be seen that the increased freedom in the placing of the motor is a very substantial asset in difficult cases.

Readers who have had no previous experience of such work may well find the prospect of obtaining correct mesh between the pinions rather disturbing. The bearing holes in the frames must be drilled just the right distance apart to engage the teeth so that they do not bind but are free from unnecessary play. It is not so difficult as it looks, but certainly calls for care and patience. The writer starts by laying the gears together on the bench so that the teeth are well engaged but do not " bottom." What this means is shown in Fig. 136. When fully engaged there is a slight clearance between the summits of the teeth and the valleys. The use of a magnifying glass is really almost essential

Fig. 136

with these small gears. Without allowing either gear to shift, measure as accurately as possible, with a finely-divided steel rule, the distance between the centres of the shaft holes. It will be easier and more certain if the measurement is made on a surface upon which a little adhesive has been spread, so that the gears are stuck in position for the time being. The measurement so obtained is transferred to the frames and the drilling centres *very carefully* centre-popped. Before drilling, check the distance between the centres to be sure the punch has not wandered. If there is any doubt about it, one of the centres may be " drifted " slightly with a punch or small drill. Make a further check after both holes have been started, but before the drill has entered them to its full diameter. If there is found to be an error, which has not been satisfactorily corrected by drifting one of the punch-marks, the only course remaining is to drill one of the holes with a smaller drill than the final size, and to file it in the required direction with a rat-tail file. It can then be cleaned up by putting through a drill of the correct size. To drift a hole in this way is not quite such an obvious and straightforward proceeding as it may appear ; it is not good enough simply to file the hole *sideways*. Unless it is filed upwards and downwards as well, so as to be approximately circular, the chances are that the drill will follow the path of least resistance and go back to the original centre, so that nothing will have been gained, as should be clear from Fig. 137. If anything, the diameter of the part of the hole which has been filed should be slightly more than the original diameter.

I have stressed the importance of correct meshing because, if gears are too closely engaged, there will be loss of power due to binding ; if, on the other hand, they are too loose, the model will be noisy. Of the two evils the second is probably the less objectionable, at least in the smaller scales. With a large machine with heavy parts a rather tight fit might not be quite so serious,

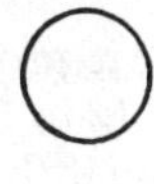

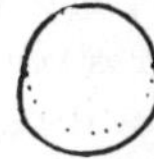

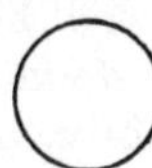

Fig. 137

because, with proper precautions as to load and lubrication, the parts would soon become run-in, but with a " OO " gauge model it might be a very long time indeed before anything of the sort happened.

The bearing holes for the jack-shaft should, of course, be drilled at the same time as those for the axles ; that is, while the frames are still soldered together.

Suitable small pinions can be obtained from some of the firms which advertise in "The Model Engineer" and "The Model Railway News", and also from some of the shops which deal in model aeroplane parts. Messrs. Bond's have a good line in small steel gears in three or four sizes ranging from a shade over a quarter-of-an-inch in diameter upwards. They are 48 pitch and, to avoid possible mistakes, this should be specified when ordering. Suitable pairs of wheels may also be found in old clocks and speedometers and various forms of timing-gear.

Fig. 139 gives details of a two-stage reduction-gear made by the writer for a model of a three-foot gauge Isle of Man locomotive. In considering the sectional end view on the right of the drawing, it is important to note that in practice the jack-shaft and axle should have practically no side-play or they will tend to move sideways so as to partly disengage the gears, resulting in noise and probably increased wear. If the wormwheel is shouldered, that can take up side-play in the jack-shaft. For the axle, washers should be placed between the wheels and the frames, or a short piece of tube can be slipped over the axle, alongside the pinion, before it is inserted in the frames. In the drawing, Fig. 139, all washers have been omitted to avoid obscuring the more important parts. Fig. 138 is a pictorial representation of the same arrangement. The jack-shaft should be a piece of steel rod. In "OO" gauge the most convenient diameter is usually ⅛ in.

It may be found that the pinions as bought are drilled for a size which is too small for the shafts on which they are to be mounted. It is not difficult to drill them out larger, because, with ordinary care, the drill will follow the original hole. Usually, the gears should be secured to the shafts by making them a force-fit. Small pinions are not as a rule provided with shoulders, so that the the use of a clamping screw is out of the question. Hence, if the gear is a sloppy fit on the shaft, the only way to make it secure is by means of solder, which is hardly to be recommended if it can be avoided. Therefore the hole should be drilled just a trifle—perhaps a couple of " thous "—smaller than the diameter of the axle, and opened out very cautiously, if necessary, with a broach. If, for example, the shaft or axle is ⅛-in. diameter, a 31 drill should be used, this being the next smaller size to ⅛-in. In no circumstances should a ⅛-in. drill be used, as it is sure to produce a hole slightly oversize. It must be understood that a broach is not an ideal tool for the purpose, since it produces a slightly conical hole, but it can be made to do the job and is likely to be the only means available. When offering the gear to the axle, to judge if the hole has been eased sufficiently, remember that the broach should be worked alternately from both ends. The hole will thus be slightly smaller at the centre than at the outside faces, and the ideal state of affairs has been reached when

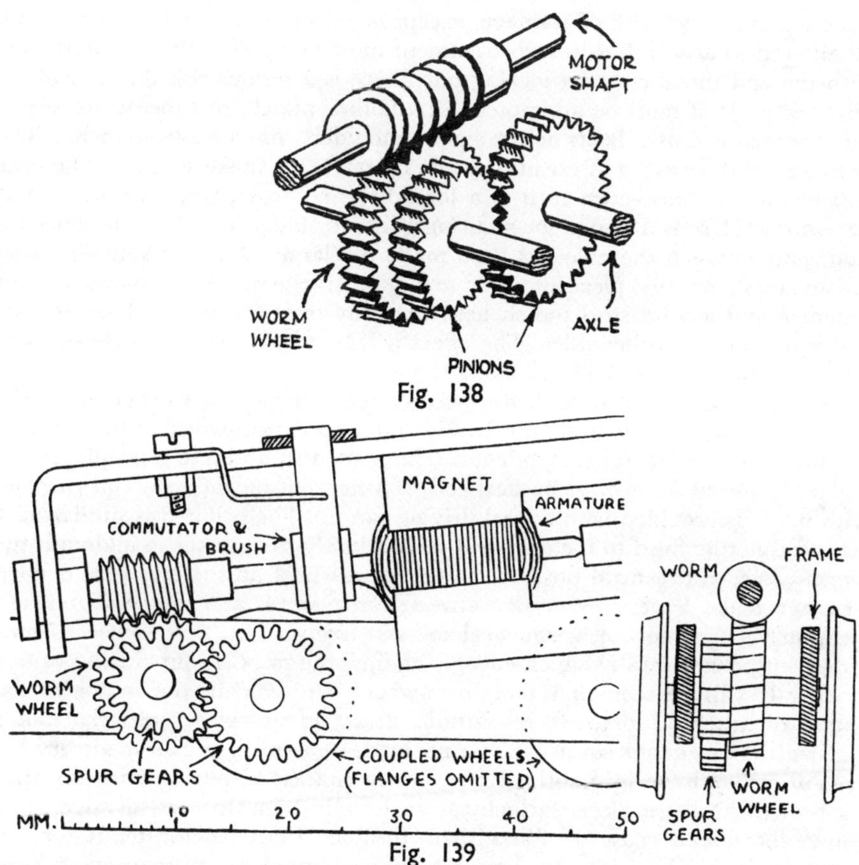

Fig. 138

Fig. 139

the end of the shaft will just enter the hole but will not pass the narrow part in the centre by hand pressure. At this point, it must be assumed that the opening-out process has been carried far enough, and the problem of forcing the gear on to the shaft without causing damage to either must be tackled. In the absence of a lathe, the best way may be to clamp the shaft upright in a vice (protected by soft packing) and to drive the gear on with a hollow punch and light taps of a small hammer. In place of a steel punch a piece of brass tube can be used, and is in fact preferable, as it is less likely than hardened steel to mark the gear. If it should be found that the size of the hole has been misjudged so that the gear cannot be forced on to the shaft without risk of damage, it may be necessary to knock the shaft out again. For this purpose the gear should be laid on top of the vice jaws, or on a piece of wood in which a hole large enough to clear the shaft has been drilled. The shaft will, of course, project downwards, and it should be tapped lightly with a centre-punch inserted in the gear until it falls out. In the case of a plain shaft this can be done without much risk of damage, except in extreme cases, which should not be allowed to arise ; but if such treatment must be applied to a squared axle, with the end threaded for a locking nut, there is a serious risk that it will be distorted. If it must be attempted use a hollow punch, or tube, which clears the threaded end and bears on the square shoulder—not a centre-punch. The best way in this case is to err on the side of safety, to make sure that the gear will fit on the axle—even if it is a loose fit—and to secure it with solder if necessary. Here is a dodge for securing gears to shafts (or wheels to axles for that matter) when the hole has been made too large. Lay the gear or wheel on an anvil, or any piece of iron, and give it several sharp blows with a hammer and a solid steel punch held centrally over the hole. Turn it over and repeat on the other side. The effect will be to close up the hole slightly, just enough, with any luck, to make the gear a firm fit on its shaft.

Mr. MacAldouie has described a " free-wheel " device for worm drive locos. which offers certain advantages. In Fig. 139A the worm-wheel is *free to revolve* on the driving axle. It must, of course, be a good fit and free from play. The collar *A*, turned from brass or steel rod, is a force fit on the axle and revolves with it. It is provided with a steel driving pin *C*. The collar *B* is similar to *A* but need not be fixed to the axle as it serves simply as a spacer to maintain the worm-wheel in a central position. The worm-wheel plus *A* and plus *B* must together make a very exact fit between the frames, allowing only enough clearance to enable the wormwheel to turn freely. The worm-wheel is provided with a steel pin *D* which engages against the pin *C* to provide a positive drive. It will be seen that the worm-wheel can overrun the motor to the extent of nearly a complete revolution. Two advantages result: the motor can start more easily since there is no load on it until it has made several revolutions and the locomotive has a better chance of getting past any spot on the track where electrical contact is defective due to dirt, or any other cause, for it can coast on for a short distance if the motor tends to stall momentarily. The writer has fitted a gear of this kind to two locomotives with satisfactorily results.

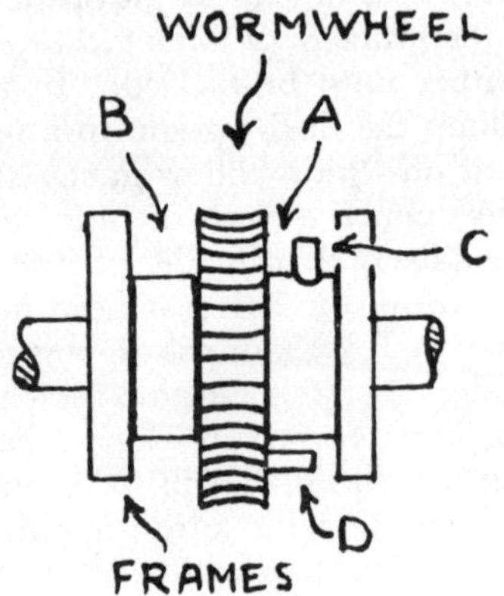

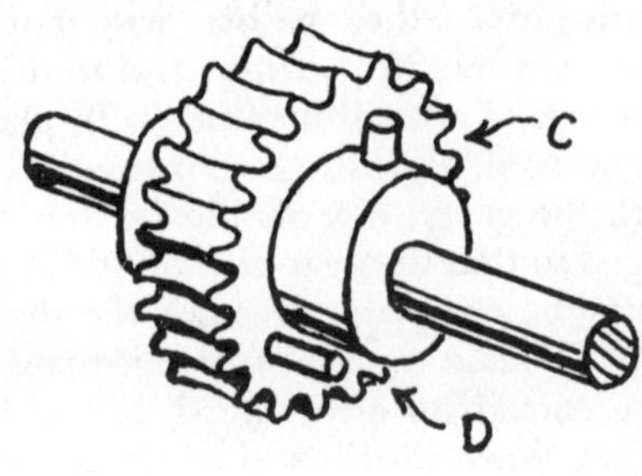

Fig. 139a

CHAPTER XIII

FLEXIBLE DRIVES, POWER TENDERS

IN a few cases, it may be difficult, or even impossible, to find room for the motor in the locomotive itself, and although this is unusual with the small motors now available it may still happen when modelling old, low-boilered prototypes. The only alternative is to put the motor in the tender, the power being conveyed to the driving-wheels by a flexible shaft or one with universal joints, rather like a motor car transmission. It is hardly necessary to say that such arrangements introduce additional complication, and should not be used unless it is necessary to do so, although successful results can be obtained if the job is carefully planned and executed. The worm, or other driving-gear, must be mounted on a shaft of its own on the locomotive frame, and means must be devised to couple it to the motor in the tender so as to allow the necessary flexibility on curves. In addition, slight lateral and transverse play between engine and tender must be reckoned with unless a very rigid form of drawbar is used.

Flexible shafts and couplings have been arranged in various ways. Some workers have used a piece of rubber tube, forced over the ends of the armature shaft and the gear-shaft on the locomotive, Fig. 140. Success depends on finding a piece of tube tough enough not to become twisted, but sufficiently flexible to allow free movement on curves. It would be an obvious advantage to attach one end of the tube to a telescopic form of coupling as shown in Fig. 141, so that the locomotive and tender could be separated without disturbing the rubber tube. Other workers have used a fine spiral spring as the flexible connection. In this case, the most convenient arrangement is to provide a spring of about the same diameter as the shafts it is proposed to connect. The shafts have a screw-thread cut on them for a distance of about a quarter or three-eighths of an inch. Provided the screw-thread has approximately the same pitch as that of the spring, it will be found that the latter can be screwed on in the same way as the expanding curtain rail sold by hardware stores is screwed to the eyelets supplied with it. This is a very neat and easily-made fitting, but the writer has not had much success with it. If the spring was sufficiently flexible to allow free movement on sharp curves, it invariably became twisted and distorted after a short period of running. It would be unwise to condemn the device entirely on this evidence, because the selection of springs may have been unfortunate. The experiments were made at a time when spring wire in different sizes was difficult to obtain, and possibly the happy mean was not discovered.

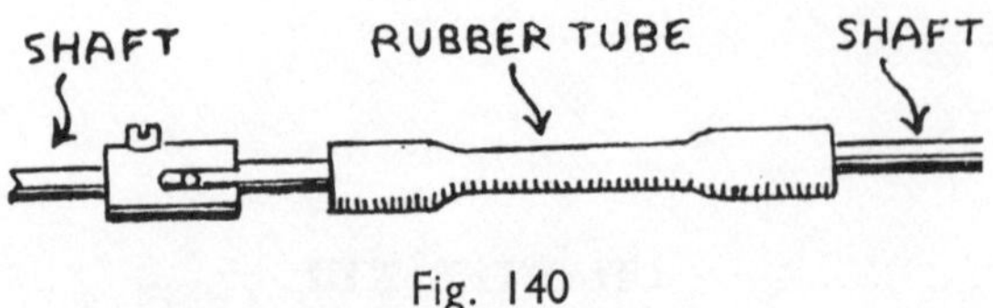

Fig. 140

A more workmanlike device, which has been found satisfactory, is illustrated in Fig. 141. Here there is a short shaft connected at one end to what is really a dog-type universal joint and at the other to a second flexible coupling which, in addition to providing some extra side movement, looks after any variation in the distance between the locomotive and tender arising from the slack in the drawbar. The couplings are easily made from brass tube or rod of suitable size and are either soldered to their respective shafts or tapped for grub-screws, as shown in the drawing. One half of the universal joint, *A*, can be filed and drilled from rod, but the other part of the " link " must be filed from flat stock, or bent from hard wire, and soldered with the two parts of the coupling in engagement, Fig. 143.

For the telescopic joint, *B*, the short middle shaft must be drilled through for a pin, as shown in the enlarged diagram, Fig. 141. The other portion, which is fixed to the motor shaft, may be $\frac{1}{8}$-in. tube. To disengage the engine and tender it is only necessary to slide the two halves of the coupling apart.

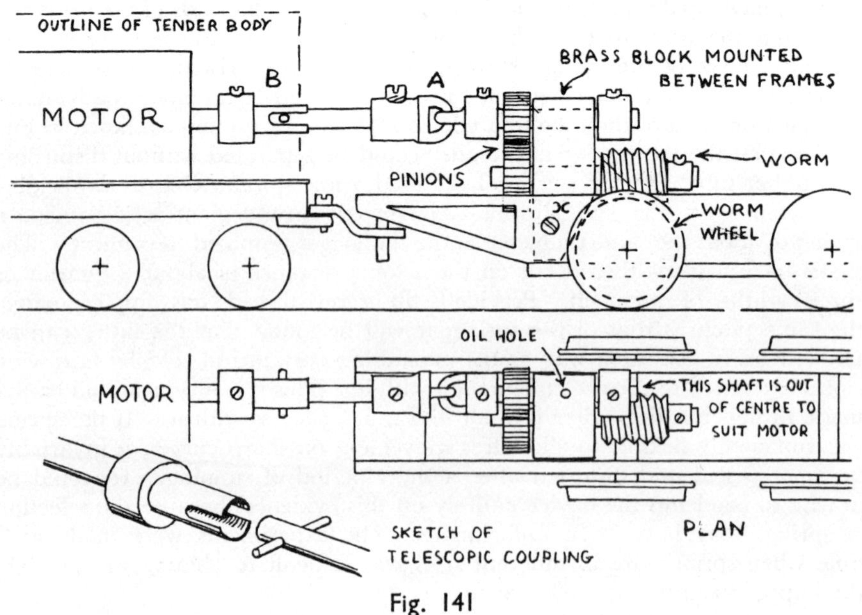

Fig. 141

Chassis for a model American 0-4-0 switcher locomotive with motor in tender as in Fig. 141

It will be seen that in this particular case a pair of spur-gears has been introduced, partly to bring the locomotive shaft up to a convenient height to line up with the motor and partly to obtain a lower gear ratio. The chassis in question was made for a 0-4-0 American switching locomotive ; its Trans-atlantic origin will be evident from the representation of bar frames ; in the photo above it is shown with the superstructure removed. Needless to say, the spur gears are not a necessary or integral part of an arrangement of

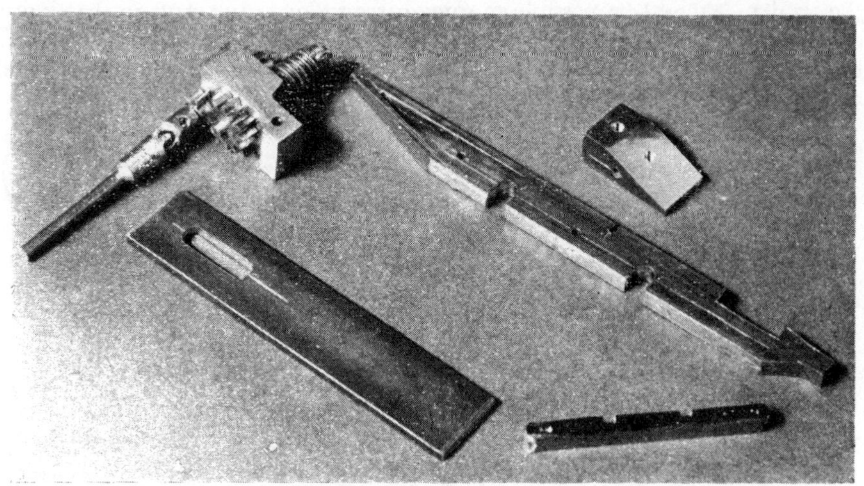

Main frames, gears and flexible coupling, keeper plate, etc., for the tender drive locomotive in Fig. 141

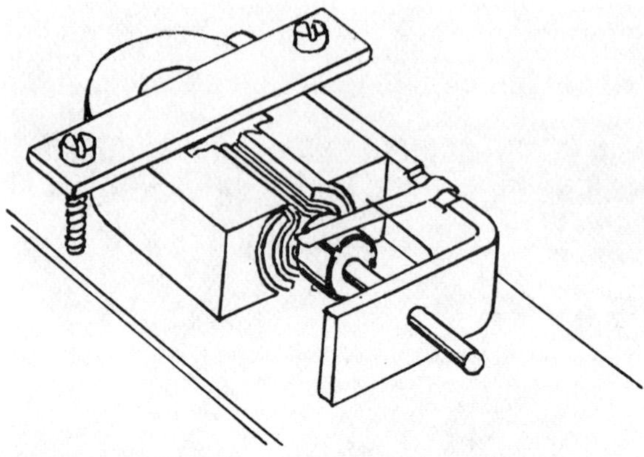

Fig. 142

his kind ; the drive could be taken direct to a worm by inclining the motor downwards at the forward end.

The method of mounting the motor in the tender must depend on the design of the former and the circumstances of the particular case. It may be advisable to place the motor on its side, as there is plenty of width, but head-room is restricted by the height of the tender sides. In most cases, something of the kind shown in Fig. 142 should be satisfactory ; the motor is clamped to the floor, or to the tender frame, by a metal plate and screws. The floor must be cut away to clear any projections on the underside of the motor. The shaft will project through an opening in the coal-plate, and will at least be rather less conspicuous than a magnet projecting back into the cab through lack of sufficient space in the firebox. By providing a pair of spur-gears in the tender, it might be possible in some cases to lower the shaft so that it was out of sight below the running-plate. The motor will be concealed by a false top, worked up to represent coal. This could be shaped from a piece of wood and treated with coal-dust as described in chapter X.

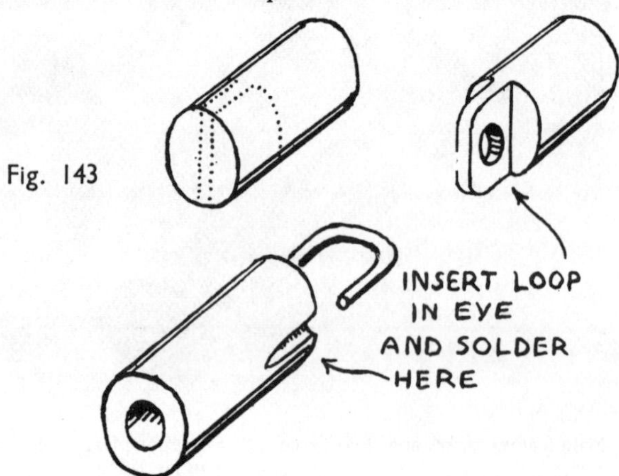

Fig. 143

Referring again to Fig. 141, it is obvious that motors such as the Zenith or the Romford, in which the ends of the armature shaft are enclosed between bearings of the pin-point type or of that in which end thrust is taken up by a single steel ball, could not be used in this manner without considerable modification. The obvious procedure with such motors would be to substitute a pinion for the worm on the shaft, as suggested in the last paragraph, and to convey the drive downwards to a second pinion on a shaft with a plain bearing, or bearings, mounted below the tender running-plate. This is illustrated—applied to a rather different case—in Fig. 146.

Alternatively it should be possible to modify such motors to give a " straight through " drive by fitting an extension shaft, coupled to the armature shaft by a substantial collar, and substituting a plain bearing for the thrust bearing. The thrust could be taken care of by an adjustable collar with a grub screw. A possible variation on this would be to shorten the bearing arm or frame which carries the forward bearing on such motors in order to bring the bearing closer to the commutator and allow the end of the shaft to project through. Naturally the makers of the motor could hardly be expected to look with much favour on such a conversion and it must be emphasised that the constructor should on no account attempt anything of the sort unless he is quite sure of his competence to carry the job through in an efficient manner. To tamper with the bearings of a small high speed motor is a job in quite a different category to most of the other operations described in this book and requires some acquaintance with the methods of the scientific instrument maker. The accurate centring of the armature in the magnet is very important, and if the new bearing is not free from end play the bearing at the other end of the shaft may show premature wear, especially if it is of the pin-point type.

A word of caution should be added as regards pin-point bearings. It is absolutely essential to the good performance of these that there should be no appreciable end play. If the hardened steel points of the shaft are allowed to chatter in the bearing cups they will very soon wear a groove and the shaft will run out of true. Wear will be progressively accelerated and the armature will probably touch one of the magnet poles. It is most important with all apparatus fitted with pin-point bearings to examine the shaft for end play from time to time, and to adjust if necessary by means of the screw-thread and locking nut on one of the bearings. The bearing cups made by the Romford Model Company for use with their own motors are obtainable separately from Messrs. Walkers & Holtzapffel*. Readers would be well advised to make use of these when bearings are required, unless they happen to be experienced in such work.

Fig. 145 shows how the arrangement can be adapted to an auto-train. The flexible couplings are similar to those shown in Fig. 141, but the drive is direct in this case, without the interposition of spur gears as in the former case. The motor can be upright as shown, or mounted on its side as in the former

* They are threaded for a hole tapped 4-B.A.

drawing. The floor of the coach can be wood or metal, and if wood should be about a quarter of an inch thick to provide the necessary rigidity for the motor mounting. The motor can be provided with a substantial metal plate which is screwed to the floor. If it is upright it will, of course, block the coach windows to some extent, but this might be overcome by sinking it in a sort of cradle so as to bring it partly below floor level.

Since the coach has only one bogie, part of its weight rests on the locomotive through the drawbar. For this reason the distribution of weight within the latter will need attention. The weight of the coach rests entirely on the end sill of the locomotive so that there will be a tendency for the latter to tip up at the forward end. This must be adjusted by the addition of lead ballast to

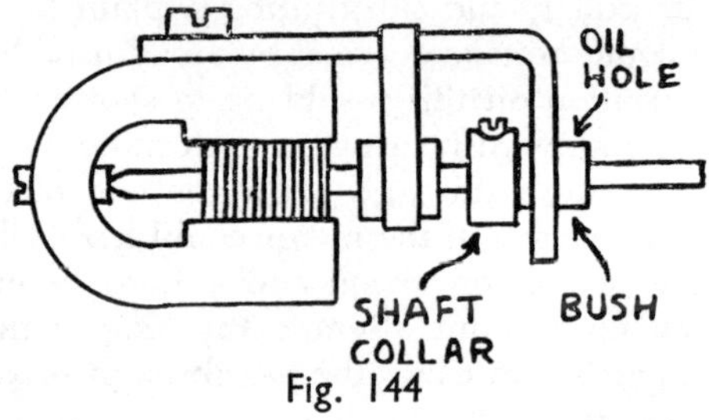

Fig. 144

make the weight approximately equal on both pairs of wheels. The ballast must be concentrated forward as far as possible, and how much is required is best discovered by trial.

As regards the current supply, if the model is designed for three-rail working collectors of conventional type should be fitted under the locomotive, an insulated flexible lead being carried to the motor. It is rather tempting to fit them under the coach floor, but it is doubtful if this would be satisfactory ; the body of a coach rocks from side to side to some extent, due to the fact that it is supported on its centre line. This would almost certainly cause short-circuiting of the collectors against adjacent running rails when passing over points. If it is for two-rail working, the simplest way would be to employ the wheels of the bogie as collectors on one side and those of the locomotive on the other. If the coach floor is made of wood the question of insulation will not arise, but if it is of metal an insulated bush must be provided for the bogie king-pin. This would be most easily provided by screwing a block of wood to the coach floor inside the body. The bogie could then be mounted exactly as if the floor were of wood. It is quite likely, however, that the constructor will want to use a bogie with insulated plastic wheels. In that case the wheels of the locomotive part should be used in the usual way. A flexible lead should be carried from the collectors which pick up current from the insulated wheels, and the return path can be by way of the drawbar which joins the coach to the locomotive. It might be necessary to arrange a light spring to press against the drawbar to ensure perfect electrical contact.

The considerations mentioned in the last paragraph do not arise when a

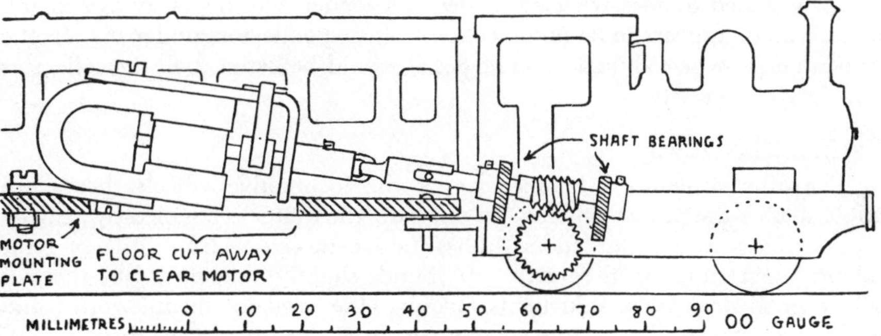

Fig. 145

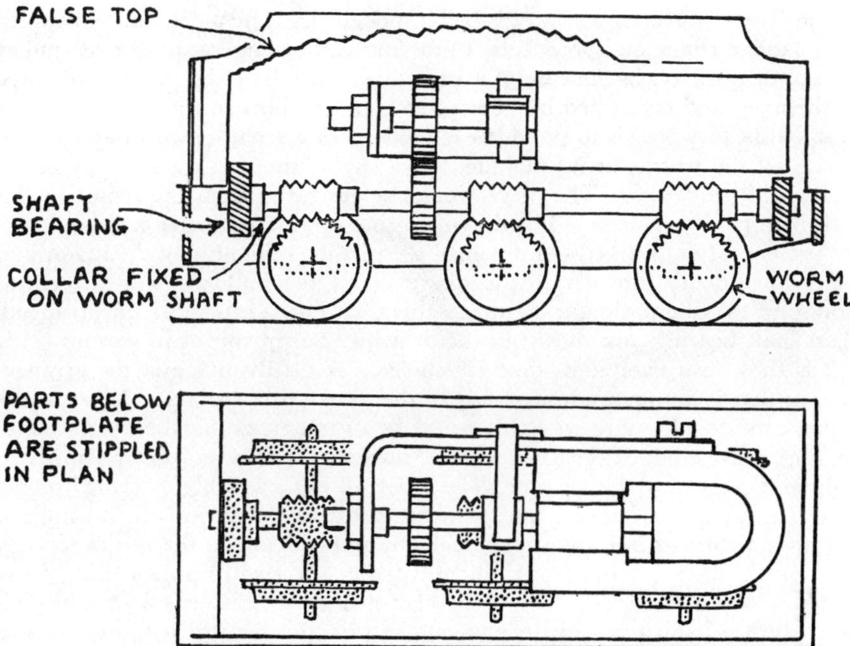

Fig. 146

motor is installed in a six-wheeled tender. A tender does not sway as a coach does and there appears to be no objection to fitting collectors under it. In the case of an eight-wheeled tender, on bogies, it would be better to fit the collectors to the bogies themselves.

POWER TENDERS

The alternative to a tender driving the locomotive wheels through a flexible shaft is the power tender. In this case, the motor is coupled by gearing to the tender wheels ; the tender pushes the locomotive in front of it, or pulls it along when running in reverse. It sounds slightly ridiculous but there is really a good deal to be said in its favour ; the need for flexible joints and couplings is abolished, and the tender becomes a self-contained power unit. The locomotive can display as much unobstructed " daylight under the boiler " as the constructor wishes. There seems to be no valid objection to this arrangement provided the locomotive is adequately weighted and that the tender is provided with enough ballast to give good adhesion. This, as a matter of fact, is more easily accomplished with a tender than with a locomotive ; the coal might be a solid block of lead filed to shape for example.

It is essential that the drive should be transmitted to more than one axle, and preferably to all of them, but the usual external coupling-rods are clearly out of the question, unless a power tender of the type used some decades ago on the Great Northern Railway is being modelled. The axles can be coupled by a ladder chain and sprockets, by a fine coil spring running over pulley wheels, or possibly, in the case of a very short wheelbase, by pinions mounted on the axles and connected by idler pinions placed betwen them. Perhaps the most satisfactory way is to provide each axle with a separate worm and worm-wheel, all the worms being mounted on a shaft running the long way of the tender as in Fig. 146. The drive would be conveyed from the motor to this shaft by a pair of pinions. The drawing is not to any particular scale and does not present a fully worked-out design ; the method of mounting the motor and some other details are left to the discretion of the builder. For the motor mounting, a clamp similar to that shown in Fig. 142 might be arranged. Plain shaft bearings are shown in the drawing, but in this as in various other details the constructor must take his choice. A disadvantage of the arrangement is that it does not admit of any of the axles being sprung. As far as the writer can see, the only way this could be overcome would be by means of floating self-contained gearboxes and universal joints in the worm-shaft. This would certainly be too complicated for all but a few highly skilled model makers, and the writer will not venture to offer any advice on the subject. Chain-drive would not appear to offer any impediment to the use of springs, but only a practical trial would show whether successful results could be expected. A chain running over a sprocket necessarily exercises a certain pull, the nature of which would depend on the direction in which the chain was running ; it is difficult to say how much this might interfere with the free action of the springs.

It would probably be simplest and most satisfactory to build a power tender on an *inside* frame chassis of conventional form, the outside frames and axle-boxes being for appearance only. The tender body, including the dummy frames, would be built as a unit, and attached to the chassis by a couple of screws. In fact the closer the job can approximate to normal model locomotive building methods the better.

CHAPTER XIV

AMERICAN LOCOMOTIVES

TO deal at all adequately with the subject of modelling American locomotives would require a volume at least as large as this one. Here we can do no more than direct attention to certain differences between them and the locomotives of the British Isles. In this country we are accustomed to a running-plate which, for modelling purposes, provides a convenient and definite line of division between the chassis and superstructure ; all external parts below running-plate level can be built on to the chassis while everything above is naturally part of the superstructure. Therefore, it is not uncommon for parts such as sand-pipes to be, in reality, in two pieces : one attached to the superstructure and appearing to pass down through the running-plate while the lower portion is part of the chassis. Similarly, it may be convenient to divide certain types of firebox, the lower part being represented by sheet-metal built on to the chassis, but arranged to line up with the principal part above the running-plate. But in American practice there is no such hard and fast line of division ; the running-plate as we know it is replaced by running-boards mounted high up on the sides of the boiler, and not directly connected with the buffer-beam, or pilot-beam as it is called in American terminology. This difference has a profound effect on the methods which must be adopted by the modelmaker. Chassis and superstructure must divide somehow differently, and it will be found that certain parts which, in British practice, apertain to the superstructure may become part of the chassis and vice versa. Fig. 147 shows how the chassis and superstructure are usually arranged on an American model. It will be seen that the smokebox saddle forms a unit with the cylinders and is built on to the chassis. The smokebox simply rests on it and is attached by means of a bolt and a nut fixed in the smokebox. At the cab end, we find that, contary to British practice, the firebox must be modelled complete, and that, in effect, it rests on the frame, which is usually downswept to conform to the shape of the ashpan. Also, modern American fireboxes are usually wider than British ones, to enable them to cope with the demands of the enormous boilers which are used over there. With very few exceptions, British fireboxes are kept narrow so that they can fit in the space betwen the trailing coupled wheels. Hence the lower part is so effectively hidden that, from the point of view of the worker in the smaller scales, there is nothing to model. In modern American practice, on the other hand, it spreads out almost to the full width of the locomotive, and is a very prominent feature. There seem to be two possible methods of dealing with this : in one, the ashpan can

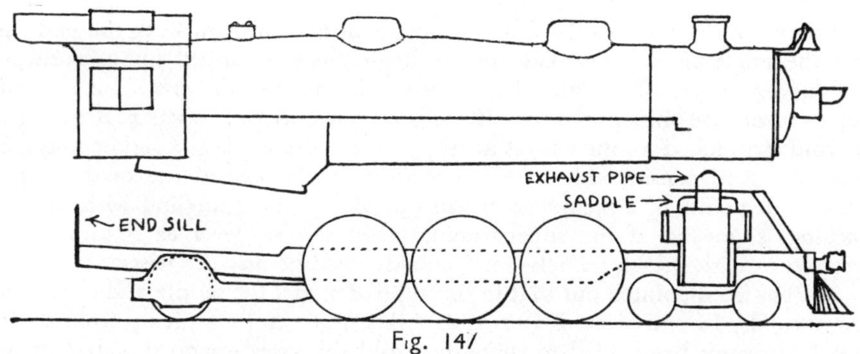

Fig. 147

be attached to the frame, as in Fig. 148A, the lower edge of the firebox sides resting on it, and the edges of the ashpan being provided with a lip to cover the joint. This method is very suitable for " O " gauge or larger sizes ; but for " OO " and " HO," where it is hardly necessary to follow the construction of the prototype with quite the same degree of fidelity, there is no reason why the sides of the firebox should not be extended and bent inwards to enclose the motor and represent the ashpan, Fig. 148B. It might, of course, be necessary to cut part of the ashpan away to enable it to clear the motor when the superstructure is removed, but few modelmakers are in the habit of worrying to that extent about whether their model conforms to the original underneath. Indeed, with a worm-wheel on the driving-axle, corresponding to nothing whatever on the prototype, any great degree of fidelity is ruled out.

The usual method of joining the superstructure to the chassis is shown in Fig. 149. The end sill (the rear end counterpart of the pilot-beam) is soldered or bolted to the chassis frame, and the squareness of the finished model will depend very much on getting this part true and level. The rear end of the cab deck is arranged to rest on the top edge of the end sill. A small angle-piece

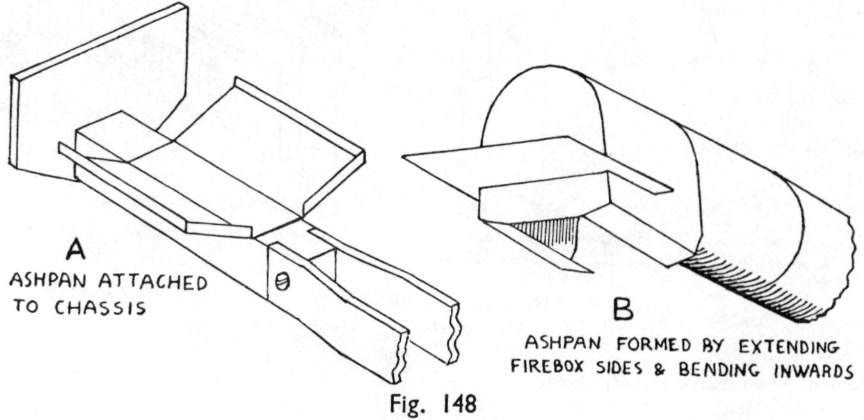

Fig. 148

is soldered under the cab deck, and a hole is drilled through both the end sill and the angle-piece. The hole in the angle-piece is tapped for a screw of suitable size, say 10-B.A., and the corresponding hole in the end sill is opened out to clearance size, Fig. 150. It will be seen that the superstructure rests on, and is attached to, the chassis at two points : the smokebox saddle and the end sill. And considerable care is necessary in the assembling of the parts since both points of attachment are in full view ; no wangling with bits of packing is possible if the superstructure does not sit level as is sometimes resorted to with British models—and nobody need be any the wiser.

It has been pointed out that in this type of model the saddle and cylinders are normally in one piece, Fig. 151, and this unit can be built up from sheet metal, the ends being filed to shape first and the sides wrapped round them and soldered a little at a time. If this method is used it is advisable to start soldering underneath and to work upwards until the junction with the smokebox is reached. A simpler but more laborious method, which is quite practicable in 3.5 and 4 mm. scales is to file and saw the cylinder-saddle unit from the solid, using white-metal or type-metal. In this case, it would be better not to rely exclusively on solder for the attachment to the frame. The cylinders should be screwed on to a cross-member fixed between the side-frames. Such parts as cylinder covers should be sweated in place before the cylinder block is

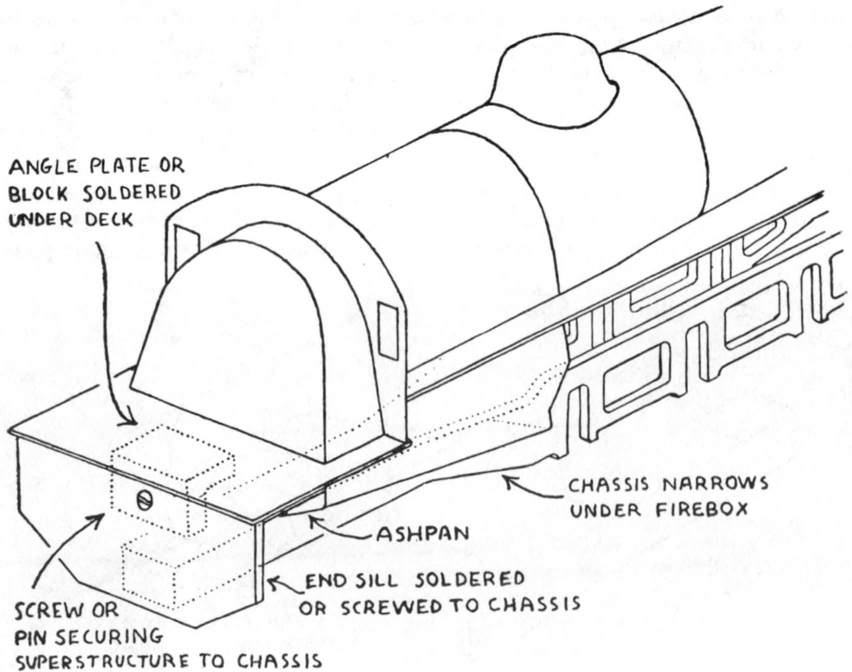

Fig. 149

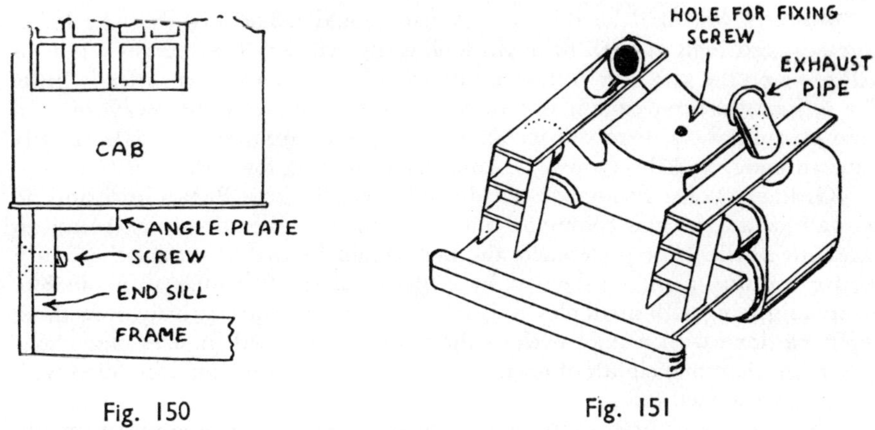

Fig. 150

Fig. 151

mounted on the frame. The writer believes that satisfactory cylinder blocks have been produced from hard, close-grained wood by means of a fretsaw. The block should be cut so that the grain of the wood runs from back to front, and it must be very well sandpapered. Particular attention should be paid to the front, where the end grain will be exposed and will be in a rather prominent position. After sandpapering, the block should be given a coat of shellac all over, and when this is thoroughly dry it should be sandpapered again, especially on the exposed end grain. In fact a second coat of shellac and another rubbing down would do no harm here. Cylinder covers and valve guide-rods are attached by the methods described in an earlier chapter when dealing with wood cylinders for British models.

Pilots—or cowcatchers, as they are usually called in this country—are not really such difficult things to make as they look, provided the job is undertaken systematically. There are various methods, but here it should be sufficient to illustrate one. What may be called the frame or foundation is cut and bent in sheet metal to the approximate shape shown in Fig. 152A, the exact dimensions depending, of course, on the particular prototype. Notches are filed in the upper and lower edges as shown. The frame is mounted on the pilot-beam as in Fig. 152B, preferably with diagonal supports, as shown, for greater resistance to accidental damage. Pins or short pieces of wire are soldered in the notches, as shown. It will be seen there is no possibility of one coming loose while another is being soldered, since each one is soldered at two widely separated points. They should, of course, be longer than is actually necessary and cut to length after they have all been soldered in place. To finish off the lower edge it is usually advisable to solder a narrow strip of thin metal so as to cover the lower ends of the pins. This method can be modified, with a little ingenuity, to suit almost any type of pilot. The fact that a pilot made in this way differs from the prototype in being solid underneath, so to speak, will never be detected when a matt black paint has been applied to that portion.

Workers who use the third-rail system should make sure that the lower edge is raised high enough to avoid fouling the third rail on curves. It is as well to be on the safe side in this matter, even if the appearance suffers a little. The writer has been caught out in this way on two separate occasions. In some circumstances, a model locomotive may rock from side to side slightly while running, and there must be some safety margin for this.

Ordinary boiler fittings do not differ materially from British ones and do not call for any special comment, but something must be said about American locomotive bells. For preference, the bell should be turned on a lathe, but a good substitute might be devised by soldering a small washer to a piece of rod and finishing with small files and emery, Fig. 153A. Alternatively, something might be done with a boot eyelet—they can be obtained in sizes down to a little more than one eighth of an inch diameter. The top would be filled with solder and rounded off.

The support or bracket is likely to be the most troublesome part to make. A fairly typical shape is shown in Fig. 153B. It should be filed from flat stock, nickel or steel, $\frac{1}{16}$ in. thick for " OO " gauge, most of the unwanted centre part being removed first with a drill, Fig. 153C. The inside should then be filed to shape before the outside is attempted. A spigot should be left underneath to be soldered into the boiler ; the base can be represented by a small washer. In actual practice such a fitting is in two parts, divided as shown in B, but since the bell is not required to ring it will be simpler to make it in one. The bell can be soldered to the bracket, but it is advisable not to rely on a simple butt joint. Provide the bell with a spigot for greater security. This can be turned if the bell is made on a lathe, or it can be a pin forced and soldered into a drilled hole. One does not necessarily drill through the bracket for this spigot. To do so would be a very delicate operation, and an alternative method is shown in Fig. 153D. A groove is filed in the bracket, with a rat-tail file, deep enough to allow the spigot on the bell to lie flush.

Fig. 154 shows in slightly simplified form the elaborate and often ornamented type of headlamp which was fitted to locomotives in the middle decades of the nineteenth century. It was one of he most conspicuous and attractive features of the period, and repays careful workmanship. The square body can be cut from brass rod, and is drilled in two places : for the lens and for the chimney on top. The lens rim can be represented by a piece of tube, soldered into the drilled hole. If the internal space is tinned to give the impression of a reflector, a lens is not absolutely necessary, but may be represented by a small transparent glass bead, or a blob of some clear transparent adhesive. The writer has used " New-Skin " quite successfully. The chimney can be turned from rod. The side panels were often raised and can be represented by pieces of thin sheet metal sweated on. The bracket is best made in one piece and bent to shape, as shown in the small sketch Fig. 154.

American smokebox fronts are more detailed and more laborious to produce than British ones. If made on a lathe they are quite a straightforward turning job, but if hand methods must be used the construction shown in

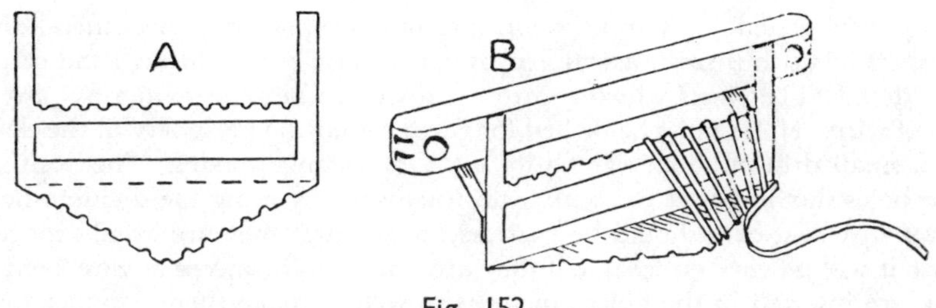

Fig. 152

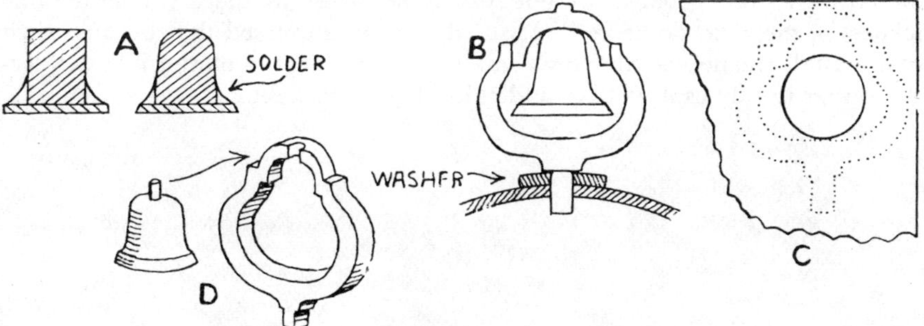

Fig. 153

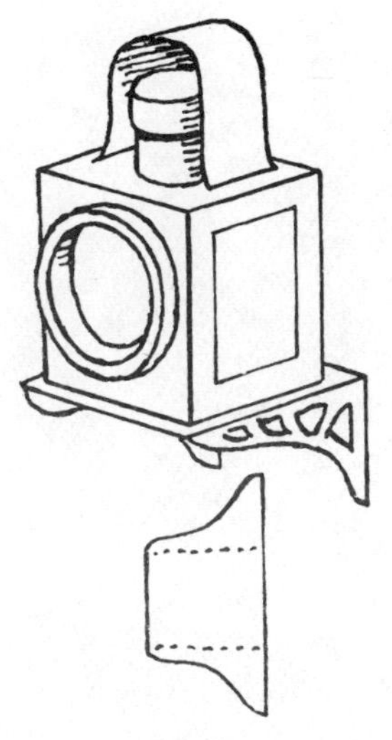

Fig. 154

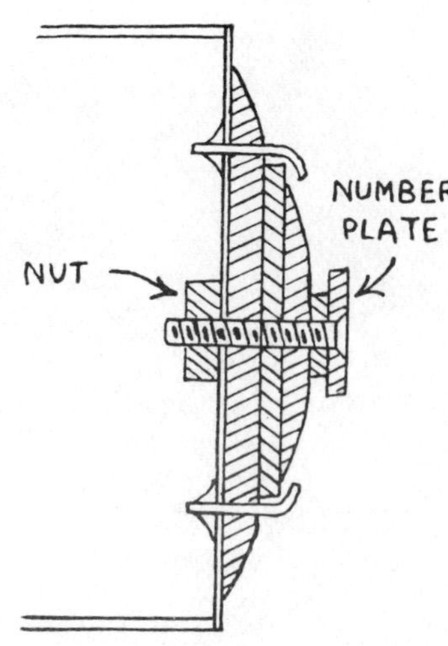

Fig. 155

Fig. 155 is suggested. The front, door, and number-plate are sheet metal discs or washers of various sizes, assembled by means of a screw through the centre and soldered. The cleets which secure the door can be represented by pins or pieces of wire. Holes must be drilled for them round the periphery of the door, using a small drill of about size 68 for a " OO " gauge model. The positions for the holes should be set out with a protractor, or by using the dividing-head of a lathe. Great care should be exercised to see that they are evenly spaced, because it will be very noticeable if they are not. Pins or pieces of wire, bent as shown, are inserted in the holes, and it is as well to make them a rather tight fit if possible as there will then be little risk of any of them slipping out of position while being soldered. The door is turned over and the shanks are soldered over on the back. A hot iron is necessary as there is considerable thickness of metal to be heated. It should not be supposed that because such jobs are small one necessarily uses a small iron ; it does not matter if the soldering is rather untidy as it will be hidden inside the smokebox.

CHAPTER XV

STREAMLINERS

THESE present a problem of a rather different order from locomotives of the traditional type. It is easy to make the mistake of thinking that they are simple to model because of the absence of the usual external details, but in fact this is very far from the case. The curves of most of these locomotives are very elusive and baffling when an attempt is made to reproduce them, and success depends on scrupulous fidelity to the original.

It seems that the method most likely to produce successful results in the hands of workers with limited equipment and facilities is that illustrated in Fig. 156. It is here suggested that the bulbous front be carved in close-grained, but not necessarily hard, wood. A recess, equal in depth to the thickness of the metal used for the boiler casing, is formed for a distance of about a quarter of an inch from the rear end, as suggested in the drawing, using files, sandpaper or a chisel. The metal casing is carefully bent to fit this recess, and is secured to the wood block with small brass wood-screws or small nails or pins. The heads of these are soldered over and filed flush. Any chinks between the wood and the metal are to be treated with a wood filler and the joint is well sand-papered to render it invisible when painted.

The best way to shape the wood block is to start by marking the *side* profile of the locomotive front on it in pencil ; with a piercing-saw, cut it to follow these lines. Draw the front elevation on the rear end of the block and shape accordingly, removing the bulk of the waste with saw and chisel and finish with files and sandpaper. It is advisable to shape a template either in metal or thin wood to the half cross-section so that progress can be checked more easily and to ensure that both sides are exactly alike. It remains to blend the various curves into one another, and great care should be exercised during this process ; the work should be examined frequently against the working drawings and any photographs which may be available. It will occur to the reader that the job is very much like the shaping of a model boat hull from the solid, except that the worker will probably have to exercise his discretion rather more since, in the normal course, he will not have closely-spaced sections to guide him, such as are usually provided by hull drawings. He will have to work by eye to a greater extent. The pencil lines for the preliminary cuts are suggested in the small sketch in Fig. 156. It will be understood that the position of the block is reversed in relation to the larger drawing ; it is the rear end which is seen.

An obvious extension of the method described here would be to use the

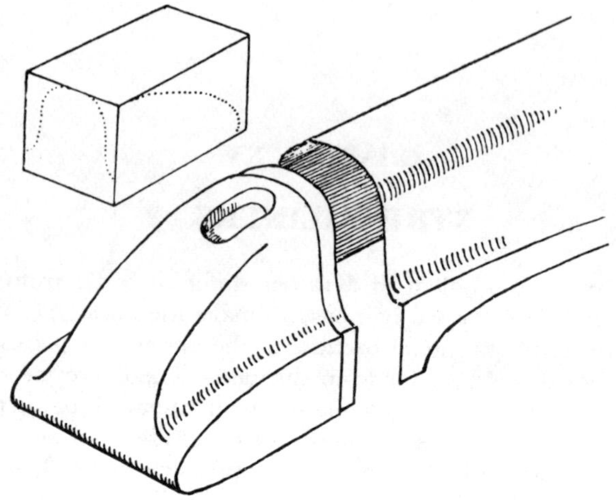

Fig. 156

shaped wood block as a pattern : to take a cast from it and to cast the actual front in metal. For preference, an alloy such as white-metal or type-metal rather than brass should be employed. This would represent a positive gain over wood as regards adhesive weight. It is doubtful if there would be any gain from the point of view of finished appearance, and some difficulty would probably be encountered in soldering to such a large mass of metal. For this reason, it would be advisable to secure the boiler casing with small screws in holes drilled and tapped in the block. The joint could then be lightly soldered over, but the solder would be required to act only as a filler, not to provide structural strength. The material known as cold solder, or Loy metal, would no doubt serve equally well.

An alternative method would be to shape the whole of the boiler-firebox unit from one piece of wood, and to hollow it out sufficiently to accommodate the motor.

In larger scales, the front could be beaten to shape in sheet copper round a former, and in anything larger than, say, 10-mm. scale, something of the sort would be practically essential. The writer does not think that such methods would produce clean and well finished results in sizes as small as " OO " gauge unless the worker was thoroughly experienced in work of this kind.

If this method is attempted, it must be understood that sheet metal can only be *expanded* by beating ; it cannot by any means be made to contract and many amateurs must have got into difficulties through ignorance of this fact. A curved shape must be made up from a number of pieces, so related to one another that in every case it is only necessary to spread the metal by beating in order to make the parts assume the required forms. The pieces are subsequently soldered together and the joints are smoothed off so that, when a suitable filler has been applied, they are invisible.

CHAPTER XVI

NARROW-GAUGE

IN view of the increasing interest among modelmakers in the stock and history of narrow-gauge railways, the inclusion of a chapter on the building of miniature locomotives of this description calls for no justification. There are indeed several good arguments in favour of a model narrow-gauge railway, and perhaps the best is that it invites the worker to a complete breakaway from the stereotyped and conventional. To those who find that the ordinary main-line locomotives begin to pall, the narrow gauges open a new world of fascinating and strongly individualised possibilities. The very fact that reliable data is often difficult to obtain, and that the worker in this field must be prepared to rely on his own resources and initative, will be an additional incentive to many. A further point which will carry weight with many is that, since locomotives and rolling-stock are smaller than those of the standard gauge the narrow gauges lend themselves rather well to operation in restricted spaces. Four- or six-wheeled tank engines can be used with perfect propriety, and passenger trains may be composed of four-wheeled stock, or short bogie vehicles the equivalent of 30 to 40 feet long, which in 4-mm. scale gives no more than 5 or 6 inches.

For any who feel that 4-mm. scale is a trifle fiddling, a very effective compromise could be arranged by employing 7-mm. scale, as for " O " gauge, in conjunction with 16.5-mm. or 18-mm. gauge and 4-mm. scale motors, wheels, track, and other parts. The 16.5-mm. gauge would then become the equivalent of 2 ft. 4 in. approximately, or the 18 mm. would give a shade over 2 ft. 6 in. An attractive feature of this combination is that the locomotive superstructures would provide considerably more space for the motor than the usual 4-mm. scale model ; the small boiler enthusiast would find himself free to reproduce practically any prototype which took his fancy. Yet, from the point of view of operation and layout, the space required for a given track plan would be practically the same as for 4-mm. scale. One would obtain most of the advantages of both " O " and " OO " gauges.

Fig. 157 shows a 2-ft. gauge locomotive of the late Lynton & Barnstaple Railway and a 3-ft. gauge six-coupled locomotive of the Isle of Man Railway. They are both drawn to 7-mm. scale with the outline of a " OO " gauge mechanism of the type marketed before the war by Romford and Hambling superimposed. It is clear that even a small low-boilered locomotive such as the Lynton & Barnstaple provides more than enough room for the motor, and vindicates the contention that, in this scale-gauge combination, room could be found for a motor in practically any locomotive, however small. On the other hand, for those who favour big locomotives, the narrow-gauge railways of the Union of South Africa, and several other overseas systems, provide prototypes which should be massive enough to satisfy anybody.

The worker who is attracted by 4-mm. scale will necessarily find his choice of prototypes more restricted until such time as smaller motors become available, or unless he is competent to build his own. But he could strike out on a new and individual line by using the gauge, wheel, and track standards which are being adopted for the new 2-mm. " OOO " scale. For track, it would be possible to use the ordinary " OO " product, or $\frac{1}{16}$-in. by 1/32-in. strip brass, or any commercial track which may be available for 2-mm. scale; and he might also employ any such parts as motors and wheels which may be marketed for " OOO."

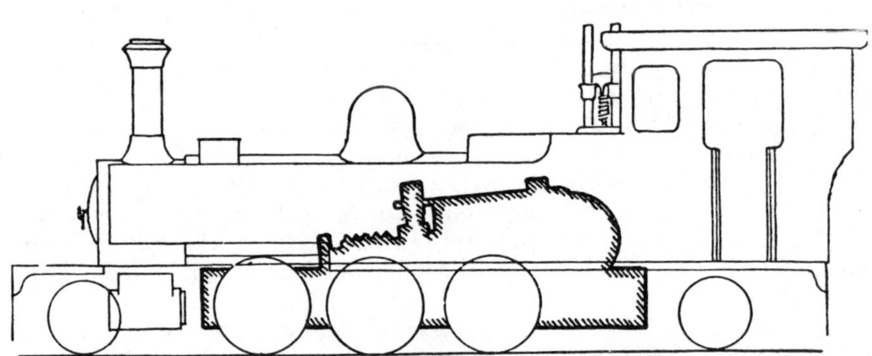

LYNTON & BARNSTAPLE 2 FT. GAUGE (ABOVE) AND ISLE OF MAN 3 FT. GAUGE LOCOS DIMENSIONED FOR 7 MM. SCALE WITH OUTLINE OF "OO" GAUGE MECHANISM SUPERIMPOSED

MM. 10 20 30 40 50 60 70 80 90 100 110 120

Fig. 157

But as some people may find the new 2-mm. scale standards a trifle "microscopic" for their taste, they may prefer to devise wheel and track standards of their own. In that event, it is suggested that the tread, flange, and check-rail, standards for "OO" gauge (either "Standard" or "Scale") could be adopted in conjunction with a gauge of perhaps 10 or 12 millimetres.

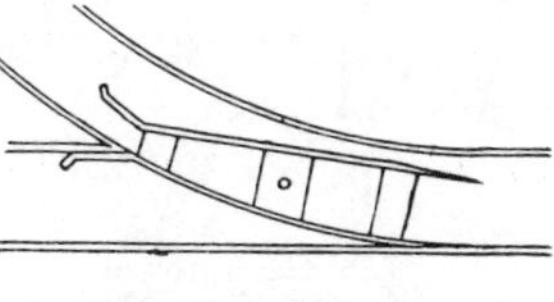

Fig. 158

As regards the back-to-back spacing of wheels, reference to the table of standard prepared by the B.M.R.S.B. shows that for Standard "OO" the back-to-back spacing is 2 mm. less than the gauge, while for Scale "OO" it is 1.5 mm. less. It is suggested that one or other of these should be adopted, preferably the second in order to allow the maximum width for the frames and gears. Thus for a gauge of 10 mm. the back-to-back spacing would be 8.5 mm. If wing- and check-rails are used the corresponding clearances would be adopted for them, but the writer is inclined to suggest that points should be made up on a system similar to that applied to tinplate track, where the switch rails are rigidly connected and arranged to pivot as a unit, Fig. 158. By this method the usual frog gap is eliminated and no wing- or check-rails are required. A more realistic form of track could be developed when experience had been gained. It is suggested, however, that short wing-rails should be provided simply to serve as stops for the switch-rail, to prevent it being pulled over too far.

If coaches and wagons are to look convincing, and have some pretension to scale proportions, something smaller than the standard 12-mm. wagon wheels will be needed ; which means that, if a suitable commercial line has not been developed for 2-mm. scale, the worker will have to produce his own, or get them turned for him. Alternatively, American "HO" gauge freight car wheels might serve if it should be possible to obtain them in this country. For locomotives the ordinary 12-mm. and 14-mm. rolling-stock wheels could be used with the addition of cranks and balance weights, and Hambling's provide plastic driving wheels 15-mm. diameter.

Fig. 159 is a suggestion for a free-lance narrow-gauge tank locomotive in 4-mm. scale, for a track gauge of 10 to 12 mm. It is designed to take the type of magnet which is being marketed by the Romford Model Company for their motors. No particular merit is claimed for the design as such ; it is introduced to show the possibilities, and also the difficulties, which will be encountered, and to suggest how the latter can be overcome. It represents the smallest locomotive which is possible with the motors available at the time of writing. It could be enlarged, with some improvement in general appearance, by the addition of another pair of wheels. For the sake of simplicity, a good

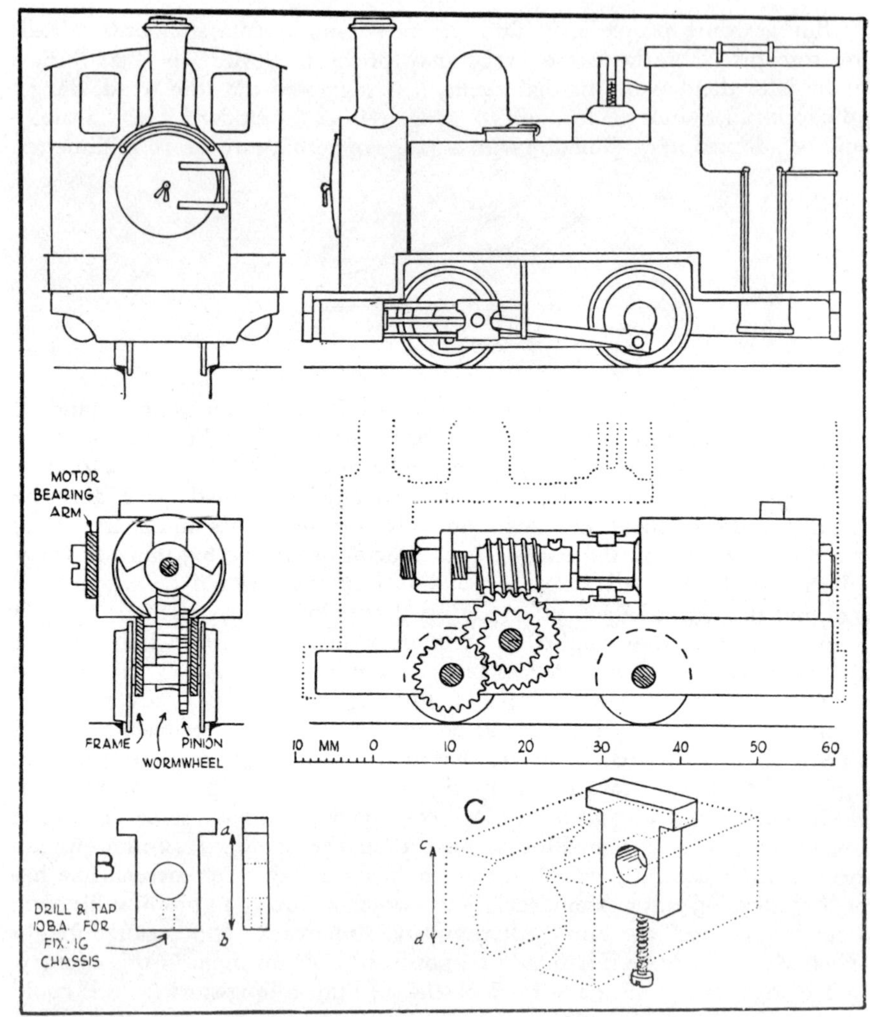

Fig. 159

many details such as brakes and brake cylinders have been omitted ; the reader can modify the design in many ways to suit his own ideas. The model made up by the writer from this drawing is shown in the two photographs opposite. It is designed for two-rail operation, the wheel rims on one side being insulated with thin fibre. The phosphor-bronze current collector, pressing on the tread of the trailing wheel, will be noted, and also the systoflex enclosed lead to the insulated brush of the motor.

It is obvious that the motor cannot be fitted *between* the wheels in the normal

Narrow gauge locomotive built to the design given in Fig. 159. The chassis and superstructure are shown separated (above) and the complete assembly is shown below

manner since it is considerably wider than the back-to-back spacing ; hence, it must be mounted high enough to clear them. This would raise the magnet too high for the fireboxes of small locomotives if it were upright in accordance with the accepted practice. To overcome this difficulty the motor has been turned on its side in the present case, as will be clear from the drawing and the photograph in which the chassis and superstructure are shown separately. There is ample space for it within the width of a side-tank locomotive. The overall width, as shown, is 30 mm. or 7 ft. 6 in., but this could be reduced to 7 ft. The wheels are 12 mm. diameter and as the worm-wheel measured nearly ⅝ in. it could not be fitted to the driving-axle, as it would have projected down below the rail level. Therefore, the worm-wheel is mounted on a jack-shaft, and the drive is conveyed to the axle by a pair of small pinions as described in chapter XII.

In selecting gears, it must be remembered that the space between the frames is very restricted, less than a quarter of an inch perhaps if the gauge is 10 mm., and for this reason it is necessary to use thinner material for the side frames than the usual $\frac{1}{16}$-in. strip. If the material is 1/32 in. thick it will be amply strong enough, and in most other respects the construction can follow the methods described in earlier chapters. It may be necessary to reduce the thickness of the worm-wheel to provide space for the pinion which is mounted beside it on the shaft. Note that there can hardly be room for a boss and clamping-screw on the worm-wheel, so that it must be a force fit on the jack-shaft. If it is not, soldering will be necessary.

The method of mounting the motor on the frame is shown in Fig. 159, diagrams *B* and *C*. The frame itself is shown in Fig. 160. A piece of brass ⅛ in. thick is filed to the shape shown at *B*. It is designed to slip into the space between the pole-pieces of the magnet at the rear end. A hole is drilled $\frac{3}{16}$ in. diameter to clear the armature and rear bearing, and, if found necessary, it can be elongated with a file to increase the clearance. A hole is also drilled into the clamping-plate from underneath, size 55 and tapped 10-B.A. for the fixing-screw which is pushed up through a hole in the frame. Note that the part of the clamping-plate between *a* and *b*, in diagram *B*, which fits between the poles of the magnet, should be slightly shorter than the thickness of the magnet, denoted by *cd* in diagram *C*. This is to enable the screw to pull the clamping-plate down tightly. *It is most important that the armature windings should not foul the clamping-plate or the insulation will be destroyed, with disastrous results.* The position of the armature can be adjusted to prevent this by means of the rear bearing-screw. Correct mesh between the worm and worm-wheel can be secured by means of metal shims under the magnet.

Every bit of available space within the model should be packed with lead or other metal to increase the adhesive weight. For this purpose the frame can be practically solid, the " cross-members " extending practically the full length of the chassis, and cut away only where necessary to clear the gears, Fig. 160.

For the attachment of the superstructure to the chassis, the usual device

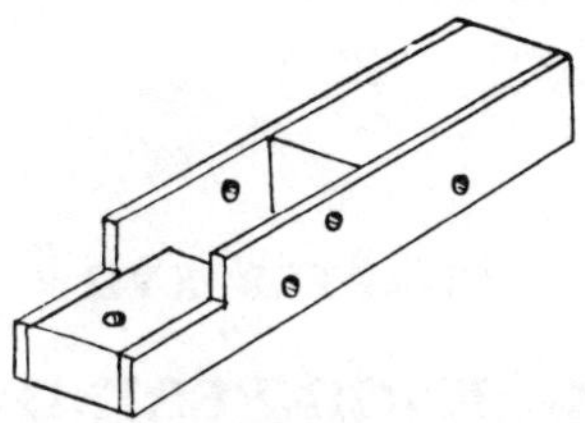

Fig. 160

of a screw passing up through the frame may be adopted at the front end. At the rear it would be more convenient to introduce a 10-B.A. screw horizontally through the buffer beam into a hole tapped in the chassis ; or a " housing " could be arranged as described in an earlier chapter.

The use of the two-rail system is strongly advised for a model railway on these lines ; the presence of a third rail would be very unsightly and rather absurd in so small a gauge.

CHAPTER XVII

RE-SCALING ENGINEERING DRAWINGS

IT appears from correspondence received by *The Model Railway News* and other journals that some modelmakers do not know how to proceed if they are obliged to work from a drawing which is made to a different scale from that of the proposed model. There is really no difficulty about it at all if the method described below is followed. It is only necessary to make a special rule which is divided so as to give direct readings off the original drawing in the required new scale. Suppose we have a drawing to a scale of, say, a

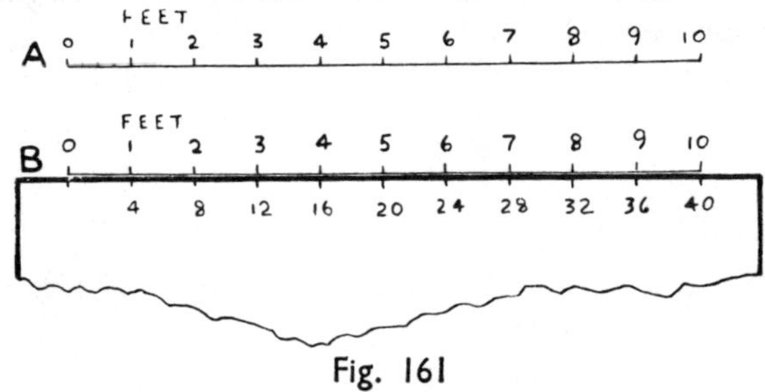

Fig. 161

quarter of an inch to the foot, and we wish to convert it to 4 mm. to the foot. Fig. 161A is assumed to be the ¼ in. to the foot scale on the drawing. Take a piece of thin hard card, such as Bristol board and lay it against the scale as in Fig. 161B. The edges of the card are indicated by the thick lines. We make ticks along the edge against the quarter inch divisions on the first scale, but instead of taking a quarter inch to represent a foot we are now going to take four millimetres to represent that unit. Therefore we mark our ticks 4, 8, 12, 16, 20, and so on. Now all we have to do is to read off dimensions on the original drawing with the rule we have made, but we transfer the figures thus obtained to the new drawing, or direct to the work, with any ordinary rule.

Of course we shall probably want to fill in some of the intermediate divisions on our card rule, and in cases where it is awkward to do this by direct measurement we can use the old school geometry dodge shown in Fig. 162. Suppose we want to divide the distance *A* to *B* into seven parts. I have taken this particular instance because the problem is likely to arise when working in 7-mm. scale, or " O " gauge, and because it is almost impossible to divide anything into seven parts by eye. Start by drawing a line to *C*. The angle it makes with *AB* does not matter within reasonable limits. Now mark off on

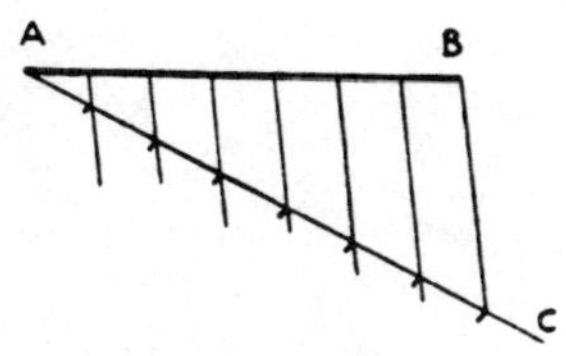

Fig. 162

AC seven quarter inches, or seven centimetres, or seven half-inches, or seven of whatevei appears to be a convenient unit. Rule a line from the last of the ticks (that is to say, the nearest to *C*) to *B*, and rule lines parallel to it through the other ticks. Thus *AB* is divided into seven equal parts.

The writer does not often use the method described above. He prefers to employ a cheap slide rule. It is usually quicker unless a very large number of dimensions have to be converted. The use of this instrument, in so far as it concerns the modelmaker, can be mastered in about five minutes ; anyone who has to undertake much scale conversion would be well advised to acquire one.